Television, Religion, and *Supernatural*

Television, Religion, and *Supernatural*

Hunting Monsters, Finding Gods

By Erika Engstrom and

Joseph M. Valenzano III

LEXINGTON BOOKS
Lanham • Boulder • New York • Toronto • Plymouth, UK

Published by Lexington Books
A wholly owned subsidiary of Rowman & Littlefield
4501 Forbes Boulevard, Suite 200, Lanham, Maryland 20706
www.rowman.com

10 Thornbury Road, Plymouth PL6 7PP, United Kingdom

Portions of chapters 1, 2, 3, and 4 appear in "Demon Hunters and Hegemony: Portrayal of Religion on the CW's *Supernatural*" by E. Engstrom & J. M. Valenzano, III, an article whose final and definitive form, the Version of Record, has been published in the *Journal of Media and Religion*, 2010, copyright Taylor & Francis, available online at: http://www.tandfonline.com/, Article DOI: 10.1080/15348421003738785, and in "Horsemen and Homilies: Revelation in the CW's *Supernatural*" by J. M. Valenzano, III and E. Engstrom in *Journal of Communication and Religion* (2013, Vol. 36, Issue 1, pp. 50-72), The Religious Communication Association.

British Library Cataloguing in Publication Information Available

Library of Congress Cataloging-in-Publication Data

Engstrom, Erika, 1964-
Television, religion, and Supernatural : hunting monsters, finding gods / by Erika Engstrom and Joseph M. Valenzano, III.
pages cm
Includes bibliographical references and index.
ISBN 978-0-7391-8475-2 (cloth : alk. paper) -- ISBN 978-0-7391-8476-9 (electronic)
1. Supernatural (Television program : 2005-) 2. Religion on television. I. Valenzano, Joseph M., 1978- II. Title.
PN1992.77.S84E55 2014
791.45'72--dc23
2013048172

♾™ The paper used in this publication meets the minimum requirements of American National Standard for Information Sciences Permanence of Paper for Printed Library Materials, ANSI/NISO Z39.48-1992.

Printed in the United States of America

Contents

Chapter One

Religion, Mass Media, and *Supernatural*[1]

Introduction

In 2005, the WB television network premiered a new show featuring monsters, ghosts, and witches and the Midwestern American family who hunted and destroyed them. The show, titled simply *Supernatural*, contemporized the classic ghost story and treated the paranormal as real and "normal," at least for the Winchesters, the family of hunters who roamed the United States on a single-minded mission to rid the land of evil. If this new program proved successful, its creator, Eric Kripke, envisioned a run of five years at most (Radish, 2010).

In May of 2013, *Supernatural* completed its eighth season on the WB's successor network, the CW, and was renewed for a ninth. Over the course of those eight seasons, the series' protagonist brothers, Sam and Dean Winchester, have died, been resurrected, prevented the "End Times" as foretold in the Book of Revelation, fought demons, vanquished three Horsemen of the Apocalypse, destroyed a wide array of monsters, met and fought with angels, gone to and returned from Hell, and traveled to Heaven—not necessarily in that order. The Winchester brothers literally have been to Hell and back.

Supernatural has consistently rated in the top three shows offered on the CW network. Though not comparable to the major networks' viewing audiences, which may reach 20+ million viewers, *Supernatural* garnered approximately 2 to 3 million viewers in its first few seasons ("Nielsen Ratings for 2005–06 Season," 2006; "Overnight Nielsen Ratings," 2008; Seidman, 2009; "Supernatural Ratings," 2007).

Beyond being a long-running television series, this program enjoys a devoted fan base. In 2012, *Supernatural* won its second People's Choice Award; its first win came in 2010. The show has garnered numerous Emmy and Saturn Award (Academy for Science Fiction, Fantasy and Horror Films) nominations ("Awards for *Supernatural*," 2012). *TV Guide* put *Supernatural* on the cover of its December 9, 2010, issue after the show received the most votes in the magazine's "Fan Favorite" contest. One can find evidence of the fan loyalty the series enjoys from its various Internet web sites, a fan magazine, attendance at science fiction conventions such as Comic-Con and *Supernatural*-only conventions known as "Salute to *Supernatural*," a series of books and *anime* (Japanese cartoons), and several nonfiction books documenting the series' "real life" basis in mythology and religion.

The wiki-based web resource Supernatural Wiki, or Super-Wiki, allows contributors to add to a range of "canonical information" about the series. Created in 2006, Supernatural Wiki had posted 2,411 articles by 2013; its home page had been visited more than seven million times as of June 2013 (Supernatural Wiki, 2013). Visitors can access episode transcripts, a library of mythologies portrayed in the show, a portal on the show's fandom listing conventions, academic articles and works, and other web sites and blogs ("Super-wiki: About," 2012). Social media sites attest to the show's popularity as well; in mid-2013, the show's fan page on Facebook counted more than 11 million "likes" ("Supernatural," 2013).

In their survey of television horror, Jowett and Abbott (2013) described *Supernatural* as differentiating itself from other television programs in the horror genre because it does not rely just on scary stories, but narrative elements borrowed from soap opera. "Thus *Supernatural* adopts a flexi-narrative that includes monster-of-the-week episodes, season arcs and ongoing relationship stories," they wrote (p. 50). Storylines incorporate both origins of monsters in ancient myth as well as a focus on character development, namely, familial themes concerning the relationship between the Winchester brothers, Dean and Sam, played by actors Jensen Ackles and Jared Padelecki, respectively. Broadcast on the CW network, whose demographic consists mainly of 18 to 34 year olds, and is known as being woman-friendly in its programming (Abbott, 2011; Villareal, 2013), the casting of two attractive stars adds to the appeal of the show. However, DeCandido (2009) pointed out, even if the show was just about "two pretty men driving a cool car, cracking wise, and shooting demons in the head" on "a fifth network," "it's much, much better than it needs to be" (p. ix).

We agree with DeCandido's (2009) assessment that *Supernatural* offers much, much more than "eye candy" or ghost stories. We saw the potential of this televisual artifact to serve as a research topic beyond examining its connection to genre, popular culture, and fandom. Our investigation into the world of *Supernatural* and its depiction of the Winchesters' adventures hunting monsters, ghosts, demons, angels, and other mythical creatures and their added discovery of the existence of angels and maybe even God, began when we discussed examining the show's depiction of religion during *Supernatural*'s fourth season. Both of us already were casual fans of *Supernatural* and enjoyed watching the show, which is always a plus when doing mass media research.

As researchers who had already done some work on media and religion separately, we saw the series' content as rife with religious-tinged data, and we began seriously examining the portrayal of religion in the stories of *Supernatural*, stories of ancient beings set in today's world. In this book, we explore the ways in which the text of this television entertainment program conveys particular viewpoints regarding religion. At the same time, we hope to show scholars who study television what this particular media product tells us about how popular culture communicates a society's values, attitudes, and beliefs.

We see *Supernatural* not as just an entertaining television series about the supernatural, but as a form of literature that reflects the culture in which it is produced, and the religious views that permeate that culture.[2] As a form of discourse, television programs are really messages, what Stuart Hall (1973) termed "sign-vehicles," that communicate *something* about a culture. We see the sum content of *Supernatural* as a sign-vehicle that provides a venue upon which to study the ways in which popular media reflect a "dominant cultural order" (p. 13). As a process, the product of mass communication is a message, and that message originates in its creators, who in turn are already members of the culture consisting of its audience. In this sense, the "circuit," as Hall put it, inherently begins with the anticipated audience of that message.

Supernatural evidently appeals to enough audience members to justify its continued renewal and existence. We seek to uncover how the guise of *Supernatural*'s plotlines and array of characters presents specific religious-based themes. What makes this television program so unique is its incorporation of a variety of characters from an array of religions, or what the show calls "lore." In a real sense, we see *Supernatural* as a platform that potentially provides viewers a basic course in comparative religions. What most interests us is how this program offers media scholars a discursive dataset for examining how television treats religion within Hall's (1973) circuit of culture.

RELIGION IN MASS MEDIA

Examinations of how theatrical films relay messages about religion include those by Jenkins (2003) and Hansen (2011) on Catholicism in the movies,

Hendershot (2010), Ostwalt (1995), and Stone (2001) on recurring Apocalyptic themes, and Cowan's examination of religious themes in horror films (2008) and science fiction (2009). As part of the cultural circuit, films, individually and collectively, provide texts for exploring how a society views religion. For example, Jenkins (2003) concluded that since the 1980s, Hollywood movies have depicted Catholics and Catholic clergy in particular as "media villains" (p. 158). Cowan (2008) examined how movies depict the religious "Other" in horror movies; in movies that depict voodoo, for example, stories reaffirm the difference between unfamiliar and familiar religions.

In *Religion and Its Monsters*, Beal (2002) explored the depiction of monsters in classic monster movies, pointing out how the monster is a "disciplinary figure" that warns humans not to disrupt the natural order of things (p. 196). The horror which ensues upon the creation of some unnatural being, such as Godzilla, which in turn wreaks havoc on humans, thus becomes a lesson to keep the status quo (the lesson of Godzilla being "do not make atom bombs"). Beal connects the notion of "monster" to portrayals of gods from an outgroup's religion; the use of the religious "Other" further reestablishes order, especially the order and rightness of Western religion and culture. "Americans and western Europeans often have made their monsters from other people's gods, that is, from the gods of unfamiliar, 'other' religious traditions," wrote Beal (p. 103). Even the classic 1939 film *The Wizard of Oz* provides an example: the Winged Monkeys under the control of the Wicked Witch of the West find their origins in the Hindu story of Hunaman, the commander of a monkey army and helper of Rama (one of the incarnations of the god Vishnu). In the Hindu legend, Hunaman is a hero, but in the movie the monkeys are portrayed as evil, and thus become a way of "othering" non-Western religious traditions.

Big-screen depictions of specific religions and characters representative of certain religions certainly offer evidence of how the circuit of culture functions through media channels. However, small-screen versions of religion provide a means by which that cultural circuit becomes more approachable, in a sense, than the larger-than-life aspects of films. As Winston (2009) contended in her edited book *Small Screen, Big Picture: Television and Lived Religion*, "Television provides a direct and (ironically) minimally mediated experience of the magic, fantasy, and possibility associated with the Divine" (p. 14). While the stories and characters on the big screen usually are confined within a single film, or at most a finite group of sequels, television programs with the same cast may run for years. Thus, Winston noted, television allows for character development and audiences to "know" them and relate to them, via parasocial interaction: "Specifically, television turns the big picture into small stories that enable audiences to see characters' growth over time" (p. 4). Television programs, regardless of genre, depict these familiar characters in day-to-day life, and may include how they experience religion in everyday life. For example, the texts examined by contributors to *Small Screen, Big Picture* ranged from primetime network dramas (*The West Wing*) to children's cartoons (*Pokemon*), as well as series in the science fiction (*Battlestar Galactica*) and fantasy (*Xena: Warrior Princess*) genres.

Even as one can find religious content on the small screen, commercial television tends to dilute religion into an "amorphous faith" that "flattens" religious traditions (Schultze, 2001, p. 40), excluding, of course, those cable networks that specifically promote or endorse a particular religion, such as the Christian Broadcast Network and the Catholic Eternal Word Television Network. Hoover (1996) observed that as a public endeavor, media can talk about religion, but must do so in a way that limits its offensiveness, maximizes its appeal, and allows it to remain seemingly neutral on dogmatic debates. Roof (1997) argued that this results in both the "flattening," or civilizing and softening, of faith, and the articulation of faith as a personal and private matter of choice in an effort to respect cultural plurality (pp. 63–65). Hunter (1983) also noted this process, stating it has "entailed a softening and polishing of the more hardline and barbed elements of the orthodox Protestant worldview" (p. 87).

Television, it appears, makes religious traditions more palatable to a generic public. Further, Clark (2003) posited, "The stories that explicitly embrace religious language and definitions are often rejected by persons who are not already members of those traditions" (p. 228). Thus, as Bird (2009) proposed, television programs that serve up a generic religiosity can succeed because they "capture the overall picture of mainstream U.S. culture today, where almost everyone professes a faith in some kind of higher being" (p. 41). In contrast, "theologically based attempts," like NBC's 2006 series *The Book of Daniel*, did not even last a full season due to the controversy surrounding its premise of a preacher who spoke to Jesus (p. 41). In short, audiences might accept and acknowledge a generic faith in stories and characters, but at the same time reject overt theology. Indeed, as Grigg (2007) contended in an analysis of the 1960s series *The Man from U.N.C.L.E.*, television could outright dismiss religion. In that program, Grigg noted, forms of religion and spirituality were universally dismissed in favor of rational explanations for supernatural phenomena.

Thus, television in general seldom deals with religion as an integrated set of religious beliefs, and explicit religious scripts are rarely presented to viewers (Roof, 1997). Rather, religion "is framed more as a moment or encounter arising out of personal experience or crisis" (p. 66). Regarding the avoidance of forwarding specific religions, in their study of primetime programs on ABC, CBS, Fox, and NBC, Skill, Robinson, and Lyons (1994) found that few characters identified with a particular religious affiliation. In addition, they found religion rarely played a central part in a program's storyline or theme; any comments related to religion, such as references to "God" or

"Jesus," tended to be ambiguous. As for the representation of religious groups, they found all to be underrepresented, except for Catholics.

When one considers the religious identification of the U.S. population, U.S. Census Bureau figures illustrate that most adults self-identify as Christian, and of those, most report describing themselves as Protestant. The latest census figures, from 2008, show that among some 228 million adults, more than 173 million (75%) identified themselves as belonging to some form of Christian religious group. In turn, of those identifying as Christian, 116 million (67%) reported belonging to Protestant and non-Catholic religious groups (including Eastern Orthodox), and 57 million identified themselves as Catholic (U.S. Census Bureau, 2009).[3] The Pew Forum on Religion and Public Life (2008), in its *U.S. Religious Landscape Survey*, surveyed 35,000 adults nationwide and presented similar results. Most respondents identified as Christian (78.4%), with a similar breakdown regarding denomination category: 51.3% Protestant and 23.9% Catholic.

More recent figures gathered by the Gallup Poll in 2012 (Newport, 2012) confirm the mostly Christian descriptor regarding religious preferences in the United States. Of 326,000 randomly chosen adults ages 18 and older, 77% reported as Christian. Of those, 51.9% reported being Protestant/Other Christian and 23.3% said they were Catholic. Of the other "major" religions, 1.7% identified as Jewish and .6% said they were Muslim. Those respondents not reporting a religious affiliation, 15.6%, outnumber adherents of the latter two religious traditions identified in the Gallup report. "The United States remains a largely Christian nation; more than nine in 10 Americans who have a religious identity are affiliated with a Christian religion" (Newport, 2012). This suggests that religious hegemony in mass media would reflect the majority view reflecting the mostly Protestant nature of affiliation with Christianity, with the Catholic faith serving as a minority viewpoint if considered a distinct form of Christianity. Non-Christian faiths, such as Judaism and Islam, then, have an even clearer distinction of being in the minority, and might then be more likely to be cast as the "Other" in U.S. media.

Studies looking at religious content of primetime network television in the United States indeed have found a generic, Christian-leaning trend. Johnson (2000) noted that more overt religious themes in programs such as *Touched by an Angel* on CBS and the "God flavor" of the PAX network seemed unexpected within contemporary mass media (p. 40). Clarke (2005) found that in 2002, fictional network TV programming offered few religious characters overall, but those that did appear tended to be Christian. Of the three top-rated comedies and three top-rated dramas on ABC, CBS, NBC, Fox, PAX, UPN, and the WB, characters considered religious in some way tended to be Protestant rather than Catholic. Clarke also found a casual use of religious language, providing support for Schultze's (2001) assertion about the flattening of religious values. Clarke also had to qualify the findings of that study due to the low number of religious characters in the sample.

A paradox emerges when one considers the "flattening" of religious content on one hand, while evidence points to a generic Christian tinge to entertainment television on the other. Even when television program content includes other religions, there appears some indication of a dominant version of religion that supports mass media's role in forwarding a particular worldview. For example, Lewis (2002) looked at the portrayal of religion in the long-running animated Fox series *The Simpsons*. While the series takes a comical view of religion overall, "good" characters, such as Ned Flanders, are associated with religion (except for Reverend Lovejoy, who represents righteous indignation and hypocrisy). Overall, Lewis concluded, *The Simpsons* "presents a mixed but ultimately respectful attitude toward religion and its important role in human deportment" (p. 154). While *The Simpsons* conveys a mostly positive view of religion, the issue of diversity brings it back into the general Christian-centered tendency of network TV. *The Simpsons* has included peripheral characters professing various religions, including Judaism, Hinduism, and Buddhism, but main characters mainly portray a generic Protestantism (Lewis, 2002).

Similarly, regarding nonfiction programming, Engstrom and Semic (2003) studied the religious nature of weddings depicted in the reality TV program *A Wedding Story* on The Learning Channel. Of the eighty-five weddings they analyzed, fifty-one (60%) were Christian, with most of those discerned as Protestant (31, or 39%). They also found a notable lack of rituals in the footage of most of both Protestant and Catholic weddings. However, the footage of weddings that featured other, more "exotic" religions, such as Hinduism and Greek Orthodox, tended to include more rituals and, thus, more screen time. Their findings led the authors to suggest that Protestant and Catholic ceremonies already might be familiar among viewers, and thus did not need or warrant as much attention.

Miles (1997) addressed the lack of diversity in primetime TV fiction's portrayal of religion by calling for not only more but also more diverse representations of characters that ascribe to religious values and commitment. Diversity of religion extends to religious-based beliefs and practices not considered mainstream. For example, the portrayal of alternative religions on television served as the focus of Massanari's (2005) analysis of the Sci-Fi (now SyFy) cable channel's 2004 reality series *Mad Mad House*, which placed ten "ordinary" houseguests in a competition set in a spooky mansion with five alternative religion practitioners. The Alts, as they were called in the show, consisted of a practicing witch, a voodoo practitioner, a "primitive," a naturist, and a vampire. Massanari concluded that throughout the show, Alts were positioned as both powerful but marginalized; the show portrayed them as strange, foreign, and not normal (p. 16). Massanari noted that the structure of reality television, such as its focus on sensationalism, emphasis on conflict, and acceptance of voyeurism, makes the content of programs in that genre "ill suited" for serious discussion about religion (p. 16). However, *Mad Mad House*'s inclusion of religions that fall outside the accepted mainstream—what we see as the "Other"—still constitutes an attempt, however flawed, to acknowledge the existence of other forms of belief. We address this theme of "Otherness" in our examination of how television programs incorporate aspects of religion, and how *Supernatural* both includes and excludes "other" religions in its storylines over the course of the series.

Television, contended Winston (2009), "has superseded church insofar as it is a virtual meeting place where Americans across racial, ethnic, economic, and religious lines can find instructive and inspirational narrative" (p. 2). It serves as a site for "creating cultural identity as well as for the 'religious' tasks of meaning making, reenchantment, and ritualization," she added (p. 2). Fictional television, a media space that holds the potential to educate as well as to entertain, becomes ever more important as a venue for researching religion in the media, especially the use of religious artifacts, themes, and mythology in popular culture.

Such exploration helps us to understand the intersection between religion and popular culture in terms of how media depict religions regarded as the "Other," or the simply unfamiliar. The conveyance of religion through television becomes even more critical when one considers how the medium of television has the ability to connect viewers to each other, to their favorite show and characters, and to the "common sense" beliefs held by a majority of society's participants. *Supernatural*'s fan base, with its online presence as previously mentioned, and the program's recognition as a "fan favorite" by the People's Choice Awards in recent years, offers evidence of this particular program's merit as *popular* culture. Within the scope of serving as a text that appears to resonate with millions of loyal viewers, it follows that one could view it as relaying at least something about the religions that serve as the source material for its religious-based storylines.

We see *Supernatural*'s longevity as a successful treatment of religion without being a religious show—and, as such, another example of how mass media companies and producers create programs that draw audiences (and, thus, advertisers) so as to turn a profit. This undoubtedly requires a negotiation on the part of scriptwriters between incorporating religion into stories in a way that does not offend viewers. In turn, the "flattening" of religion becomes a device that allows for its use as the origin for various characters encountered by the show's protagonists, but in a way that does not "preach" to its audience.

Members of the show's production team have noted this balance regarding the philosophy of *Supernatural*, stating that the main focus of the series is on horror and scary stories rather than religion. In a 2008 *TV Guide* interview, series creator Eric Kripke emphasized the core of the show's narrative as being rooted in "the really fun, bloody, gory stories with a twist at the end" that reflected aspects of American culture (Surette, 2008). Moreover, Kripke was "attracted to the idea that America had its own mythology, as really fleshed out as any world mythology, and it just wasn't that well publicized" (Surette, 2008). *Supernatural* became Kripke's effort to publicize American mythology.

This approach was reiterated by writer, executive story editor, and showrunner Sera Gamble, who left the series at the end of its seventh season. She maintained the show is more about humanism than about reliance on a higher power. In an online article by Newitz (2009) on the web site io9.com, a "daily publication that covers science, science fiction, and the future," Gamble explained: "We've been careful to leave room for agnosticism when we talk about God. There's no direct line to answers about His existence—at least not in the first four seasons. And in my mind, there's been lots of room for atheists to stay on board. First of all, no one's trying to convince anyone of anything; we're just here to entertain you. Second—even some of the angels doubt God's around, so join the club." The showrunners and scriptwriters assert they use biblical stories such as the Apocalypse more for the horror and terror the texts invoke, rather than any explicit theological purpose. The background of the production team also becomes salient when considering this perspective; several of the writers worked on or moved on to write for other television series in the science fiction, horror, and drama genres, including *True Blood* (HBO), *Being Human* (BBC), *Legend of the Seeker* and *Revolution* (NBC), *Mad Men* and *Breaking Bad* (AMC), and *Ringer* (CW) ("Category: Writer," 2013).

Though the spokespersons for *Supernatural* characterize an avoidance of imbuing the show with religious instruction, and instead maintain they rely on religion(s) as a narrative source, we seek to explain how this television show itself becomes a conduit through which explanations and adaptations of certain myths and rituals—based in specific religious traditions—nevertheless emerge. Thus, our project is primarily rhetorical, and as such we utilize *Supernatural* to examine how popular culture promotes and enacts a particular stance regarding ingroup religions (from the viewpoint of the culture in which it is produced), outgroup religions, and the mythology associated with "America," as explained by Eric Kripke, the show's creator.

With this in mind, we approach *Supernatural*, a television series that incorporates religious traditions, stories, and practices, with the perspective that it does offer a means for conveying messages about American culture and its primary religion *vis à vis* other cultures and their religious traditions. Thus, we ask: How does religion become part of the subtext of horror and the fantastic without portraying characters as religious themselves? This serves as our central research question, and guides our analyses of *Supernatural* over its thus-far eight-year existence.

SUPERNATURAL: COMBINING THE HORROR GENRE AND RELIGION

Kane (2006) contended that horror is "the longest lived of any genre" of film (p. 3), with Hollywood "churning these out for over 90 years" (p. 14). Though a mainstay of cinema, Hills (2005) maintained that television studies scholars have "marginalized" the horror genre, because television viewing takes place within the domestic sphere in the home via glances as opposed to the gaze required for watching films (p. 112). In addition, the television industry's self-censorship and practices of production have rendered horror on TV "relatively invisible," Hills claimed (p. 111). Since television programs require a certain level of viewership, niche programming such as horror inherently would eliminate some portion of the general audience. Hence, horror programs, like *Supernatural*, would invoke what Hills called "the expert fan audience" and the label of cult TV (p. 126). Indeed, *Supernatural*'s cult TV label is evidenced by its fan following, and its inclusion in academic treatments such as *The Essential Cult TV Reader* (Peirse, 2010).

Supernatural as a media artifact provides a multifaceted discourse visually, musically, and textually which makes it rife with material for commentary and analysis. For example, *The Mythology of Supernatural: The Signs and Symbols behind the Popular TV Show* (Brown, 2011) provides viewers a guidebook to the myths, legends, and biblical sources presented in the program that one also can find in "the real world." In edited compendia, such as *In the Hunt: Unauthorized Essays on* Supernatural (Supernatural.TV, 2009) and *TV Goes to Hell: An Official Road Map of* Supernatural (Abbott and Lavery, 2011), fans and scholars alike have addressed the layered meanings embodied within the storylines and production values of the show. These range from the symbolism of the show's characters and props, familial themes, and the underlying fight between the Winchesters (good) and the forces of darkness (evil) to its incorporation of folklore and religion. Indeed, in *TV Goes to Hell: An Official Road Map of* Supernatural, Giannini (2011) contended that the "bricolage of religions and traditions" keep the show from connecting itself to any particular religion (p. 164). We revisit this topic in chapter 2, Plurality of Religion. These treatments offer further evidence of this program's appeal to scholars, both in terms of formal and informal commentary.

In *Supernatural*, demons and angels are real, and ghosts do harm the living. The horror genre, which characterizes *Supernatural* as literature, serves as a means by which storytellers infuse aspects of theology into entertaining stories about monsters, witches, and ghosts. In *Paranormal Media: Audiences, Spirits, and Magic in Popular Culture*, Hill (2011) noted, "Resurgence in paranormal beliefs gives momentum to representations of ghosts, supernaturalism, angels, and fringe science, across multimedia environments" (p. 7). Among examples of this normalization of the weird and fantastic, Hill mentioned primetime network series such as *Medium*, *The Ghost Whisperer*, and *Supernatural*. Indeed, even reality television programs treat ghosts and hauntings as "real," with the SyFy series *Ghost Hunters* and the Travel Channel's *Ghost Adventures* featuring "detectives" who search for spirits using a documentary approach. Hill also found that while the paranormal—extrasensory perception, hauntings, witchcraft—has become a part of mainstream media, it remains a neglected area of media and communication studies.

Clark (2003) described "stories of evil, demons, and apocalyptic battles," precisely the material that *Supernatural* deals with on a regular basis, as the "dark side of evangelicalism" (p. 13). Popular teen-aimed television programs from the recent past like *Buffy the Vampire Slayer* and its spinoff *Angel* illustrate how the good-versus-evil underpinnings of evangelicalism become folded into tales of the occult, noted Clark. These sign-vehicles serve as the platform for telling stories that evoke notions based in traditional religions; stories are set in a world that affirms "the existence of demons, witchcraft, and manifestations of evil in the material world" (p. 73). Horror stories, she noted, "contain elements that may be dramatic and highly entertaining, and thus their use extends beyond the pedagogical goals of religious conversion" (p. 14). Indeed, Clark further explained, evangelical Protestants long have used the horror genre to introduce the gospel to the "unchurched" (p. 17).

We see *Supernatural* serving a similar role, deliberate or not, which makes it a logical venue for exploring the relationship between religion and media. Clark's 2003 book, *From Angels to Aliens: Teenagers, the Media, and the Supernatural*, pre-dates *Supernatural* the series, but her observations regarding the entertainment value of horror stories and their utility as conduits for evangelicalism apply to this particular media artifact quite clearly. The horror genre, Clark wrote, "has elements of human drama and futuristic imaginings, a battle between good and evil, horrific consequences for some, and a happy ending for 'the good guys'" (p. 33). Further, younger audiences, which *Supernatural* the series draws, seem to embrace the openness and possibilities that entertainment media in this genre offers, noted Clark (2003).

Even as the paranormal has found popularity, as documented by Hill (2011), the tying of the supernatural to a specific religious tradition might not go over so well (Clark, 2003). The 2005 NBC miniseries *Revelations*, observed Bird (2009), tied biblical references to the paranormal, and combined

Roman Catholic imagery with elements of fundamentalism. It was an explicitly religious horror program, but Catholics, Evangelicals, and horror fans turned away. Bird explained that rather than attracting a "religious horror" audience (à la the classic film *The Exorcist*), its slow pace and "tame" style resulted in its failure (p. 24). This example appears to support Hills's (2005) contention that horror had failed to take a stronghold on television because "textual agency" is denied to creators of horror (p. 117).

The characteristics of the horror/occult genre listed by Clark (2003) include the possibility of the existence of angels who give advice and guidance, humans who possess supernatural powers to fight evil, and the return of loved ones from the dead to bring peace for the living (p. 228). These elements allude to belief in supernatural beings and the notion of an afterlife. Over the course of its run thus far, *Supernatural* the series has incorporated all of these in individual episodes and season story arcs, and has even used specific religious language and artifacts, as we later describe in this book. Analyzing the religious overtones and undertones presented in the text of this particular media artifact and what differentiates it from other attempts at interweaving religion into the horror genre serves as the purpose of our inquiry.

THEORETICAL FOUNDATIONS

The 2001 Gothic horror film *Frailty*, released four years prior to the television appearance of *Supernatural*, provides a markedly similar premise: a motherless family of demon hunters from blue-collar origins. In *Frailty*, the Meiks family lives in rural Texas. The father, known simply as "Dad," is a car mechanic raising two young boys on his own; the boys' mother died giving birth to the younger son. One day, Dad announces to his sons, Fenton and Adam, that "demons are taking over the world." He reveals to the boys that God came to him in a vision and told him the names of demons that needed to be destroyed.

It appears Dad has lost his mind, as the so-called demons God told him to find appear as ordinary people, not the monsters one might expect. The twist in this initially apparent crime drama comes when the viewer learns that Dad was right all along: the people the Meikses were abducting, then killing in their specially built demon holding cell turned out to be murderers; the family was indeed ordained by a higher power to mete out justice and destroy demons. *Frailty* came complete with heavenly visions of angels as well, when Dad experienced a visitation from an angel-warrior while underneath the car he was repairing.[4]

In *Frailty*, the Meikses sought out evil humans identified as demons. In *Supernatural*, the Winchester family of Lawrence, Kansas, seeks out demons disguised as humans. But in the world created by *Supernatural*, the demon-fighting family also takes on all manner of unnatural creatures. Though originally spurred to find and destroy the demon that killed Mrs. Winchester, the family becomes part of a secret, loosely connected network of "hunters" and "men of letters" (introduced in season eight)—all of whom see their mission as ridding the world of evil. The Winchesters' prey gave form to mythic beings from a range of religions and folklore, including those from Judeo-Christian tradition.

The filtration of a religious perspective into mass mediated fictional programming further demonstrates the interconnected nature of religion and American society. Even as the series' writers and producers have relied on material directly from the New Testament, as in the overarching storyline that had the Winchesters involved in "The" Apocalypse in seasons four and five, *Supernatural* somehow continues to avoid an overtly religious or proselytizing tone that may alienate its core audience and other potential viewers. The Winchesters regularly consult the Bible as a reference in their "family business," but they do not practice any particular faith, nor do they attend church.

The Bible and other religious books are used as serious evil-fighting tools, however, and the brothers interact with beings like angels and even Lucifer. Indeed, the author of a review of the show in *The New York Times* concluded, "More often than not *Supernatural* seems to be God loving yet utterly without an agenda, its mythology too digressive and ad hoc to feel as if it carried much stealth intention" (Bellafonte, 2011). This avoidance of directly casting the main protagonists as religious may help to explain the show's success in light of the failures of other television offerings based on biblical material.

In this book, we aim to explain how religion appears in popular culture in the early twenty-first century. In studying *Supernatural* as a cultural artifact and its place among the milieu of fictional entertainment television that touches on religious themes in some fashion or other, we employ the following theoretical foundations that inform our analyses: hegemony, homiletics, civil religion, and core cultural myths which comprise a composite American mythos. In terms of how *Supernatural* contains a certain viewpoint regarding religion, we employ hegemony theory to explain the emergence of a predominance or validity of certain religions over others—or, to put it another way, uncover the mediated representation of a hierarchy of faiths in American culture. Homiletics, the practice of relating lessons from Scripture through storytelling, becomes important when analyzing how *Supernatural*'s texts operationalize certain passages from Scripture that also convey moral lessons for everyday life. Regarding the American mythos, the notion of being "chosen by God" marks American Exceptionalism. Its related concept, the Frontier Myth, extends the notion of a divine destiny by placing Americans into a mythic story in which they explore the frontier (in various forms), and tame it. In turn, the newly subdued land becomes assimilated, fulfilling this special nation's destiny. Additionally, practicing these cultural myths reflects and reinforces a specific civil religious identity for Americans.

We use each of these theoretical approaches to address different angles from which we view *Supernatural* as a text that conveys, whether effectively and accurately to viewers or not, themes regarding (a) a recognition that a variety of religions exist and that their entities have power, (b) there is a hierarchy of religions based on the strength of that power, (c) moral lessons based in religious texts from the faiths at the top of the hierarchy, and (d) values associated with the contextual culture of the program (the United States of America). Each of the descriptions of these theoretical foundations pertain to these viewpoints, with the purpose of relying upon them to carefully deconstruct specific aspects of the show regarding the plurality of religions depicted, the hegemony of religion emerging from that plurality, the utilization of Bible Scripture for moral instruction, and how the religious-like imperatives associated with the notion of "America" and its self-appointed purpose on the international stage emerge and are reinforced or reframed. Ours is not a treatment limited to just one of these theories as overarching or as a continual theme throughout the analyses. Rather, we purposively limit each of the theoretical perspectives to facets of the show's text, thus illustrating the uniqueness that *Supernatural* brings to the study of religion in mass media.

Hegemony

Hegemony theory as used today by critical and cultural scholars stems from the writings of Italian philosopher Antonio Gramsci. Gramsci sought ways to rectify gaps in Marxist theory, by presenting a two-level explanation for how power functions in a society.[5] The state, or legal, authority serves as one of these levels, and "civil society" serves as the other. Gramsci (1999) explained how power functions in a civil society, which provides a level of "governance," so to speak, that teaches us "rules" that are not necessarily enforced but ones to which we give our consent without really knowing that we are doing so. Civil society thus functions through

> The "spontaneous" consent given by the great masses of the population to the general direction imposed on social life by the dominant fundamental group; this consent is "historically" caused by the prestige (and consequent confidence) which the dominant group enjoys because of its position and function in the world of production. (p. 145)

Because hegemony resides primarily in the realm of civil society, it includes religion and mass media, wherein a "philosophical and moral outlook" is "actively supported and articulated by subordinate and allied groups" (Mumby, 1997, p. 48). Eventually, Van Zoonen (1994) noted, a dominant ideology forwarded by those groups becomes invisible, unquestioned, and appears as the natural, unpolitical state of things accepted by everyone. Common sense, "a multifaceted representation of social life under determinant conditions" (Landy, 1994, p. 78), serves as a manifestation of this natural state. Lears (1985) used the term "spontaneous philosophy" to describe hegemony as the proper ways of acting and seeing things that we all "know"; this spontaneous philosophy includes language, conventional wisdom (common sense), and popular religion and folklore (p. 570). Gramsci was interested in the workings of popular culture because he saw revolutionary change as a process in which popular thinking and behavior became transformed, as Forgacs explained in *The Antonio Gramsci Reader* (Gramsci, 2000, p. 363).

Hegemony results through "the establishment of cultural norms, rituals, and traditions"—of which religion serves as a perfect example—that in turn perpetuates beliefs that justify its dominance (Zompetti, 1997, p. 73). As with other manifestations of hegemony, a religion, or even a few religions, eventually becomes dominant within a society at a certain time (for example, the United States in the early twenty-first century). Femia (1981) explained that hegemony, including that of dominant, or major, religions within a society or culture, "is a predominance obtained by consent rather than force of one class or group over other classes" (p. 24).

People do not always explicitly provide that consent, however, but may imply it through the passive reception of a message. This predominance arises from the communication of certain recurrent, accepted, and "shared beliefs," rather than the imparting of information (Carey, 1989, p. 18). As a conduit for those shared beliefs, media provide a cultural function of providing a selective construction of social knowledge, which Hall (1977) called a "world of the whole" (pp. 340–341). Thus, the totality of mass media messages, rather than a purposive conveying of a certain viewpoint, reflects what people generally think of as either the truth/reality or a representation of it. Continuation of those beliefs depends on the receivers' acceptance or "tacit approval" of them as common sense or at least as not threatening to already held beliefs (Dow, 1990, p. 262).

Because media serve as a mirror of cultural views, the intersection of religion and television becomes an ideal site to examine hegemonic notions about religion. Within American culture, there exists a dominant core of cultural beliefs, values, and practices, and television serves as a primary manifestation of what one generally can consider the cultural mainstream (Signiorelli & Morgan, 1996). For example, Cowan (2010) noted a "cultural hegemony of Christianity" among science fiction films and television shows, pointing to the Christ allegory in the film *The Matrix* as an example. Hegemony theory becomes useful as an explanation for the dominance of Christianity on U.S. network television because it accounts for why certain ideas, attitudes, and values become prevalent.

In order for hegemony to continue, it needs something to compare itself to: alternative ideologies that threaten the ones that have come to be accepted as common sense (what "everybody knows"). Thus, it also allows for the inclusion, even if only symbolic and temporary, of other worldviews. This acknowledgment of non-hegemonic, alternative ideas, values, and "reality" (as far as one can ascertain from media messages) serves as a necessary component of hegemony, in that hegemony needs resistance in order to keep functioning. The inclusion of other points of view reinforces what is already known and accepted because the "Other" is different and unfamiliar: "In this process, one protects the dominant ideology from radical change by incorporating small amounts of oppositional ideology" (Dow, 1990, p. 262).

Related to this requirement of hegemony theory to include counterhegemonic viewpoints, Hoover (2002) noted that scholarship on the intersection between the social institutions of religion and mass media has formed along the lines of demarcation between mainstream and other marginal forms and practices. Thus, according to Hoover, mass media "are significant for the ability to bring marginalized voices (both domestic and foreign) into contexts where they have traditionally not been accessible" (p. 5).

The inclusive-yet-exclusive nature of religious plurality on television becomes acute when we consider how the diversity of religious portrayals holds the potential to widen viewers' awareness of other religions aside from those most often depicted in mainstream media. Yet, that inclusion simultaneously also has the power to reinforce the dominant worldview offered by mass media as a whole, even if that viewpoint does not necessarily reflect the state of things as they are.

Homiletics

As mentioned earlier, Clark's (2003) analysis of the horror genre and its relevance to the purpose of evangelicalism pre-dated *Supernatural*, but we see her observations as highly applicable to how this particular television series both reflects and contradicts, to a degree, past "recent" programs in this genre. In particular speaking to the religious-based, but not really religious, horror series *Buffy the Vampire Slayer* and *Angel*, Clark wrote, "Like most fictional stories in popular culture . . . they are not only at some distance from organized religion, but approach its claims and its traditions with irreverence and ambivalence" (p. 73). This is true of *Supernatural* as well. Indeed, several episodes have leaned decidedly toward the comedic side. In addition to an overall or general stance regarding various lore and religious-based entities encountered by the Winchesters, certain storylines forward lessons based in religious writings, namely, the Bible, and, specifically, the New Testament.

Bullock (1994) pointed out that in order for a religious message, or homily, to strike a chord with an audience, it must actually create an experiential encounter between scripture and the audience. Homiletics thus refers to the audience-centered practice that encourages audience members to see their own lived experiences through the lessons found in religious scripture (Fiorenza, 2003; Swearingen, 2005). We see *Supernatural*'s more serious side in terms of religion and lessons of morality evoked through the use of homiletics, the practice of relating "real" life to the lessons of Scripture.

Regarding the association between rhetoric and homiletics, religious studies scholars argue that homilies should not be considered rhetoric, while rhetoricians typically define everything as potentially rhetorical. This schism offers a modern-day manifestation of the Platonic perception many original Church fathers held of rhetoric as dangerous and not religious in nature (Murphy, 1960). Despite the fact that many of those same early church leaders learned how to preach in Roman schools of rhetoric, it was not until Augustine of Hippo and his book *De Doctrina* (*On Christian Doctrine*) (1958) that someone clearly articulated a way of bridging the differences between religious discourse and rhetoric.

In the Augustinian tradition, rhetoric seeks meaning in a text, and for one to properly understand a text, whether sacred or secular, one must view it within the particular cultural context in which the rhetor produced it. Augustine, in *On Christian Doctrine* (1958), asserted that in order to construct an effective homily, the rhetor must have an education in sacred Scripture, since homilies aim to teach Scripture to an audience. He called for a balance between scriptural interpretation, on the one hand, and the mode in which the message itself is delivered, on the other: "There are two things necessary to the treatment of the scripture: a way of discovering those things which are to be understood, and a way of teaching what we have learned" (p. 7). With regard to the latter point, Augustine firmly believed that the narrative structure and truth inherent in the Bible remains intact throughout history, but its lessons, principles, and values can apply to a variety of different contextual situations over time.

Indeed, fictional mediated stories as reflections of contemporary culture in a given context can serve homiletic purposes, whether narratives rely on Scripture or not. For example, *Star Trek*, in its various permutations on television and specifically in the film *The Final Frontier*, incorporated religions and mythology into its storylines that did not specifically invoke or invite belief or conversion. Rather, it forwarded lessons about dealing with the unexplainable or unknown. As Kraemer, Cassidy, and Schwartz (2003) explained, the *Star Trek* universe may contain godlike beings and practitioners of religions, but does not forward "God" as "some kind of Western monotheist notion" (p. 56).

Hills's (2005) work on the pleasures of horror also relates to how homiletics becomes useful in analyzing the content of religious-related mass media. Hills asserted that in addition to offering "fascination and curiosity at impossible, monstrous beings," the themes or lessons of horror can involve "disclosure plots that resemble the 'proofs' of philosophy" (p. 23). In *Sacred Space*, Cowan (2010) focused on science fiction's ability to reflect and appropriate the Bible, and how science fiction movies and television programs may not depict lived religion, but center on "mystical answers" to the big question of humans' place in the universe (p. 258). Related to homiletics, Cowan further saw that storylines may contain elements of contemporary popular culture that "reflects or approximates" aspects of biblical teachings, such as those found in the Gospel (pp. 268–269).

Using Divine Authority: Combining Secular and Religious Identities

Americans have long thought of themselves as special, unique, and different from the rest of the world. Scholars have identified this belief as the myth of American Exceptionalism, which finds its roots in the Puritans of the seventeenth century. "A Model of Christian Charity" by John Winthrop contains the now-oft quoted statement that America is like a "city on a hill" (Winthrop, 1630). Ideas about America and Americans—ones framing them as different and better than other nations and peoples—that germinated at the inception of the United States continue today, with politicians from former Speaker of the House Newt Gingrich to President Barack Obama openly debating the special nature of the United States. Taken together, these notions about America's place on the world scene have given scholars an entire area of study known as American Exceptionalism. These notions appear in both political and, to a lesser degree, popular culture texts (Edwards & Weiss, 2011; McKrisken, 2003; Hodgson, 2009; Soderlind & Taylor, 2011).

American Exceptionalism embodies three distinct emphases: (a) The United States is a special nation with a special destiny ordained by God; (b) the United States is qualitatively different from the Old Europe, which was beset by corruption; and (c) the United States will escape the ruinous fate of other great civilizations because of its divine mission and perpetual state of improvement. These notions manifest in two entirely different ways in the political arena. Although there may exist a common and accepted belief regarding the exceptional nature of the United States, the two main avenues for putting this belief into policy look at this "responsibility" as either serving as an example for others to emulate, or actively intervening and promoting "American" values elsewhere. Regardless, the idea of the special nature and destiny of the United States has become a core component of American culture, whose roots originate in a sense of the divine. As G. K. Chesterton (2009, originally published in 1922) famously quipped, the United States is a "nation with a soul of a church" (p. 10).

The idea that the nation is special has evolved into specific approaches to policy, such as westward expansion, which in turn spawned new powerful cultural myths for the American people. The Frontier Myth encapsulates this notion; its most clearly seen manifestation became the idealized American West, a story which explains how America conquered from sea to shining sea, so to speak, and now serves as a justification for movement in other social contexts. Bercovitch (1978) traced the roots of the Frontier Myth to the Puritans in early New England, in much the same vein as American Exceptionalism. The popular story of the Puritans tells a tale of a group that emigrated to the New World in the hopes of creating a community that respected freedom of religion. As Bercovitch pointed out, this story creates "a moral framework within which a certain complex of attitudes, assumptions, and beliefs can be taken for granted as being not only proper, but right" (p. 41). On screen, one finds the iconic hero of the Frontier Myth in the archetypal "cowboy" who, astride a horse, violently fights against those who would do harm to the American way of life.

These mythologies serve to tie America to God and goodness, and they also serve to contribute to another, more potent and perceivable aspect of American culture and identity. The United States, as a divinely ordained nation blessed by God, also has its own civil religious elements. The Constitution, for example, serves as the equivalent of the Bible, while figures such as George Washington and Abraham Lincoln take on a divine identity in American history. Certain Christian holidays are often celebrated as national, state, or local holidays as well—and yet in this civil religion God becomes "flattened" in much the same way as Christianity is in successful mass media. Presidents and, in effect, the American people, tie their cultural and national identity to religion without being religious.

We see these elements, which inform the American mythos, as a way to view *Supernatural*'s protagonists, the American demon hunters Dean and Sam Winchester, whose destiny to save the world from demons and other nefarious forces mirrors the self-perceived view of America as saving the world from evildoers, especially those that originate from outside the Judeo-Christian religious tradition that accompanied the Puritans when they arrived in the new land and who sought religious freedom. In *Supernatural*, as we illustrate, the Winchesters serve as stand-ins for America writ large, and wander the country protecting the supernatural and religious frontier from evil Others in the same way America asserts an interventionist exceptionalism at times with its foreign policy. By doing so, they also convert those they save or set on the "straight and narrow" path to seeing the world their way: the American, Judeo-Christian way.

SUPERNATURAL AS NEXUS

As "America's central institution for storytelling" (Thorburn, 1987, p. 172), television becomes a way that civil society disseminates a social hegemony, a common-sense thinking about ways of life. As a popular culture artifact, *Supernatural* offers richly layered texts for analyzing the complexity *and* simplicity of the human condition. Set in a world where the fantastic is real, its horror stories reflect what Clark (2003) called "today's plural religious landscape" where a range of religious traditions "may be viewed as equally possible and plausible—or equally fictional" (p. 228). We seek to uncover how its composite discourse illustrates a religious hegemony by presenting a religious plurality.

Even as it offers a multi-faith landscape that brings to life ancient religions, *Supernatural* manages to simultaneously incorporate homilies based in New Testament passages that provide commentary on contemporary life. The creative ways in which Bible lessons become part of the series' narrative illustrate how hermeneutics and homiletics function, even within a secular text. The "Americanism" embodied by the protagonists of the *Supernatural* story, the Winchester family of "hunters," forwards a hegemonic civil religion informed by the myths of America: the Frontier Myth and American Exceptionalism. In these ways, we aim to add to the understanding of how hegemony functions through media messages that not only entertain but also to instruct.

Our investigation into how popular culture achieves the "gentle persuasion" explained by hegemony starts with chapter 2—Plurality of Religion, in which we provide an overview and history of *Supernatural*. The show's main storyline had viewers following the adventures of Sam and Dean Winchester as they travel the country hunting demons and monsters. The show originally featured antagonists from pagan cults and urban legends, and incorporated various religions and lore into its episodes. These encounters with pre-Christian deities have continued even as the Winchesters have dealt with "real" angels as found in the Judeo-Christian tradition. In addition to an overview of the series, we explain how its religious-oriented themes and storylines present a plurality of religions.

In chapter 3, Hegemony of Religion, we delve into the findings of our analysis of the series' variety of religions and folklore that find their origins in "real life" and historical documentation. We discuss how a religious hegemony that forwards Christianity, and notably Catholicism, emerged over the course of the series as the main and most powerful opponent of evil. Non-

Catholic, non-Christian religions and their associated villainous characters, in contrast, are vanquished by the protagonists, thus contributing to the series' and U.S. television's hegemony of religion.

Supernatural's fourth and fifth seasons featured a story arc that had the forces of Heaven and Hell recruiting the Winchester brothers to serve as combatants in an eventual Christian Apocalypse. In chapter 4, Horsemen and Homilies, we look at how episodes from this story arc, informed by Revelation 6:2-8, provide homiletic messages about life grounded in episodes depicting the Four Horsemen. We argue that as a "new church," television offers a cultural space where homiletic messages can reach audiences through the filter of programs such as *Supernatural*, thus actively enacting a hegemonic faith tradition.

The application of hegemony carries over into chapter 5, A Divinely Ordained Civil Religion, when we analyze the religious origins related to the Winchesters' family business of "saving people, hunting things." We discuss how *Supernatural*'s demon-hunting heroes themselves embody a Christian-based American mythology throughout the show. We explore how these two characters serve as modern manifestations of the iconic cowboy character central to the secular Frontier Myth in American culture. We further explore how the characters serve as a vehicle to promote an interventionist interpretation of the myth of American Exceptionalism that also reinforces the idea that the United States is a nation chosen by God. We argue that the Winchester brothers represent a particular understanding of how special Americans are and what that status requires of them in the world. In this role the Winchester characters gradually assert even more authority than any other religious tradition, and thus bring a new message about God to viewers—a message that serves as a metaphor for America's place in the "real" world.

We review our findings in chapter 6. In our conclusion, we summarize this unique series' ability to present religious themes via entertainment by relying on a combination of horror and fantasy genres to convey a Christianity without Christ. In addition to reviewing the findings of our analyses, we discuss how this particular program provides a conduit for religious messages, messages that speak to the continued role of faith in today's "modern" world.

NOTES

1. Portions of this chapter appear in "Demon Hunters and Hegemony: Portrayal of Religion on the CW's *Supernatural*" by E. Engstrom & J. M. Valenzano, III, an article whose final and definitive form, the Version of Record, has been published in the *Journal of Media and Religion*, 2010, copyright Taylor & Francis, available online at: http://www.tandfonline.com/, Article DOI: 10.1080/15348421003738785, and in "Horsemen and Homilies: Revelation in the CW's *Supernatural*" by J. M. Valenzano, III, and E. Engstrom in *Journal of Communication and Religion* (2013, Vol. 36, Issue 1, pp. 50-72), The Religious Communication Association.

2. We attribute our approach to mass media scholar Jane Marcellus, who inspired us to view *Supernatural* as literature. As literature, it is thus deserving of criticism and treatment as a literary artifact.

3. The 2008 figures also appear in the U.S. Census Bureau's *Statistical Abstract of the United States 2012*, in the table "Self-Described Religious Identification of Adult Population: 1990, 2001 and 2008." Retrieved from http://www.census.gov/compendia/statab/2012/tables/12s0075.pdf.

4. Directed by Bill Paxton, who played the role of "Dad," *Frailty*'s surprise ending has one of the Meiks boys actually revealed to be a demon. During the course of the film, the young Fenton Meiks continually questions Dad's motives and serves as the conscience of the story, allowing the viewer to sympathize with him and wonder if Dad is indeed a deranged psychopath. The younger brother Adam, however, never questions Dad—he grows up to become a sheriff (played by Matthew McConaughey) and destroys his brother, who has become a serial murderer. Film critic Roger Ebert called the film "an extraordinary work," noting how the production team created "a complex film with the intensity of a simple one" (Ebert, 2002). *Frailty* is available on DVD through Lionsgate Home Entertainment.

5. Forgacs, as editor of *The Antonio Gramsci Reader* (Gramsci, 2000), provides a historical context for Gramsci's theoretical work. In 1928, during his trial for violating "parliamentary immunity" along with other Communist party leaders—basically, he was a political prisoner—the prosecutor who argued for Gramsci's imprisonment allegedly said, "For twenty years we must stop this brain from working" (p. 21). Such was the threat Gramsci's writings posed.

Chapter Two

Plurality of Religion[1]

The narrative of *Supernatural* centers on Sam and Dean Winchester, two brothers from Lawrence, Kansas. Their father, John, has raised them as "hunters" of paranormal creatures, notably demons who possess humans. Their mother, Mary, was killed by a demon when the brothers were very young. John then became determined to find the demon that killed Mary, starting the Winchesters' journey on the roads of America. After the death of John in season two, the brothers, now in their twenties, are left on their own as they take on "jobs" around the country, which they find via news reports of strange happenings that occasionally also coincide with portents of evil. Helped by "Uncle" Bobby Singer (played by Jim Beaver), their father's friend and fellow demon hunter, the altruistic brothers roam the land protecting and saving innocent people from evil.

Many episodes during the first three seasons were essentially ghost stories, in which the brothers served as "ghostbusters," either exterminating vengeful spirits, or helping spirits of those wrongfully murdered to "find peace." Though the program at first did not make clear the destination of ghosts who do "move on," an underlying sense of an afterlife hinted at some kind of reality beyond the rational world. The existence of Heaven, Hell, and Purgatory became revealed in later seasons, however, affirming that there exists somewhere to "go" once a spirit releases itself from its earthly dimension. Other storylines had the brothers encountering monsters and creatures with origins in folklore, either local or from other cultures and eras.

The series reifies to urban legends as well, such as "Bloody Mary," the "Hook Man," and the story of the ghostly appearance of a "woman in white." All three became the focus of episodes in the series' first season. One may recall these familiar tales of urban legends and ghosts as spooky campfire stories common in childhood. For example, a children's game, popular among young girls, invokes "Bloody Mary" by looking into a mirror at night and repeating the name "Bloody Mary," in hopes of witnessing her appearance (if the reader has ever tried this, it does not work, but creates a sense of dread nevertheless). In the season one episode "Bloody Mary" (Episode 1.5), the brothers dispatched her after discovering she was a ghost inhabiting a mirror.

The "Hook Man" legend involves variations of a story that has an escaped psychopath with a hook for a hand roaming the countryside in search of victims. At the end of the story, he somehow or another leaves his hook on the car door of a young couple, who is usually making out while stranded in the woods or some remote locale. The Winchester brothers encounter a vengeful spirit that appears as this legendary figure in "Hook Man" (Episode 1.7).

The story of the "Woman in White" usually centers on a young woman who walks along remote roads and gets picked up by sympathetic passersby who only later find out she is really a ghost. One of the authors remembers being told that this was a true story on the island of Oahu, Hawaii; however, one can probably trace this legend to just about anywhere in the United States. The woman in white ghost story serves as the plotline in *Supernatural*'s premiere episode, the generically titled "Pilot" (Episode 1.1).

As evidence of the series' purposeful use of "actual" myths, ghost stories, and monsters from the so-called real world, several popular books explore the "lore" and legends depicted in *Supernatural,* with explanations for their origins. These serve as handbooks for fans and include *The* Supernatural *Book of Monsters, Spirits, Demons, and Ghouls* (Irvine, 2007) and *The Mythology of* Supernatural: *The Signs and Symbols Behind the Popular TV Show* (Brown, 2011).

Supernatural Magazine, the "official" magazine for the show (Edwards, 2009a), also provides fans with what one might consider educational material regarding the origins of the urban legends and monsters featured in episodes. The article "Know Your Legend" (2008) gave readers information about various pagan gods, such as Druids and Norse gods; mystical objects related to the winter solstice (the beginning of Christmas traditions) monsters such as the Native American *wendigo*, which the article explains comes from an Ojibwe legend and various urban legends, such as the aforementioned Bloody Mary and the Hook Man. The season three episode "The Magnificent Seven" (Episode 3.1) centered on demons embodying the Seven Deadly Sins. In "Know Your Legend," the reader learns that the demons represented the seven deadly capital sins from the early Catholic Church "formalized by Pope Gregory the Great in the 6th century" (p. 53) and described in literature by Dante Alighieri in his epic poem *The Divine Comedy.*

Expanded explanations of the creatures and monsters prominent in episode narratives that comprise "Myths & Legends," a regular feature in *Super-*

natural Magazine, include the origins of these entities as based in folklore, historical accounts and books, and religious teachings, such as those from the Catholic Church, as well as the Bible. Readers learn that sirens come from Greek myth, notably Homer's *Odyssey* (Mathews, 2009b). In an article on ghouls, readers learn that ghouls have origins in Japanese folklore, and a fascination and revulsion regarding treatment of the dead helped to account for the sensationalism surrounding crimes involving cadaver suppliers in 1820s Scotland (Nelson, 2009–2010). Japanese folklore and myths serve as the bases for a variety of ghosts, monsters, and shape-shifters with evil intent, including the *kitsune* and *shojo* (Nelson, 2013), which served as "monsters of the week" in season six. In an article on Samhain, the Celtic "commander of demons and spirit," Mathews (2009a) cited an 1827 book titled *The Celtic Druids*. Other articles in the "Myths and Legends" column inform readers that fairies derive from British and Scottish folklore (Nelson, 2011a), while vampires and werewolves have origins in European folklore (Nelson, 2010a; Nelson 2010c).

Supernatural Magazine adds to an impression of authenticity for program episodes, even though one easily could find out about the "real" stories of the creatures, demons, and gods on the show from other sources. This becomes enhanced when the curious viewer/fan finds that the official magazine for *Supernatural* includes citations from religious sources or ties the creatures depicted on the TV show to "real" religions. Specific biblical references in "Myths & Legends" articles provide background for episode storylines and overarching season narratives. These include items on the Anti-Christ, Armageddon, the "Beast," and the Whore of Babylon as described in the Book of Revelation (Nelson, 2011b). "Cures" for werewolves, according to Nelson (2010c), included "converting the sufferer to Christianity" as well as exorcism (p. 30).

Several creatures are specifically associated with Catholicism and the history of the Catholic Church in some way. Connections to Catholicism appear in articles on demons (Nelson, 2009a), witches (Nelson, 2010b), and the rugaru, a creature from Cajun lore that hunted down Catholics who broke the rules of Lent (Nelson, 2009b). In *Supernatural*, the Winchesters fight demons or expel them from their human hosts and send them back to Hell via exorcism. As depicted on the show, this process requires artifacts such as holy water and Latin incantations based in the Catholic rite.

The inclusion of Judeo-Christian mythology requires a suspension of disbelief—or just belief—that relies on the existence of Hell, and implying, but not explicitly acknowledging the existence of a Heaven or Paradise. In the *Supernatural* world, Heaven does exist, as the Winchesters discovered in the season five episode "Dark Side of the Moon" (Episode 5.16). In the version of Heaven depicted in the episode, the Axis Mundi appears as a road that leads the brothers to their fondest memories, what they considered "heaven" to them. In Heaven, they meet their old fellow hunter friend Ash, who tells them he has met Albert Einstein, adding, "That man can mix a White Russian [cocktail]" (Dabb, Loglin, & Woolnough, 2010). Thus, along with ghosts, depictions of the afterlife become part of the reality in the world of the Winchesters.

In this chapter, we explore the supernatural world of *Supernatural* and the range of religions, mythologies, and lore that presents to viewers a plurality of faiths and beliefs. Our investigation relies on two separate analyses: one conducted using the first three seasons of the show, the second using all episodes aired as of the conclusion of the eighth season. We present our findings using simple frequency counts to provide a context for discussion of how certain religions and folklore become framed as either familiar or the "Other." Although many episodes of *Supernatural* may not contain or allude to religion at all, those that do invite the critical viewer (us) to conduct a closer reading that may reveal a certain viewpoint. This in turn allows for an application of hegemony theory, which we offer after presenting our findings.

RANGE OF RELIGIONS: SEASONS ONE THROUGH THREE

In an interview on TV.com, series creator Eric Kripke emphasized the cross-cultural aspect of the show's inclusion of religious/folkloric-based creatures: "We borrow from every world religion, every culture . . . So you really have this cross-pollination of different demons, different creatures, all from different religions" (Surette, 2008). When asked about the series' direction toward a Christian-based portrayal of demons fought by the protagonists, Kripke countered that characterization: "We don't really consider it a Christian demonology as much as it is just more of a focus in demonology" (Surette, 2008).

As with the urban legends and folklore that serve as bases for scripts, the show's writers report that Kripke was "keen on getting the facts straight" regarding myths, legends, and even religions (Knight, 2008). In a *Supernatural Magazine* article on the show's writing process, staff writer Cathryn Humphris related the importance for Kripke to ground the series as much as possible in reality, to ensure "everything we're doing comes from a real urban legend or just finding out the reality behind these stories" (Knight, 2008, p. 35). This includes the use of religious artifacts. For example, several episodes show demon hunters frequently using a religious diagram used to bind demons, known as the Devil's Trap, which, according to Humphris, "is a real thing we found in some ancient text" (p. 35).

Prior to the Bible-based narrative that has permeated the series over its last five seasons, the program focused mainly on how its protagonists dealt with a variety of enemies drawn from tales of the weird and otherworldly. To track how the series treated religion prior to the introduction of more overtly religious-based elements, such as the existence of angels based in Judeo-Christian theology, we conducted an exploratory content analysis of *Supernatural*'s first three seasons. Both of us were familiar with the series as casual, infrequent viewers prior to deciding to seriously conduct research on the show. Regarding familiarity with religious images and practices that informed our reading of episodes, we both identify as Roman Catholic; one is currently practicing, the other is not.

In our first study of *Supernatural*, we examined religious portrayals in the first three complete seasons using the total of 60 episodes aired from 2005 until 2008 (Engstrom & Valenzano, III, 2010).[2] We identified main antagonists or enemies of the Winchesters as being creatures or monsters, such as vampires, shape-shifters, or witches (21 episodes; 35%); ghosts or vengeful spirits (16 episodes; 27%); demons from Hell (13; 22%); humans (8 episodes; 13%); or curses or cursed objects (2 episodes; 3%).

Of the 60 episodes, we ascertained no mention of religion in 29 (48%) of them; these were usually stories about ghosts or vengeful spirits, vampires, and humans. We found 34 (57%) episodes that included specific and discernible depictions or mentions of specific religions and "lore," a term used in the series by Sam Winchester to refer to the history and legends behind the creatures and monsters encountered by the brothers that may or may not have actual religious origins. Several episodes contained imagery involving multiple religions or lore, such as "Mystery Spot" (Episode 3.11), which contained Catholic-related images as well as lore from several cultures.

We grouped religious-based depictions into three categories: non-Christian, which includes established religions, such as Hindu and Islam, and practices that involved rituals, such as black magic, hoodoo, paganism, and other beliefs embodied in lore; Catholic; and Protestant Christian. We identified non-Christian religions/beliefs in 19 (32%) episodes. Regarding Christianity, we found Catholicism evident in 12 (20%) episodes, based on the depictions of specific artifacts/weapons used repeatedly to fight demons, such as holy water, Latin incantations, rosaries, or the depiction of priests in some way. We identified three (5%) episodes as depicting nonspecific, Protestant denominations through the imagery of a church or minister we determined as being non-Catholic. Episodes could contain multiple religious references; thus, percentages may not equal 100%.

Regarding specific, discernible religions, we found that over the course of seasons one through three, non-Christian religions tended to involve portrayals of villainous creatures that required their destruction. Of the 60 episodes from the series' first three seasons, 31 episodes that involved religion in some way featured either villainous characters drawn from recognizable, currently practiced religions, or a specific culture's folklore. In turn, 19

(51%) of those 30 religion-related episodes featured characters that were villainous or posed a threat to the Winchesters or humans. For example, Hinduism was represented by the flesh-eating *rakshasa* in "Everybody Loves a Clown" (Episode 2.2), and Islam by the life-draining *djinn*, a creature mentioned throughout the Koran, as noted by Sam in "What Is and What Should Never Be" (Episode 2.20). Though not mentioned specifically as such, we determined that Buddhism was represented by the *tulpa*, a "thought" form or golem-type creature associated with meditative practices of Tibetan monks, in "Hell House" (Episode 1.17). The season one episode "Shadows" (Episode 1.16) included a reference to Zoroastrianism as the source of shadow demons called *daevas*.

We noticed that none of these religions was represented by benign or friendly creatures, nor any kind of helper to assist the brothers in fighting them. We found the absence of such assistance telling, in that the Winchesters must discover the methods needed to fight these creatures themselves. That no helpful characters from these religions are introduced in the episodes results in the impression that nobody representing these religions can, or would want to, help them, consequently leaving the brothers to fight them on their own.

During the first three seasons, black magic, explained in the series as originating in early Christianity, appeared in three episodes (5%). The use of black magic is not reserved for its true believers, as both witches ("Malleus Maleficarum," Episode 3.9) and ordinary, non-witch humans ("Hollywood Babylon," Episode 2.18; "Faith," Episode 1.12) practice it. In all these cases, those who employed black magic—witch or not—were portrayed as evil, using the dark arts for selfish or unsavory purposes.

Throughout the first three seasons of *Supernatural* we also indentified incorporation of non-Christian traditions, ones that depicted gods that required some form of sacrifice in order to be appeased or to simply exist. Norse paganism became manifest as a *vanir*, a pagan god that demands human sacrifice, in "Scarecrow" (Episode 1.11). In "A Very Supernatural Christmas" (Episode 3.8), the Winchesters had to fight a pair of pagan gods who had become used to eating humans as part of the rituals practiced by their followers prior to the arrival of a new faith, one that worshipped Jesus Christ.

If not associated with some kind of religion or religious practice, creatures may originate in "lore," the term regularly used by Sam Winchester to refer to historical legends and myths. When the brothers investigate a case, Sam usually conducts research either online on his laptop or by visiting a local library to determine what creature the brothers are dealing with and how to destroy it. Their Uncle Bobby, who holds an encyclopedic knowledge of supernatural creatures and has his own library of religious and occult-related books, and their deceased father's journal serve as other sources of information.

Myriad monsters from legend appear on the show that the brothers, mainly Sam, identify as rooted in cultural histories. For example, Sam finds out that the Native American *wendigo*, a cannibalistic creature, originates from a Cree legend ("Wendigo," Episode 1.2). A Yuchi tribe curse causes insects to attack people ("Bugs," Episode 1.8). The *shtriga* is a soul-sucking witch based in Albanian and ancient Roman lore ("Something Wicked," Episode 1.18). The *crocotta* is a human-eating creature actually based in ancient Greek legend, though its origins are not specifically mentioned in the episode in which it appears ("Long Distance Call," Episode 3.14). In "The Kids Are Alright" (Episode 3.2), the brothers kill a changeling that goes after mothers by taking the place of their children. The Trickster serves as the only recurring supernatural enemy besides demons. He confronts Dean and Sam in two episodes ("Tall Tales," Episode 2.15; "Mystery Spot," Episode 3.11). When the brothers first encounter him, fellow demon hunter Uncle Bobby tells them that the Trickster is known as the Norse god Loki and as Anansi in West Africa.

We concluded after our initial examination of *Supernatural*'s first 60 episodes that the show illustrated a religious hegemony regarding Christianity. Of the episodes that referenced religion in some way, which we determined occurred in 34 episodes, we identified 15 (44%) as having to do in some way with Christianity. Of those episodes, Catholicism appeared in almost all of them (12 episodes; 80%).

We identified as Catholic those episodes that featured demons from Hell, the presence of Catholic-based artifacts, and priests. Catholicism serves as the origin and source for weapons used to fight evil on *Supernatural*. The Winchesters and their fellow hunters regularly use holy water and Latin in their "profession" of hunting. The Winchesters use these artifacts against demons, the main and most powerful agents of evil they fight, which led us to contend that Catholicism appeared to have "the edge" over other religions and faiths.

Even though we indentified a Catholic-oriented slant, we saw *Supernatural* as making a serious effort at being inclusive regarding religion, as Miles (1997) had suggested. However, our initial analysis led us to contend that *Supernatural* portrayed characters drawn from other faiths as generally evil. No positive characters appeared as originating from these "outside" religions. Combined with the lack of help from anyone practicing or familiar with these other forms of faith, the resulting impression we got regarding non-Christian, and specifically non-Catholic, religions suggested a marginalization of the "Other." That is, this "Otherness" emerged when we considered the nature of the creatures associated with particular religions.

Online posts have addressed the way the series has portrayed religion, noting how the show moved toward a positive portrayal of Christianity as it stayed on the air. For example, Vollick's (2008) web post on the site Telewatcher.com provides an informal comparison between how the show portrayed pagan gods and witches and the validation of Christian objects as effective weapons against demons. This, Vollick contended, is because the "use of Christian symbols and villains most likely get better responses because Christianity is so culturally ingrained in American society," while negative portrayals of pagan gods and witches "is due to the fact that the majority of Americans are Christians." Considering the nature of the portrayals of non-Christian characters, the plurality of religions included on *Supernatural* tends to lead back to the centrality of Christianity, similar to what Lewis (2002) found.

RANGE OF RELIGIONS: SEASONS ONE THROUGH EIGHT

Beginning in season four, *Supernatural* introduced angels with biblical names. These angels used terminology such as "Our Father," "the Lord," and "Perdition," a direct Christian reference to *Purgatorio* as found in Dante's *The Divine Comedy*. A major story arc developed during season four that involved an impending confrontation wherein the forces of evil would engage humankind in an all-out war: Armageddon. Just as it had previously explained the origins of the monsters and creatures from past seasons, *Supernatural Magazine* eventually included explanations of the origin of angels. In the "Myths and Legends" article on angels, Edwards (2009b) explained that in the Old Testament of the Bible, angels serve as guards and warriors of God; Roman Catholic texts associated certain angels with days of the week; and categories of angels include archangels, seraphim, cherubim, thrones, and lower ranks. Edward also referred to the books of the Bible that mention them. For example, "nephilim" appear in the Book of Enoch,[3] "thrones" in Daniel, and other angels in the New Testament Book of Ephesians (p. 28).

In their chapter in the edited book *TV Goes to Hell: An Unofficial Road Map to* Supernatural, Wimmler and Kienzil (2011) addressed the Judeo-Christian origins of the angels who have become a permanent part of the cast of characters on the show. The use of phrases such as "angel of the Lord" and names of angels found in the Old and New Testaments of the Bible and other sources add to the authenticity of religious portrayals in the series. Wimmler and Kienzel's explanation of the sources for the portrayals of angels on the show reflect an amalgamation of Jewish, Protestant, and Catholic influence. They further noted that non-religious sources have been incorporated into categories of good and bad angels, notably regarding Lucifer. As a "fallen angel" he nevertheless retains the supernatural powers associated with archangels. They explained that additional sources can account for this: "While the idea of good and evil angels is absent from the writings of the Old Testament, at the time of the New Testament the concept of a fallen army of angels was a popular folk theme that occupied an important place in subsequent Christian beliefs" (p. 180).

As of the spring of 2013, *Supernatural* had been on the air for eight seasons, resulting in a total episode count of 172. We wanted to determine the range of religions and religious influences that would give a composite picture of the show's portrayal of religions. The season four introduction of angels and the Apocalypse story arc that ended with season five resulted in a more pronounced presence of characters based in the Judeo-Christian tradition, including biblical references as well as accompanying religious material on the hierarchy of Heaven. Further, seasons six and seven continued to include an overarching narrative based in dogma and heavenly hierarchy; the Winchesters learned of the existence of Purgatory and tablets containing "the word of God" that had the power of closing Hell and Heaven.

We conducted a follow-up analysis that used frequency counts to find out whether or not the results from our original study of the series' first three seasons held when we considered all 172 episodes.[4] Viewing of episodes from seasons four through eight included watching them during initial airings, then subsequently on DVD (seasons four through seven), and, for season eight, as recorded on DVR or VCR.[5] As we did in our initial study, we based our coding of episodes from subsequent seasons on imagery and mentions of religions or origins of characters in the episodes themselves.

For this new analysis, we determined the presence of religion using the categories "Catholic," "Christian," "non-Christian," and "none." In order to ascertain how the series reflected a religious aspect in general, episodes might include elements of more than one category, so we determined which category best reflected the episode's narrative and imagery. Regarding the category "Catholic," we considered an episode as relating to Catholicism either as a main aspect of the narrative or as relating to Catholicism if we detected the following: holy water, use of Latin (as used in exorcisms against demons or other purposes, such as incantations), holy oil/holy fire, rosaries and crucifixes, priests, or Purgatory. These determinants were used based on their origination and use in the Catholic Church, or, as in the case of Purgatory, a central tenet in dogma. Purgatory became prominent during season seven, when Dean "died" and found himself in Purgatory.[6]

In addition to coding for religion, we again identified antagonists featured in episodes; these included those fought directly by the Winchesters or those who posed a threat in some way to either the brothers, or the world in general. We extended our initial coding scheme to include new types of enemies that appeared after season three, specifically, angels from Heaven and gods from non-Christian religions and traditions. Of the 172 episodes in the population of episodes from the eight seasons, we determined that the main antagonist or enemy was a creature or monster, which included vampires, shape-shifters, and witches (56 episodes; 33%); demon (35 episodes; 20%); ghosts or vengeful spirits (27 episodes; 16%); gods (14; 8%); humans (15 episodes; 9%); angels from Heaven (14 episodes, 8%); or curses or cursed objects (5 episodes; 3%). Although episodes could include mentions of more than one type of enemy, for purposes of describing the nature of *Supernatural*'s treatment of evil or bad things that appear, we decided to limit each episode to one of these categories.

We also considered some antagonists as not accurately falling into these general categories. Specifically, these included Lucifer, who technically would be considered an angel given his origin, and the Four Horsemen of the Apocalypse, who appeared in special episodes in which plots revolved around finding and vanquishing them.[7] Though Lucifer appeared in several episodes in seasons four and five, we categorized him as the main enemy of one episode, "Swan Song," when the Winchesters actually had to do battle with him. The Four Horsemen played prominent roles as part of the Winchesters' efforts to avert the Apocalypse; we saw them as main opponents in four episodes. What sets *Supernatural* apart from other horror or science fiction shows is that angels from Heaven are depicted as being just as, or even more, evil than demons from Hell. When considered as a type of enemy, then, our counts show that angels appear as main enemies (14; 8%) as often as gods from non-Christian religions and mythologies (14; 8%) and humans (15; 9%).

Of the 172 episodes in our follow-up analysis, we found 62 (36%) as mentioning no religion; 52 (30%) as specifically Catholic or related to Catholicism, which included the use of Latin; 38 (22%) as having to do with Christianity, excluding Catholicism; and 49 (28%) as non-Christian, which included portrayals or mentions of practices such as black magic, Wiccan, paganism and pagan mythologies, and established religions such as Islam, Shinto, or Judaism. In that episodes could include imagery or mentions of multiple religions, percentages could exceed a total of 100%. For example, of the episodes categorized as having protagonists or main plotlines that do not reflect a particular religion, we found four that had some aspects of Catholicism. Black magic appeared in 11 episodes either exclusively or in addition to another general religious category.

Of the 172 total episodes, we found 27 in which a ghost of some kind appeared as the main antagonist. Vengeful spirits represented people whose souls came back to seek revenge on the living. The typical weapons used by hunters against ghosts include salt and iron; eradication requires burning the remains of the person whose ghost has returned. As Cowan (2008) noted, ghost stories serve as common narratives in most cultures. Even though the ghost stories in *Supernatural* largely reflect a non-religious aspect, not relat-

Table 2.1.　Frequency of Religions, Seasons 1-3 and Seasons 1-8

	Seasons 1-3 N = 60 episodes	Seasons 1-8 N = 172 episodes
No mention of religion	29 (48%)	62 (36%)
Non-Christian religions	19 (32%)	49 (28%)
Catholicism	12 (20%)	52 (30%)
Protestant Christian	3 (5%)	38 (22%)

ing specifically to a particular religion (we categorized 16 of the 27 as having no religions or practices mentioned), the very nature of the idea of a soul or spirit that returns to the world of the living speaks to the concept of life after death. In this manner, Cowan observed, "the soul is an explicitly religious concept" (p. 6).

We found that seasonal story arcs in seasons four through eight involving aspects of the Judeo-Christian tradition incorporated antagonists of the Winchesters; "enemies" with whom the brothers had to do battle included angels from Heaven, including archangels as found in the Old and New Testaments, such as Uriel, Raphael, and Michael. Their main opponent, of course, was Lucifer, the fallen angel who defied God and sought to bring the destruction of Heaven as well as the earth. Reference to "super" demons and monsters also became part of this narrative. For example, during season six, the brothers fight "Eve," the mother of all monsters named for the mother of all humankind who appears in the Book of Genesis and whose origins, according to the show, date back 10,0000 years. The Leviathan, a creature also born from passages in the Old Testament ("Bible Verses About Leviathan," n.d.), is unleashed from Purgatory, and also plays a major adversary over the course of season six. The *Supernatural* version of Leviathan has it depicted as a legion of monsters; individually the Leviathan somehow contain themselves within human vessels after devouring them and taking on their form. When they do reveal themselves, they are shown as having enormously large, sharp teeth. The abject evil and depravity of the Leviathan becomes manifest when they eat each other as punishment, or are punished for their own mistakes by their leader, who has taken the form of a corporate mega-mogul named Dick Roman: a Leviathan must literally consume itself by eating its own vessel while still in it ("How to Win Friends and Influence Monsters," Episode 7.9).

While demons serve as a sort of a staple enemy throughout *Supernatural*'s run, the appearance of "major" demons—aside from Azazel, the demon that killed Mary Winchester—becomes more prominent after season four. During season eight, the brothers encounter a "Knight of Hell" known as Abaddon, a demon mentioned in the Old and New Testaments (Maas, 1907).

The character of Crowley, the self-described King of Hell who assumed power after Lucifer's "capture" by the Winchesters at the end of season five, poses the major recurring enemy of the Winchesters and their angel ally Castiel.

When compared to the Winchesters' enemies and their associated religions and lore that appeared during *Supernatural*'s first three seasons, as described previously in this chapter, later seasons appear to introduce a wider range of enemy types that draw from non-Christian religions, practices, or lore. After season three, the Winchesters began to encounter antagonists or characters that included gods or creatures from Greek, Egyptian, and Norse mythologies, most of whom they defeated either by destroying them or essentially making them "go away." For example, over seasons four through eight, the Winchesters vanquished or rid the world of the power of the Celtic god Samhain ("It's the Great Pumpkin, Sam Winchester," Episode 4.7); the Egyptian god Osiris ("Defending Your Life," Episode 7.4); the Mayan god Cacao ("Heartache," Episode 8.3); and Tiamat, the Babylonian god of chaos ("Wishful Thinking," Episode 4.8). They killed Leshii, a pagan god of the forest ("Fallen Idols," Episode 5.5); Veritas, the Roman goddess of truth ("You Can't Handle the Truth," Episode 6.6); Chronos, the Greek god of time ("Time After Time After Time," Episode 7.12); and even Zeus, the Greek god of gods in "Remember the Titans" (Episode 8.16).

The Winchesters encountered gods representing several religions and lore in the season five episode "Hammer of the Gods" (Episode 5.19). The episode featured a sort of convention of the gods, including Balder and Odin from Norse myth and Kali from the Hindu tradition. In this episode, the brothers weren't responsible for the gods' demise. Instead, Lucifer, representing Judeo-Christian mythology literally killed the gods—symbolizing a displacement of other religions. We explain this episode and its implications in more detail in chapter 3, Hegemony of Religion.

As we found in our initial study of the first 60 episodes, black magic makes a few more appearances in subsequent seasons; we identified nine episodes in particular that featured black magic between seasons four and eight. These featured the dark arts as practiced by witches and warlocks ("The Curious Case of Dean Winchester," Episode 5.7; "Man's Best Friend with Benefits," Episode 8.15; "Shut Up, Dr. Phil," Episode 7.5; "Everybody Hates Hitler," Episode 8.13). Humans who used black magic for evil or selfish purposes always met a bad end, specifically, death ("Criss Angel Is a Douchebag," Episode 4.12; "Swap Meat," 5.12; "The Mentalists," Episode 7.7; "Plucky Pennywhistle's Magic Menagerie," Episode 7.14). Taken together, this demonstrates that those who "play" with black magic, as opposed to those who are experts (such as witches), can expect a poor outcome. In others words, the message implies the familiar adage heard in television programs featuring dangerous stunts: "Don't try this at home."

"Wiccan" was mentioned or depicted in two episodes in our sample of 172. While black magic connotes nefarious intent, the use of Wiccan, we observed, tended to be used or uttered for good intent or by a good character. Specifically, though not central to the plot, Wiccan (or "white magic") appeared in the episode "Repo Man" (Episode 7.15); it was practiced by an ally of the Winchesters, a woman trying to track down the demon that possessed her own son. In "Man's Best Friends with Benefits" (Episode 8.15), Dean Winchester posed as a Wiccan to investigate a case involving witches and their familiars—pets that can take human form but are loyal to their owners. In these instances, the representation of Wiccan was associated with "good" characters; those using it or identified as practitioners employed it in fighting nefarious forces. In the WB television series *Charmed*, the protagonists are identified with Wicca, which Meyer (2007) explained is a subsection of witchcraft. Similar to the mission of the Winchester brothers in *Supernatural*, the sister-heroes in *Charmed* "take up the crusade against the demonic population of their home city of San Francisco" (Beeler & Beeler, 2007, p. 1). In this way, one can view Wicca as a force against evil and therefore on the side of good.

Creatures killed or driven away by the Winchesters over seasons four through eight continued to represent a variety of religions and lore. *Djinn*, creatures based in Islamic mythology, made two more reappearances ("Exile on Main St.," Episode 6.1 and "Pac Man Fever," Episode 8.20). The brothers encountered arachnes, spider-like monsters based on the Greek myth of Arachne, in "Unforgiven" (Episode 6.13). They also dealt with creatures based in Greek myth again in "The Slice Girls" (Episode 7.13), when they encountered murderous Amazons, and in "Sex and Violence," when they dispatched a siren. In "Adventures in Babysitting" (Episode 7.11), the brothers killed a pair of *vetalas*, human-eating creatures from Hindu myth, with the help of a young hunter-in-training. Shinto was represented in "Party On, Garth" (Episode 7.18) with an alcohol spirit known as a *shojo*, and in "Weekend at Bobby's" (Episode 6.4), when Uncle Bobby killed an *okami*, a monster that feeds on young women.

In the humorous episode "Clap Your Hands If You Believe" (Episode 6.9), the Winchesters first thought they were investigating aliens from outer space. They later discovered they were dealing with fairies—complete with Irish accents—the source of which we determined as being based in Celtic myth. The fairies caused trouble for some humans; the Winchesters took the advice of a local "fairy expert," who told them fairies could be temporarily stopped from doing harm if one dropped salt or sugar in front of them because they would be compelled to count every grain. The anti-human attitude of these mythic and religious-based creatures also applies to the angels of Heaven, who essentially work against the brothers and humanity rather than protect them the way many current popular versions of angels portray them.

While these creatures had some religious aspect to them, some creatures did not represent particular faiths but did relate to specifically mentioned folklore. The Japanese fascination with horror and ghostly tales, which manifests with apparent regularity in *Supernatural*, appeared in an episode featuring the *buru-buru*, a ghost that instills incredible fear in humans that had Dean running for his life from a tiny Yorkie dog in "Yellow Fever" (Episode 4.6). Examples from Japanese folk tales included the *kitsune*, a shape-shifting creature featured in "The Girl Next Door" (Episode 7.3). Of the various creatures mentioned in "Weekend at Bobby's" (Episode 6.4), the *lamia*, a type of vampire, originates in Greek folklore.

The Winchesters, of course, continued to do some "regular" jobs not associated with the Heaven-and-Hell narrative that began in season four; these had them contend with vengeful spirits and ghosts, vampires, shape-shifters, and evil humans in episodes that we determined did not convey a religion. However, the creatures and gods representing varying religions and mythologies that the Winchesters encountered continued to be cast as evil, either trying to wreak havoc in some way, or harm, kill, or even eat humans. We did find an exception, however, which we see as notable, given the religion the "monster" in question represented.

FINALLY, AN ALLY

We concluded after our first study of the series' initial three seasons that the Winchesters tended to receive no assistance from representatives of the various religions and lore associated with the monsters they had to fight. Starting in season four, the Winchester found a powerful supernatural ally in the angel Castiel, whom we see as representing Christianity, when they began their quest to avert the Apocalypse during seasons four and five. However, their list of allies remained rather sparse; the angels of Heaven play a similar role to the generally evil monsters, creatures, gods, and demons in making the Winchesters' lives difficult as they pursue their own agenda to bring on the end of the world.

In terms of a non-Christian religion or tradition, we finally detected a sympathetic and favorable portrayal of a monster in the season eight episode "Everybody Hates Hitler" (Episode 8.13). The golem, a creature from Jewish folklore, serves as the story's "hero," of sorts. Made from clay and animated with a Hebrew spell, in this episode the golem plays a central role in defeating evil when the Winchesters and the golem's master, a young man named Aaron (a reference to the brother of Moses, as mentioned in the Bible), fight against Nazis who are using black magic to create zombies.

In the episode, the Winchesters investigate the mysterious death of a rabbi ("Rabbi Bass," played by Hal Linden) who has discovered a log book detailing supernatural experiments conducted by a group of Nazi occultists known as the Thule; the log book also contained the names of the Thule members. Luhrssen (2012), in the book *Hammer of the Gods: The Thule Society and the Birth of Nazism*, traced the history of the actual Thule Society and the ideologies it promoted, which included anti-Semitism and Pan-German nationalism. According to Luhrssen, the use of the swastika as the Nazi symbol is attributed to the Thule. Its members, some of whom later became prominent Nazis, also had a "neo-pagan fascination with the old Nordic gods" (p. 15).

The lack of accurate historical scholarship on the Thule, noted Luhrssen, has created a "vacuum" of facts, providing material for entertainment media: "Related ideas of Nazism and its occult roots have found their way into the imaginative literature of fantasy and science fiction" (p. 15). For example, the 2004 film *Hellboy* featured a storyline based on the occultist nature of the Thule-Nazi connection, with imagery associated with the forces of good specifically representing Catholicism (Hellboy himself carries a rosary and crucifix).[8] The Nazis' search for and nefarious use of supernatural artifacts with biblical origins (the Ark of the Covenant) appeared in the 1981 classic film *Raiders of the Lost Ark*; the film served as the inspiration for *Supernatural*'s season-eight story arc (Prudom, 2012).

In *Supernatural*'s treatment of the Thule-Nazi connection, the inclusion of a Jewish weapon used against the forces of evil bolsters the association between the Judeo-Christian religious heritage and the "good" side of World War II. The backstory of the golem in "Everybody Hates Hitler" started during that war, when Rabbi Bass was part of a protective order of rabbis known as the "Judah Initiative"; the group's charge was to protect the Jewish people in times of crisis. The golem, referred to in the episode as "clay of Adam," was used by the Judah Initiative against the Thule in wiping out the Nazi compound in Belarus where they were using black magic to reanimate the dead. In the episode, the evil Thule returned, tracked the rabbi to present day Pennsylvania, and killed him with black magic.

Before his death, the rabbi had bequeathed the golem to his grandson, Aaron, now the last descendant of the Judah Initiative. Aaron had neglected his Jewish religious training, which left the golem "ownerless" and essentially dangerous, prone to breaking and destroying furniture in Aaron's apartment. Seeing the golem as an uncontrollable threat, the Winchesters initially tried to "neutralize" it, but were unsuccessful. Eventually, the brothers team up with Aaron to fight the Thule members who are after the golem. The golem, in essence, becomes part of the team and thereby secures its status as "good" within the *Supernatural* assemblage of monsters and creatures.

The golem plays the part of a weapon against evil. He also has knowledge of Hebrew and Jewish practices. He scolds Aaron for not keeping kosher when he complains to the Winchesters that Aaron "does not perform mitzvahs [worthy deeds], labors on Sabbath, and dines on swine" (Edlund & Sgriccia, 2013). Regarding the depiction of religion on TV, Roof (1997) concluded that fictional television rarely presented audiences with religion as "inherited tradition," and lacked any depictions of spiritual depth or transcendence (p. 66). Here, we see that *Supernatural* succeeds in incorporating a specific inherited tradition: the golem's knowledge of Judaism and subsequent admonishment of one who did not follow its tenets provides an example of how a fictional, or science-fictional, television program can present its audience with some degree of religious instruction in an entertaining way.

Initially reluctant to take on the responsibility of being a member of the Judah Initiative, Aaron finally accepts his duty to take ownership of the golem to continue fighting the Thule. Thus, the golem appears as an ally in the fight against evil, against the Thule and the world in general. In that the golem specifically represents the Jewish faith, we see this as presenting Judaism as the only other established religion besides Christianity, Catholicism in particular, that offers the Winchesters assistance in their battle against threats to humanity.

In addition to the golem and Aaron in "Everybody Hates Hitler," we found two episodes in which allies, or apparent allies, of the brothers represented Judaism. In the season six episode ". . . And Then There Were None" (Episode 6.16), the Winchesters and Uncle Bobby team up with their longtime friend and fellow hunter Rufus Turner. In this episode, Rufus is killed by Bobby, who was possessed by "Eve," the mother of all monsters. After Eve's defeat and Bobby's recovery, the brothers and Bobby bury Rufus. The Winchesters learn that Rufus was in fact Jewish. However, Bobby, tells the brothers, "He didn't exactly keep kosher" (Matthews & Rohl, 2011). Although cremation serves as the common funereal practice among hunters in *Supernatural*, the Winchesters and Bobby instead bury Rufus in a Jewish cemetery. By connecting Rufus, a "good" hunter, with Judaism, this particular religion thereby becomes "good" as well in the world of *Supernatural*. We revisit this episode in terms of its religious aspects in chapter 5, A Divinely Ordained Civil Religion.

We found an additional instance of the portrayal of Judaism as a helpful and "good" religion in the season seven episode "Defending Your Life" (7.4), when the Winchesters encounter the Egyptian god Osiris, who is responsible for a rash of strange deaths. They discover that Osiris has been meting out justice on the perpetrators of crimes on behalf of their victims. The brothers find out from Bobby that they need to stab Osiris with a ram's horn in order to vanquish him (at least temporarily). Sam then goes to a local synagogue to obtain the weapon, after finding out on the Internet that "Jewish people blow through them once a year." Although the temple is closed, Sam breaks in, and finds the ram's horn in the rabbi's office. The rabbi catches him, but does not appear angry. Instead, seeing Sam holding the relic, he quips, "I'm guessing you're not here for bar mitzvah lessons" (Glass & Singer, 2011).

Shortly thereafter, Sam next appears in a scene in which he stabs Osiris with the ram's horn; the god drops dead after apparently becoming mummified and crumbling to dust. The viewer must assume that instead of calling the police, the rabbi had let Sam take the weapon after hearing Sam's explanation for why he needs it. The power of Osiris and the danger he poses becomes even more emphasized because he has chosen Dean to punish; while Sam obtains the ram's horn, Dean is about to be killed by a ghost, who is working under Osiris's power (Dean survives, of course).

The implication that the rabbi understands Sam's motive and Sam may even have the rabbi's blessing in using the ram's horn to defeat Osiris further enhances the goodness of a Jewish character. A closer reading points to the irony of the episode regarding the two forces that appear as "combatants" in this episode. Judaism helps to defeat an Egyptian god, which could be read as an allusion to the biblical story of Moses and the Exodus of the Jews from Egypt in which Moses essentially defeats the pharaoh.

The framing of the golem as a monster that fights on behalf of the Jewish people—against Nazis, no less; the fact that Rufus was Jewish; and the apparently sympathetic rabbi who lends Sam the ram's horn all combine to present a favorable treatment of Judaism as an ally of the Winchesters. When compared to the other established religions associated with the creatures the Winchesters have encountered, Judaism poses the only one not of nefarious intent. Based on our reading of these three episodes that specifically incorporate Judaism in some way, we see a tendency for the show to depict the Judeo-Christian religious tradition as assisting in the Winchesters' battle against the forces of darkness. In particular, Judaism and Catholicism stand out as offering effective weapons against formidable enemies.

RELIGIOUS PLURALITY: LEGITIMIZING THE "OTHER"

Regarding an overall depiction of religions, we see *Supernatural* as making a serious attempt to incorporate other religions and lore into its episodes. Though diversity of religious portrayals holds the potential to widen viewers' awareness of other religions aside from those most often depicted in mainstream media, that inclusion also has the power to reinforce the dominant worldview media offers. Over the past eight seasons, the Winchesters have encountered entities or persons representing Hinduism, Shinto, Islam, Zoroastrianism, Wiccan, Judaism, and Christianity, as well as a slew of other ancient faiths no longer practiced.

The inclusion of non-hegemonic, alternative ideas, values, and "reality" (as far as one can ascertain from media messages) serves as a necessary component of hegemony, in that resistance to hegemony is essential to maintaining it. If one considers Christianity as the most prevalent religious affiliation of the show's intended audience, that is, the U.S. television viewing public, we contend this particular storytelling medium gives legitimacy to pagan religions and mythologies associated with ancient Greece, Rome, and Scandinavia. In other words, *Supernatural* reifies the representations of a wide range of practices and faiths: these representations take on tangible form and make a difference in the lives of the people depicted in the show. The Winchesters, although almost always defeating them, must contend with their physical power with risk to their own safety.

In this sense, we see *Supernatural* as treating the "Other" in a serious way—the gods of old still hold some dominion over the world, even in the twenty-first century. However, the gods in these episodes acknowledge that they no longer hold the same level of power over humans as they once did. For example, in "Remember the Titans" (Episode 8.16), Zeus blames Prometheus for the downfall of the Greek gods. Prometheus gave humankind the gift of fire, which symbolically gave light to the darkness, the unknown. "He's the reason they have forgotten about us," Zeus says (Loflin & Boyum, 2013). Similarly, in "A Very Supernatural Christmas" (Episode 3.8), the pagan gods lament that their time as revered and feared gods has passed, no thanks to the appearance of a new god, Jesus Christ.

Despite the displacement of the once-powerful gods of the pre-Christian era, we find it telling that while gods such as Osiris and Zeus appear among humans in the modern world, the Winchesters have yet to find the Judeo-Christian God, the one the angels call their Father. Indeed, even the angels acknowledge the absence of God. In "On the Head of a Pin" (Episode 4.16), the archangel Uriel confirms that even the archangels have no proof of their Father's existence. Castiel tells Uriel that for his part, he still serves God. "You haven't even met the man!," retorts an angry Uriel (Edlund & Rohl, 2009). A deeper reading of the way *Supernatural* depicts an unseen, unknown God suggests that as a matter of faith, this is the one god that requires belief in Him despite the absence of physical evidence and when He takes no corporeal form. Thus far on *Supernatural*, pagan gods, demons, and angels have all made their acquaintance with the Winchesters. But the brothers have yet to meet the God of the angels and of Heaven, even though Death assures them of His existence, as we explain in more detail in chapter 4, Homilies and Horsemen.

The legitimacy of the "Other," portrayed through the reification of and power exhibited by characters associated with religions outside those considered the "main" faiths in the wider U.S. culture surrounding *Supernatural*, points to the ability of entertainment to provide some modicum of religious instruction. In that the "lore" the viewer learns about via Sam's research and other sources in the narrative relies on its writers' own research and desire to convey accurate information, we see the show as inclusive regarding religion. However, even as there may not appear an overwhelming majority of episodes we considered as "Christian," we must acknowledge that a hegemony of religion emerges when considering the nature of the portrayals of non-Christian antagonists.

Depicted as murderous and evil, the *djinn* based in Islamic lore, the *rakshasa* and *vetala* from Hindu myth, and the *okami* and *shojo* associated with Shinto all posed threats to humans and the Winchesters. In opposition to these portrayals, the instances in which Judaism plays a role in the episodes described here results in a favorable portrayal of the Jewish religion. When combined with the reliance on material based in Judeo-Christian tradition, this positive impression of Judaism highlights a certain viewpoint that presents some religions as "good" and others as "bad."

Regarding the functioning of hegemony, television assists in the reaffirmation of hegemony through the incorporation of radical (read: "different") ideology; the inclusion of other points of view reinforces what is already known and accepted because it is different and unfamiliar. Based on our frequency counts of the show's 172 total episodes presented earlier in this chapter, we found 49 episodes (28%) related in some way to non-Christian religions or traditions. Further, the frequency of appearance of *individual* and *specific* non-Christian religions is low, which suggests their importance in the overarching narrative of the show. In this sense, the "injection" of religions such as Islam, Hindu, and even Judaism, and practices such as black magic and Wiccan provide the small amounts of oppositional ideology required for a hegemony to stay in place.

The "Otherness" presented by non-Western religions and non-Christian religions in particular thus allows the ingroup (here, Christians and Christianity) to remain the preferred and valid way of worship and source for decisions regarding right and wrong, good and evil. Beal (2002), in *Religion and Its Monsters*, observed, "Like the monsters of Gothic horror, the representation of another god as monstrous has a disciplinary effect, pulling its viewers away from it and back into the center of the order of things, encouraging them to shore up their own identity in terms of established religious norms" (p. 116). Thus, the inclusion of other, monstrous gods and putting them in the role of antagonist reaffirms and reinforces what "good" means—and in the case of *Supernatural*, that good becomes aligned with Christianity generally, and Catholicism specifically.

SUMMARY

Combined with the generally evil depiction of creatures associated with "other" religions, *Supernatural* becomes part of the media-created and perpetuated "terrain of ideology" (Lewis, 1992) that discounts outside religions, such
as those depicted in single episodes. The tacit approval of content, indicated
by viewership, thus contributes to a hegemonic notion regarding the legitimacy and credibility of some religions over others. Of the religions associated with particular monsters and creatures, we found that non-Christian traditions tended to present evil entities that required the Winchesters to extermi-
nate them. However, one creature, the golem from Jewish tradition, actually
served as an ally against evil others.

   While *The Man from U.N.C.L.E.* portrayed religion as irrational (Grigg,
2007), and the 1990s Fox network series *The X-Files* sought to find explanations for the paranormal, *Supernatural* presents a world in which the occult,
ghosts, mythical creatures, angels, and demons are real and combatable with
religious artifacts, Christian or not. We find compelling *Supernatural*'s assumption that all religions, no matter their origin or era, "count" and thus can
do actual physical harm to humans. As a media product, it provides a text
that not only entertains but also can enlighten viewers about myths, folklore,
and religion.

   Even when we detected no discernible religion, folklore, or practices
associated with episodes that included ghosts and vengeful spirits as the
enemy or antagonist, the notion of souls that can return after death and make
a presence nevertheless supports a religious viewpoint. In that *Supernatural*
treats ghosts and spirits as "real," the presumption that souls do exist and can
physically affect the living in some manner perpetuates at least a belief in the
afterlife, itself a religious belief (Cowan, 2008). In that it is based on the
implicit understanding that humans are more than their corporeal existence,
the notion of the soul becomes further emphasized when Death, which appears as a real and manifest entity on *Supernatural*, explains to Dean in
"Appointment in Samarra" (Episode 6.11) that the human soul "is more
valuable than you can imagine" (Gamble, Singer, & Rohl, 2010). The Winchesters themselves "die" several times over the course of the series, yet still
exist in the realm of the dead. [9] The assumption that one can die yet still exist,
the underlying foundation of the classic ghost story, thus imparts a certain
belief that life does not end with physical death.

   In this chapter, we examined the plurality of religions and folklore offered
by *Supernatural*. We identified how creatures and entities related to this
plurality become the means by which a hegemony of religion emerges, notably, that of Christianity. Most prominently, the weapons associated with
Catholicism appear as those capable of defeating the main and recurrent
enemies of the Winchesters—demons from Hell. While Christianity plays

the role of "dominant" religion comparatively speaking and considering specific religious traditions and practices, the nature of even this "major" form of religion becomes further demarcated in *Supernatural*. We find it bears noting that when angels refer to God as "our Lord," they implicitly endorse Catholic doctrine regarding the Holy Trinity. In Christian tradition, "Lord" often is used to reference Jesus Christ; thus, the name Lord implies both God *and* Christ—who are essentially the same deity. This very subtle implication further underscores the place of Catholic and Christian traditions in American popular and religious culture.

As we discuss in the next chapter, the hegemony of Christianity unfolds on *Supernatural* in the way that other religions, especially ones that pre-date Christianity, become displaced. In addition to displacement of other traditions, the references to Christianity itself become a venue for the unpacking of what it means to be a Christian, particularly in terms of how that faith becomes manifested by its adherents. While one may profess Christianity, the nature of professing one's faith—that is, how one goes about showing one's belief in the philosophy and approach espoused within the general label "Christian"—becomes a means by which *Supernatural* offers a specific viewpoint regarding what it means to be "Christian."

NOTES

1. Portions of this chapter appear in "Demon Hunters and Hegemony: Portrayal of Religion on the CW's *Supernatural*" by E. Engstrom & J. M. Valenzano, III, an article whose final and definitive form, the Version of Record, has been published in *the Journal of Media and Religion*, 2010, copyright Taylor & Francis, available online at: http://www.tandfonline.com/, Article DOI: 10.1080/15348421003738785.

2. Number of episodes per season: season one = 22; season two = 22; season three = 16. Fewer episodes were produced for season three due to the 2007–2008 Writers Guild of America strike.

3. From the Apocrypha, not included in standard versions of the Old Testament.

4. Of the 172 total episodes from the 2005-2006 season through the 2012-2013 season, episode counts are as follows: season one = 22; season two = 22; season three = 16; season four = 22; season five = 22; season six = 22; season seven = 23; season eight = 23.

5. The DVD set for season eight was not yet released at the time of this analysis. Additional information regarding content related to coding of religious mentions for the episodes "Blood Brother" (Episode 8.5) and "A Little Slice of Kevin" (Episode 8.7), initially viewed but not recorded on VCR, were obtained from online episode descriptions.

6. In *Supernatural*, Purgatory appears as a wooded wilderness that holds the souls of various creatures, including vampires and Leviathans. During his time in Purgatory, Dean befriended the soul of a vampire named Benny Lafitte.

7. As part of the Apocalypse story arc, based on material drawn from the Book of Revelation in the New Testament, the Winchesters vanquish three of the Horsemen: War, Pestilence, Famine. The only one they cannot defeat is Death, who reappears in several episodes after the Winchesters avert the Apocalypse. We discuss the Horsemen episodes in particular in chapter 5, Homilies and Horsemen. We see the Winchesters' ineffectiveness against Death as one of the homilies provided by the Horsemen stories depicted in *Supernatural*.

8. Hellboy's "father," Professor Broom, identified himself as Catholic, as well as other religions. The *Hellboy* series of comic books by Mike Mignola portrays Hellboy as a devout

Catholic, according to several web forums ("The Religious Affiliation of the Comic Book Character Hellboy," retrieved from http://www.adherents.com/lit/comics/Hellboy.html; "Hellboy on Cartoon Network," retrieved from http://forums.catholic.com/showthread.php?t=145320). The 2004 movie's opening scenes, set during World War II, feature images of Catholic artifacts carried by Professor Broom that suggest a hegemony regarding Catholicism as *the* counter-force to the evil conjured by the Nazi/Thules, who seek to access another dimension containing demons and monsters.

9. Episodes in which either Sam or Dean or both "die" and encounter other souls or Reapers, entities that escort the dead to their destiny, include "In My Time of Dying" (Episode 2.1), "Death Takes a Holiday" (Episode 4.15), and "Dark Side of the Moon" (Episode 5.16).

Chapter Three

Hegemony of Religion[1]

The overarching storyline of *Supernatural* during its initial season centered on Sam and Dean Winchester's twofold quest to find their father, John, and to kill Azazel, the "yellow-eyed demon" who killed their mother as depicted in the very first episode. Seven of the 22 episodes in season one involved plots focused on the fight against this particular demon. The Winchesters fight Azazel, a demon mentioned in the Book of Leviticus (Jastrow, Jr., et al., 2009) and in the 1998 film *Fallen*, and other evil spirits who seek to corrupt and eventually destroy humankind. This classic "good vs. evil" plot structure invokes Christian/Judeo-Christian themes based on biblical references to specific angels and demons mentioned in the preceding chapter.

The centrality of this plotline in the fictional world of *Supernatural*, where elements and characters from different religious lore exist, also creates the impression that Christianity holds a higher status in the hierarchy of religions. In this chapter, we expand our discussion of the hegemonic aspects of Christianity forwarded through episodic and seasonal narratives. Specifically, we focus here on the ways in which *Supernatural* portrays Christianity, and Catholicism in particular.

We address three major themes that provide evidence for what we see as an overall hegemonic version of a particular religious foundation that leads us to view *Supernatural* as conveying a positive portrayal of Catholicism: the depictions of pre-Christian religions, ones we term today as "mythologies"; Christianity as presented in different denominations and modes of expression; and the casting of Catholicism as allied with the Winchesters in their fight against evil. When assembled, these themes combine to create a hegemony of religion even as we had identified *Supernatural* as a venue for presenting a plurality of religions.

CHRISTIANITY AS SUPPLANTING PAGAN GODS

Supernatural presents religious beliefs and traditions from ancient times as existing, at least in some form, in the present day, with Christianity holding a higher status in terms of power to both preserve and eradicate the world. This becomes evident in episodes in which the God of Judeo-Christian tradition has usurped ancient paganism. Several episodes over the course of the series have the Winchesters actually vanquishing pagan and other gods who reveal themselves in human form. The appropriation of holidays from the pre-Christian era celebrated today as Christmas, Easter, and Halloween become ways to educate audiences about their origins as well as imply that the ancient gods associated with their practices no longer have any power.

"A Very Supernatural Christmas" (Episode 3.8) includes a lesson in how Christmas originated in pagan customs. While researching a series of murders during Christmastime, Sam informs Dean, "Pretty much every Christmas tradition is pagan" (Carver & Tobin, 2007). In a rare reference to Christ, Dean replies, "Christmas is Jesus' birthday." Sam corrects him, saying that Jesus was probably born in autumn, and that the pagan winter solstice was "co-opted by the Church." Other remnants of paganism, he continues, include the yule log, Christmas tree, and "Santa's red suit." Dean alludes to Easter as well, sarcastically asking Sam if the Easter Bunny is Jewish.

Though initially thinking the murderer was Holdenacar, the pagan god of the winter solstice, the brothers eventually find the real culprits: the Carrigans, a pair of pagan gods who have been collecting "tribute" in the form of humans. The gods had "assimilated" into human society and now appear as a stereotypical Ozzie and Harriet. Mr. Carrigan, while preparing a captured Dean and Sam for tribute, tells the brothers that "Back in the day, we were worshipped by millions." He goes on to say, "All of a sudden, this 'Jesus' character's the hot new thing in town. All of a sudden, our altars are burned down and we're being hunted down like common monsters" (Carver & Tobin, 2007). Clearly the pagan gods are both aware of, and upset by, the popularity and now preeminence of Christianity.

The brothers manage to escape their bindings and kill the Carrigans using evergreen branches from the couple's own Christmas tree. Ironically, evergreen was the only ancient weapon effective against these gods. The *Christmas* tree used to kill them symbolizes the final death of paganism at the hands of Christianity, reinforcing the dominance of the Christian interpretation of the holiday by eradicating the pagan elements of its origin. Further, while the pagan characters are referred to as gods, they are capable of physically dying, unlike the Christian or Catholic God, whom viewers never see on the show. In fact, during season five, it is hinted that the only thing capable of destroying the Judeo-Christian deity is Death itself ("Two Minutes to Midnight," Episode 5.21).

When combined with the other episodes in which non-Christian creatures and gods are vanquished, "A Very Supernatural Christmas" further underscores the tangential relevance of these evil characters and the religions they represent to the main plot of the *Supernatural* story. These negative, one-shot depictions relegate them to the sidelines, and make them appear less powerful, less important, and less influential than Catholicism. Additionally, their lack of invincibility, which one might expect in gods, implies the falsity of the religions that worshipped these entities. Because the Winchesters ultimately defeat and destroy them, we see the show as placing these particular faiths on a lower tier in the hierarchy of religions within the overarching story's universe, serving as distractions from the Winchesters' main quest of vanquishing demons.

In the season four episode "It's the Great Pumpkin, Sam Winchester" (Episode 4.7), the brothers investigate a series of strange deaths occurring around the time of Halloween in a small town. Someone or something has been hexing people: a man sneaks some Halloween candy only to find himself coughing up razor blades, and a high school girl bobbing for apples at a party drowns. The brothers soon discover that Samhain, the Celtic god of death, has manifested as the local high school's art teacher. Sam researches the lore of Samhain, and explains to Dean that Halloween originated in the Celtic religion: candy and sweets were offered to appease the god, people wore masks to hide from him, and pumpkins were used to honor him. Even though Samhain was believed to have been exorcised "centuries ago," his return is revealed to be one of the seals that needs to be broken in order for Lucifer to rise from Hell—part of the season arc involving the impending Apocalypse.

Two followers of Samhain had been awaiting his return, it turns out, and one successfully brings the god back to inhabit her brother's body. During the scene in which Samhain is brought back, the Winchesters lay prone, almost powerless. Then Sam remembers the use of masks to hide oneself from the god. He and Dean then smear blood (from Samhain's human vessel, whom they have shot) on their faces, disguising themselves and averting the god's gaze—he cannot recognize them and leaves. Samhain walks among trick-or-treaters in his bloodied vessel, eventually appearing in a crypt at a cemetery where a large group of high schoolers are holding a Halloween party. The brothers confront Samhain and Sam uses his temporary demon-expelling powers to exorcise Samhain from his human vessel; the black smoke of Samhain's essence leaves the man's body and appears to go to Hell. This depiction implies that he is not the god the Celts thought, but just an evil emissary from the depths of the Judeo-Christian Hell. In the world of *Supernatural*, Samhain is portrayed as a demon that can be defeated by the brothers, another in the contingent of demons from Hell.

The successful defeat of the seemingly all-powerful and terrifying Celtic god by Sam Winchester further illustrates the displacement of pagan gods. Today's version of Halloween has become juvenile-oriented, in that the celebration of All Hallows Eve now largely has become a children's "holiday," when they can feast on candy and wear cute costumes. Further, the celebrations shown in the episode of children trick-or-treating and high school teenagers dressed in costumes and having parties frames the practices associated with avoiding Samhain's wrath as fun, rather than a time of dread. Halloween thus has evolved from the one night when children needed to stay indoors to avoid Samhain into a celebratory festival for children.

Samhain joins the literal pantheon of gods that the Winchesters defeat, symbolizing their displacement in the modern world in which Christianity holds the most power, at least in the *Supernatural* universe. Even as the series presents these older gods as "real" and tangible entities, their destruction in terms of being killed or sent back from whence they came puts them firmly within the realm of near-triviality. Gods from Old World and ancient Middle East traditions include Leshii, a pagan god of the Balkan forest whom the brothers destroy in "Fallen Idols" (Episode 5.5), and the Babylonian god of chaos, Tiamat, whom the brothers defeat in "Wishful Thinking" (Episode 4.8) when they find the magical coin that embodied the god's magic.

Even gods from what one would consider the "major" religions of ancient Greece and Egypt find they are no match for the two boys from Kansas. Those defeated, albeit with quite a bit of effort on the part of the Winchesters, include the Egyptian god Osiris in "Defending Your Life" (Episode 7.4). The brothers vanquish several major Greek gods as well, including the god of time Chronos in "Time after Time after Time" (Episode 7.12), and Zeus in "Remember the Titans" (Episode 8.16). Even New World gods cannot escape their fate when the brothers encounter them. In "Heartache" (Episode 8.3), the Winchesters kill the recipients of organs cursed by the Mayan god of maize, Cacao, once worshipped by athletes through blood sacrifice of human hearts. An ancient Mayan athlete had made a deal with Cacao to live forever, but had decided he could no longer handle immortality. The athlete killed himself, but his organs were donated to various patients who were then possessed by Cacao's power. As with their other enemies, the Winchesters destroyed the remnants of Cacao's curse by killing the possessed organ recipients. Even though Cacao's power remained strong enough to eventually result in the deaths of humans millennia after his assumed demise, his power as a god is nevertheless trivialized when Dean refers to Cacao as "a 1,000-year-old god of corn" (Buckner and Ross-Leming, 2012).

Much in the way that H.L. Mencken's (2007) short essay, "Memorial Service," provides a commentary on the passing away of gods throughout history, the adventures of the Winchesters reifies the notion of old gods making way for the new, or becoming obsolete at the hands of humans.

Mencken listed 136 "dead" gods, which he assured the reader had all once been "worshipped by millions"; they had temples built to them, sacrifices made in their name, and "to doubt them was to die" (p. 144). Mencken concluded his eulogy with this reminder to the reader about the obsolete gods of eons past:

> They were gods of the highest standing and dignity—gods of civilized peoples—worshipped and believed in by millions. All were theoretically omnipotent, omniscient, and immortal. And all are dead. (p. 146)

Supernatural complicates the notion that such gods are dead by creating consequences for their reappearance, notably, that people can still die by their hand or through the actions of their current worshippers. These gods gain the attention of the monster-hunting Winchesters through the strange deaths they leave in their wake, which implies that they do still have power in contemporary times. Within the plurality of religions depicted in the series exists a legitimization of their power; the pre-Christian gods still hold sway over humans, and thus require some kind of intervention on the part of those who can protect people. The Winchesters become that intervention, smiting the old gods, thereby putting an end to them once and for all.

Even as these gods are given their due, at least until they are vanquished, they simultaneously become trivialized through the way in which they are portrayed or referred to by the brothers. For example, in "Fallen Idols" (Episode 5.5), a wax museum replica of the tabloid celebrity Paris Hilton, of famous-for-being-famous fame, plays the vessel for the god Leshii. Comical treatments of some episodes that involve ancient gods or their influence in human events and actions further reinforce their position in theological terms. "Wishful Thinking" (Episode 4.8), the episode involving the Babylonian god Tiamat, features humorous consequences for those whose wishes come true due to Tiamat's power, wielded through a magical coin. A little girl wishes her stuffed teddy bear were alive gets her wish, only to have the bear kill himself because he becomes depressed after watching a television newscast. The coin's owner wishes that the woman he has a crush on will love him in return; she does, but becomes so obsessed with him that he can no longer tolerate her affections.

Three of the funniest episodes of the series' run thus far had the Winchesters befuddled by the Trickster, a recurring character who vexed the brothers; their efforts to vanquish him posed a challenge to their usual efficiency. In "Tall Tales" (Episode 2.15) the brothers learned that they were dealing with one of the archetypes of myth, the trickster. Known as Loki in Norse myth and Anansi in the folklore of West Africa, the Trickster proved elusive and immune to the Winchesters' hunting prowess. In "Mystery Spot" (Episode 3.11), Sam repeatedly witnesses Dean's death à la the 1993 film comedy

Groundhog Day; each of Dean's many "deaths" were comical—he died from a falling piano, choking on breakfast sausage, eating "funny"-tasting tacos, and electrocuting himself. These, of course, turned out to be bad dreams concocted by the Trickster. The first two times the Winchesters encountered him, the Trickster got away.

In the season five episode "Changing Channels," Sam and Dean meet the Trickster again, only to discover his true identity: the archangel Gabriel. They learn that Gabriel had put himself in a self-imposed "witness protection program," taking on the identity of pagan gods to hide himself from his heavenly brothers. The revelation, so to speak, of the Trickster's true identity further serves as a means by which a hierarchy of gods and religions becomes established over the course of the series' first five seasons. Rather than just another funny Trickster episode, "Changing Channels" was folded into the season five story arc involving the Apocalypse. In the episode, the Trickster/Gabriel places Sam and Dean in various realities modeled after television program genres: a wacky Japanese game show, a silly sitcom, a police drama similar to *CSI: Crime Scene Investigations*, and a *Grey's Anatomy*-style medical show. By doing so, he was trying to persuade the brothers to say yes to their "destiny"—serving as the human vessels for the impending showdown between Lucifer and the archangel Michael. The power of the Trickster, one of the few enemies that the Winchesters cannot defeat, becomes a way of emphasizing that his abilities originate in his identity as an archangel of Judeo-Christian mythology.

This subsuming of the pagan religions into an overarching, more powerful Judeo-Christian tradition became the narrative for the subsequent episode involving Gabriel/Trickster, "Hammer of the Gods" (Episode 5.19). Also part of the Apocalypse story arc of season five, this episode featured a slew of non-Christian gods at a summit meeting to discuss how to deal with the impending end times to be instigated by the angels and Lucifer. Realizing they needed to work together against Lucifer and the angels, the gods from Norse, Hindu, Chinese, and voodoo religions and mythologies gather at a luxury hotel in the middle of nowhere called the Elysian Fields—itself a reference to the afterlife paradise of Greek myth. Sam and Dean find themselves seeking shelter there, and soon confront the group.

As with other depictions of pagan gods, human sacrifice features prominently in this episode, as the gods sit down for a group dinner and feast on human flesh. The use of name badges typically used at conferences (which typically read: "Hello, my name is . . .") creates an almost-pedestrian portrayal of this gathering of the gods: Ganesh and Kali the Destroyer represent Hinduism; Odin, Balder, and Loki (Gabriel) represent Norse myth; Baron Samedi represents voodoo; and Zao Shen (the "Kitchen God") represents Chinese mythology. As Balder announces to the group that "the Judeo-Christian Apocalypse is upon us," the gods start arguing about who is the most powerful and ancient. Kali invokes an East-versus-West debate, as she declares contemptuously, "Westerners. You think you're the only ones. There are billions of us, and we were here first. If anyone gets to destroy the world, it's me" (Dabb, Loflin, & Bota, 2010).

Kali tells the group that together they can kill Lucifer. Lucifer then makes an appearance after the gods squabble amongst themselves about who "was here first." Lucifer makes known his status as the ultimate and most powerful threat to the world known by calling the gods "pagans," implying their minimal and now-extinct power. To make clear the superiority of the Judeo-Christian tradition, symbolized throughout season five as a battle between Lucifer and his demons and the archangels and the host of Heaven, Lucifer tells them: "No wonder you forfeited this planet to us." Lucifer then proceeds to kill all the gods as well as Gabriel, his brother angel. In "Hammer of the Gods," even Kali the Destroyer is destroyed. The combined efforts of the gods failed to stop Lucifer. His way now clear, Lucifer's plan to bring on the end times becomes the plot for the rest of the episodes, leading to the season finale in which he and Michael meet to determine the fate of the world.

The season eight episode "What's Up, Tiger Mommy?" (Episode 8.2) follows in a similar vein the confirmation of a hierarchy of religions and beliefs illustrated in "Hammer of the Gods," one that again puts a Judeo-Christian God at the top of the theological ladder. The episode carries the narrative of a story arc involving the discovery of a stone tablet known as the "demon tablet," which contains secret instructions for closing the gates of Hell. Its keeper and translator, a college student named Kevin Tran, who also turns out to be a "prophet of the Lord," lost possession of the tablet. The Winchesters, Kevin, and Kevin's mother (the tiger mommy referred to in the episode title) track down the tablet, which had made its way into an auction of religious and mythological artifacts run by Plutus, the Greek god of greed.

Among the items up for bid is the Norse god Thor's hammer, and the finger bone of the Norse frost giant Ymir. The Winchesters' archenemy, Crowley, the King of Hell who took over after Lucifer was returned to his cage in Hell at the end of season five, is in attendance at the auction and describes the demon tablet as the word of God, "with a capital 'G'" (Dabb, Loflin, & Showalter, 2012). The tablet had been written by Metatron, an archangel who served as the scribe of God. The description by Crowley of the tablet as being the word of God with a capital G implies that among the various gods and religions associated with the artifacts at the supernatural auction, the Judeo-Christian god associated with the tablet is superior to all the others.

In season six, the episode "My Heart Will Go On" (Episode 6.17) presented a similar displacement of pre-Christian religions and mythology by an overarching, superior Judeo-Christian one. The episode involved the interference of the angel Balthazar in human history, namely, saving the *Titanic* from sinking. Balthazar had gone back in time and prevented the ship from hitting the iceberg that sealed its fate. By doing so, he incurred the wrath of the goddess Atropos, one of the Fates from Greek mythology whose duty was to cut the thread of humans' lives. Atropos, depicted in the episode as an accountant, then begins to ensure that the descendents of the *Titanic*'s survivors die so as to correct what Balthazar did.

In the episode, Atropos says that "God" gave her a job, implying that she works for the Judeo-Christian God associated with the angels and the Apocalypse, which had been averted by the Winchesters. Apparently Atropos, one of the Fates from Greek myth, has become an "employee" of the monotheistic God. In addition, the angel Castiel actually fires her, thereby firmly placing Atropos under the command, so to speak, of the God with a capital G. When considered with the other episodes that feature gods and religions from the pre-Christian era, especially Greek and Norse, this episode exemplifies their status as not only being obsolete, but subordinate to the Judeo-Christian tradition and subject to the authority of its delegates, the angels.

The appearance of the angel Castiel during season four marked a turning point in the series, in that the Winchesters worked under the assumption that they and their fellow hunters were alone in the universe to hunt demons. The weapons they used contained some divine power: holy water and Latin served as their main defense against demons that originated from Hell. However, in the season four premiere, "Lazarus Rising" (Episode 4.1), the rules changed. Dean had been sent to Hell when he died in the season three season finale; his deal with a crossroads demon to spare Sam's life in exchange for his soul finally was sealed. However, in "Lazarus Rising," he was resurrected by some unknown force and returned to life on earth. When he found his way back to Uncle Bobby, Bobby tested him by splashing Dean with holy water to make sure he was not possessed by a demon. All the "usual" weapons are shown in this episode, including the holy water, a silver knife, salt, and iron; this array illustrates the variety of items that make up the hunter's arsenal.

During the episode, an intolerable sound would be heard, accompanied by the breaking of any glass in the vicinity. The Winchesters and Bobby ask a psychic named Pamela Barnes to summon the new entity. As they perform a séance to summon it, Pamela demands that the entity show itself. She learns that the entity's name is "Castiel." It warns her to stop the ritual, but she refuses—then her eyes light on fire, leaving her blind. The brothers continue their search for the entity, and find out that even the local demons are afraid of it.

To summon this new, unknown entity, Dean and Bobby use everything in their hunters' knowledge, "Traps and talismans from every faith on the globe," as Bobby put it, when they go on a stakeout in an abandoned building (Kripke & Manners, 2008). Dean reviews their arsenal, which contains every weapon used against every creature he's ever heard of: "Stakes, iron, silver, salt, the [demon-killing] knife." Bobby then uses Latin in a summoning spell. After a brief wait, the building starts to shake and the lights explode. A scruffy man in a trench coat enters, as the building's large doors open by themselves. Dean and Bobby shoot salt at him, with no effect. Dean asks the man who he is, to which the man replies, "I'm the one who gripped you tight and raised you from Perdition." Dean stabs him with the special demon-killing knife, which also has no effect on the man.

In a scene that changes everything that the Winchesters and Bobby have known their entire lives, the man in the trench coat finally tells Dean who and what he is: "I'm an angel of the Lord" (Kripke & Manners, 2008). Dean tells him there is no such thing. When Castiel reveals himself, shadows of his enormous wings appear briefly, as if to confirm his true identity and leave no doubt in Dean's, or the viewer's, mind. Castiel had saved Dean, bringing him up from Hell; his handprint was seared onto Dean's arm. Castiel tells Dean that God commanded him to save Dean because, he explains, "We have work for you." That work, the boys learn, is that they are to serve as the vessels for the two ultimate fighters in the Apocalypse: Lucifer and Michael.

In addition to introducing angels as another form of supernatural beings, "Lazarus Rising" establishes the position of the Judeo-Christian tradition within the *Supernatural* universe. While their foremost powerful enemies were demons from Hell, especially Azazel, the Yellow-Eyed Demon who killed their mother, the Winchesters now encounter a force that even demons fear. The ineffectiveness of the various weapons used for destroying monsters, spirits, and demons and all the talismans from every faith on earth against the angel Castiel not only demonstrates his power, but the power of the Judeo-Christian God whom he serves. Furthermore, the episode's title refers to the story of Lazarus in the New Testament, underscoring that the "ultimate" religion of the *Supernatural* universe is not only based in the Judeo-Christian tradition of monotheism, but Christianity itself. When considered with previous and subsequent episodes featuring antagonists from other religions and traditions, "Lazarus Rising" thus creates the trajectory for the unfolding of the Apocalypse story arc as well as the preeminence of a Christian-based theology, one that relies heavily on material from the New Testament.

MARGINALIZATION OF NON-CATHOLIC FAITHS AND ERRANT CHRISTIANITY

Prior to the introduction of angels in season four, individual episodes already had incorporated Christianity in some fashion. However, even within its treatment of Christianity as another form of lore, a hierarchy or at least a form of "good" and "bad" forms of Christianity emerge. Similar to the dichotomy between non-Christian/pagan forms of belief and Christianity, our scrutiny of storylines and themes of episodes in which this form of religion appears results in the impression that Christians come in a variety of forms— not all of which are good. Thus, even as *Supernatural* presents a plurality of religions based on a progression from pagan pantheism to monotheism according to a Judeo-Christian tradition, our analysis points to a valence-oriented comparison between denominations within Christianity itself.

In particular, we see a demarcation between Protestant versions of Christianity and Catholicism. Based on imagery and visual cues, such as the lack of, or appearance of, artifacts associated with Roman Catholicism, the viewer often can discern whether characters or churches are Protestant or Catholic. Furthermore, specific denominations may be explicitly mentioned by characters who identify as certain being of certain faiths or describe certain denominations or sects. In general, we found that non-Catholic denominations tended to be portrayed as less sympathetic than Catholicism. In the following episode descriptions, we deconstruct these portrayals to reveal the nuanced ways in which the show presents religion in terms of a Christian hierarchy.

We found several episodes in which the characters representing non-Catholic denominations were typically portrayed as fraudulent, sinful, or evil. The episode "Faith" (Episode 1.12) in particular offers a negative portrayal of faith-healing based in Christianity. In this episode, Roy LeGrange, a blind faith healer, runs an evangelical revival tent. The sign on the tent reads, "The Church of Roy LeGrange, Faith Healer, 11 a.m.-2 p.m., Witness the Miracle." Roy claims to heal the sick and dying. He proclaims, "It is the Lord who does the healing here, friends, the Lord who guides me in choosing who to heal by helping me to see into people's hearts" (Gamble, Tucker, & Kroeker, 2006). He goes on, "It is the Lord God who rewards the good and punishes the corrupt." The revival-tent setup and terminology used by LeGrange make it clear that his character represents an evangelical Christian preacher.

Roy does in fact heal the sick, but not due to faith or God. Rather, the Winchesters discover that Roy's wife is using a black magic ritual involving a Coptic cross to bind a reaper (a version of the "Grim Reaper," as found in almost every culture and lore on earth, Dean notes), who kills people she considers immoral. As the reaper goes after victims identified by the wife, Roy simultaneously heals sick people, including a heart-damaged Dean. By debunking and uncovering the evil behind the so-called faith healing power of Roy, the non-Catholic, evangelical-based religious convictions of his congregation turn out to be false and its true source corrupt, thus denying the power of that religion/ritual. Not only is Roy's power illicit, but the Coptic Christian cross used as a source of his abilities implies its use as a corrupting tool, thus discrediting two proverbial Christian birds with one episode. Additionally, the "Church of Roy LeGrange" further underscores the fakery of a self-named church (as opposed to referring to *the* Church, as in Catholic). Logically, one could take the analogy further and read the episode as associating faith healing with black magic. Amplifying the distaste the Winchesters have for religious dishonesty, Dean makes a reference to this particular episode when he later mentions "skeevy faith healers" in the season four episode "Death Takes a Holiday" (Episode 4.15).[2]

The episode "Hook Man" (Episode 1.7) portrays Protestant ministers in a negative light. The vengeful spirit of Jacob Carnes, a preacher who in the 1860s used a hook to kill thirteen prostitutes in a small town's red light district, is killing young people in the present day. In addition to the depiction of a preacher as insane and evil, the story also includes the overprotective and adulterous Reverend Sorenson, the father of Lori, a young woman who wears a silver necklace made from the melted down silver of the vengeful preacher's hook. The portrayals of the hook man as a violent moral crusader and the adulterous reverend as corrupt present a stark contrast to the seemingly incorruptible Catholic priests in other episodes.

During season five, the Apocalypse story arc included an episode that addressed the dangers of blindly following religious beliefs, especially when killing in God's name. In "99 Problems" (Episode 5.17), the Winchesters come upon a small town, Blue Earth, Minnesota, where they see the townspeople use militia-like tactics to wipe out a group of demons; specifically they use water pumps that spew holy water and recite Enochian incantations (Enochian refers to a mythic language of the angels). The brothers befriend the group, who call themselves the "Sacrament Lutheran Militia." They attend a wedding at the group's church, and notice that the congregation members have brought guns into church. The townspeople are preparing for war with the demons, as if they were a "regular" army; even the town's children prepare salt rounds as ammunition. The brothers ask the minister why the townspeople haven't called the National Guard to help them, to which he replies they were told not to—by his daughter, a young woman named Leah Gideon.

Leah apparently recognizes the Winchesters, and reveals that she learned about them "from the angels." As a prophet, Leah also says that the angels tell her where to find demons and how to fight them with Enochian exorcism spells. Every time Leah has a vision, the townspeople are summoned to the church to learn the location of the latest demon attack. The minister leads the people in prayer, asking God's protection as they go into battle.

Sam learns some disturbing details about the town, after a night of drinking with Paul, the owner of the town's bar. Not only does the town have a curfew, but all communications such as cell phones and the Internet have been terminated. "Total cutoff from the 'corruption of the outside world,'" Sam explains to Dean. Dean doesn't see the problem, until Sam explains, "Don't you get it? They're turning this place into some fundamentalist compound." When Dean says he doesn't care, Sam becomes the voice of reason, asking him, "At what point does this become too far for you? Stoning Poisoned Kool-Aid?" (Siege & Beeson, 2010). Sam's criticism points to the destructive power of fanaticism and blind faith, notably that which characterizes fundamentalist religious practices and cults and sects, and, more famously and subtly referenced with Sam's "Kool-Aid" comment, the Jonestown massacre of 1978, when hundreds of followers of the "Reverend" Jim Jones committed suicide by drinking Kool-Aid laced with cyanide.

When the prophet Leah reveals that the angels are angry because some of the townspeople haven't been listening to their commandments, a group of townspeople go to the bar and tell Paul he has to leave town. One woman named Jane says, "This is a town of believers, Paul. You are not a believer." Even though Paul has been a friend and a fellow combatant, they demand he leaves. Dean comes to Paul's defense, but Jane shoots him. Leah had told the townspeople that they could not go to Paradise because of the non-believers. Jane kills Paul in order to see her son in Paradise. Leah assures Jane that murdering Paul was okay because "he was a sinner."

As this is going on, Sam has summoned Castiel to the town, telling him what has been going on and about the prophet Leah. Castiel tells him that she is not a prophet, because the names of the all the prophets have been "seared" into his brain. It turns out she is a false prophet, which the Book of Revelation calls the Whore of Babylon, a creature that rises "when Lucifer walks the earth." The Whore of Babylon has been sending the demons to attack the town, and the Enochian exorcisms used by the townspeople are fake.

Castiel tells the brothers that the Whore can only be slain by a "true servant of heaven." Naturally, Leah's father, the minister, comes to mind. He even questions Leah when she preaches to the townspeople that they must slaughter their own friends and even some children. Castiel and the Winchesters tell him he is the only one who can kill her, but he is reluctant to kill his own daughter. The minister agrees to help them, but it is Dean who finally kills the Whore with a special weapon, a stake of cypress from Babylon. The irony here is that Dean, far from the ideal "servant of heaven," given his penchant for drinking and womanizing, apparently *is* a true servant of Heaven, the only one who can wield the special weapon and destroy the Whore. The assumption that a minister would be a true servant of heaven based solely on his occupation thus turns out to be false; the lesson here points to the artifice of piety as an indicator of who can or who cannot serve heaven.

"99 Problems" portrays a fundamentalist version of Christianity in which alcohol and other "evil" influences of the world are deemed wrong and sinful. The blind willingness of the townspeople to follow Leah simply because she invokes the (false) authority of the angels points to the lack of critical thinking that can lead to death and destruction committed "in the name of God." Additionally, the directives to kill come from a false prophet who has blinded the people, causing them to do unspeakable things on the promise of going to "Paradise" and seeing their dead loved ones again.

Several times throughout the series, allusions to specific versions of Christianity forward an attitude that they do not truly reflect what Christianity as a philosophy really means. If one takes the teachings of Jesus Christ as philosophy, the tenets of forgiveness and love become a way of living—replacing the commandments of the Old Testament. The directive stated in John 13:34, "love one another," was ignored, indeed rejected, in "99 Problems." Hints regarding the legitimacy of those who claim to follow Christ's teachings and religions that have evolved from the beginnings of the Catholic Church come from authorities such as angels, and, especially, the Winchesters' heavenly ally and friend Castiel.

Proselytizing is portrayed in a negative tone in the series, as seen in "The End" (Episode 5.4), when Dean encounters a man on the street who asks him, "Have you stopped to think about God's plan for you?" (Edlund & Boyum, 2009). It turns out the man, whom Dean calls "the Bible freak," is working for the angels. The angels at this point have become the Winchesters' antagonists; they are trying to bring the Apocalypse to fruition and can only do so when the brothers give Lucifer and Michael permission to possess them. Dean later tells Castiel to "stay away from Jehovah's Witnesses from now on." As the statement comes from Dean, one could read this as a general rule of thumb in his or her own life being conveyed by the episode writers.

In the same episode, visitations to certain non-Catholic but Christian religious groups by the angels create a connection between the enemies of the Winchesters and Christianity—mainly, forms of the faith associated with fundamentalism and those outside what could be considered "the Church" (Roman Catholicism). The archangel Zachariah has been trying to coerce the Winchesters to accept their fates as the vessels for Lucifer and Michael for several episodes. In "The End," he tells Dean that he and the angels have been using informants, such as the Bible freak who accosted Dean, to find Dean and Sam. "We've been making inspirational visits to some fringier Christian groups," says Zachariah, implying fundamentalists and fanatics may be easily duped into obeying the orders of an unquestioned "higher power."

The use of "fringier" Christian groups by the angels implies that their members may be unbalanced and susceptible to accepting that (a) angels are real and (b) angels have visited them specifically and chosen them to do the bidding of God. This casts people who actually have been visited by Zachariah's comrades as unstable, which by extension calls into doubt the legitimacy of their denominations. One could describe those groups as cultish. However, the Winchesters themselves are never portrayed as "fringy" or unstable, even though they, too, have been visited by angels of the Lord. Indeed, their best friend is Castiel. The notable aspect of Zachariah's admission is that those who have been visited are members of fringe groups, rather than those one might consider non-fringe, i.e., Catholics, Episcopalians, Methodists, or even Lutherans. That is, his statement could be read as meaning that extreme forms of Christianity would not question the directives of angels, but would follow them blindly. Those who may be members of extreme sects thus would be "easy pickings" for any nefarious purpose the angels may recruit them for. This further becomes associated with the notion that zealots do not represent "true" Christianity, but rather harm the credibility of Christianity as a religion.

Though the Winchesters and Uncle Bobby don't profess or practice any religion, some hunters have been portrayed in the series as holding religious views. However, those who professed or showed zealotry met a bad end. For example, in the season three episode "Bad Day at Black Rock" (Episode 3.3), a hunter named Kubrick becomes obsessed with killing Sam, after another fanatical hunter named Gordon convinces him that an impending war with demons is related to Sam, whom he says is pure evil and must be killed.[3] Kubrick apparently is a devout Christian; he wears a cross on a necklace and his camper home is decorated with a large painting of Jesus, a ceramic *tchotchke* with Jesus' face painted on it, and a crucifix. Kubrick believes he is doing "God's work" by killing a captured Sam. Just when Kubrick is about to shoot Sam, Dean comes to the rescue. As a lesson about the dangers of fanaticism, both Kubrick and Gordon eventually come to bloody, grisly demises in "Fresh Blood" (Episode 3.7): Gordon becomes a vampire and kills Kubrick by eviscerating him. Then Sam kills Gordon by decapitating him with barbed wire.

In contrast to these examples of "true believers," religious teachings associated with a quiet, reflective version of Christianity become manifest through hints as to how a true Christian would behave. We found one of the more illustrative examples of this in the season five episode "Point of No Return" (Episode 5.18). At this point in the season, Sam and Dean are hiding from the angels. Dean encounters another street proselytizer, a young bearded man dressed in a suit standing in front of a bar, shouting, "The end is nigh! The Apocalypse is upon us! The angels talk to me and they ask me to talk to you!" (Carver & Sgriccia, 2010). Dean tells the man to pray to "your angel buddies" and let them know where he is. Apparently the man is a member of one of the fringe groups to which Zachariah referred. The man then kneels and starts reciting the Lord's Prayer aloud. Castiel suddenly appears and tells the man, gruffly, "You pray too loud," then puts his hand on the man, who falls unconscious.

Although Castiel quieted the man in order to keep the angels from hearing him and locating Dean, the brief interaction alludes to the verse in Matthew 6:5 about how hypocrites pray "in the corners of the street" so that they may be seen doing so. Instead, prayers should be made in private: " . . . when thou prayest, enter into thine inner chamber" (Matthew 6:6, English Revised Version). Castiel's admonishment forwards a certain message regarding the expression of religion, one which tells the viewer that a true Christian does not make a public scene, but instead prays quietly behind a shut door. In short, to call attention to oneself, such as praying loudly in public and making sure others know that one is a Christian, is not what Christianity is about. This scene also provides a visual enactment of the verse, suitable even for Bible instruction.

The angel Castiel becomes a conduit for conveying a certain version of Christianity and religion in subsequent episodes; as an angel, the show presents him as a kind of authority on religion. In a way, he represents a credible source regarding the "real" story behind the Bible. Further, he forwards a more general notion about religion, one that emphasizes the separation between faith and ideologies of extremism. Specifically, Castiel communicates a version of Christianity that embodies tolerance, acceptance of evolution, and an almost humorous explanation for Bible stories that may have exaggerated the facts. In "The Man Who Would Be King" (Episode 6.20), Castiel recounts biblical history by comparing it to "actual" human history. The episode opens with a scene titled "Cass' Story," a monologue in which Castiel, seated on a park bench, prays to God. Castiel says he has been around a very long time, and remembers how life on earth began. His story serves as a voiceover for images of a darkened earth, with lightning flashing over a roiling ocean. Castiel recalls "watching a little gray fish heave itself up on the beach" (Edlund, 2011). An angel, older than Castiel, told him not to step on that fish, because there were "big plans" for it, hinting at evolution. The image of what looks like a mudpuppy crawling in mud provides visual support that points to the notion that evolution is unquestioned in *Supernatural*'s religious world; this subtly illustrates disdain for creationists who believe the Bible is actual history and thus deny evolution.

The human penchant for explaining disasters as acts of God receives a humorous take when Castiel then skips to the story of the Tower of Babel, with a scene from an old black-and-white film accompanying his voiceover. According to Castiel, it was 37 feet tall, which he supposes was "impressive at the time." When the Tower fell, the people attributed it to "divine wrath." But, according to Castiel, it was probably more an error in engineering, as he says, "dried dung can only be stacked so high." Biblical stories get a bit of credibility as Castiel tells the viewer he remembers "Cain and Abel, David and Goliath, Sodom and Gomorrah."

Recalling the ending episode of season five, Castiel further explains that the Apocalypse was averted by "two boys, an old drunk, and a fallen angel," referring to the Winchester brothers, Uncle Bobby, and himself. What was left in the wake of their success in saying no to destiny was now freedom and choice. If taken as a parable, the story of the non-ending of the world as portrayed in *Supernatural* points to humans' power to create their own destinies, rather than leaving their destinies to a higher power. In this manner, even though the Bible may hold some truth, according to Castiel, it is ultimately up to the individual to decide how to live his or her life.

In an ironic twist to Castiel's message regarding free will, he becomes "God" in season seven, in the episode "Meet the New Boss" (Episode 7.1). The episode's title refers to the song "Won't Get Fooled Again" by The Who, whose lyrics tell the listener, "Meet the new boss. Same as the old boss" (Townshend, 1971). Castiel believes he is God, and decides to get humankind into line, punishing or threatening to punish those who do not follow his directives. The irony of the song lyric-based title of the episode becomes revealed as Castiel says he is better than his Father. However, even as Castiel declares he is better, his tactics of fear and intimidation to get people to obey him actually make him as equally or even more wrathful as he says God is. Further adding to the multi-layered messages in this episode, although Castiel presents an almost-totalitarian version of God, his admonishments and proclamations actually demand tolerance and reversal of fundamentalist attitudes.

For example, at the "Lady of Serenity" church, a preacher sermonizes, "Plenty speak for them and their so-called lifestyle. Media. Hollywood" (Gamble & Sgriccia, 2011). In a clearly contemptuous tone, he refers to Lady Gaga, who "won't shut up."[4] The man goes on to tell his followers that they need to raise their voices "and picket their so-called weddings and their funerals," a reference to religious protesters who have gained attention in the news in recent years.[5] The viewer understands that the preacher espouses an anti-gay attitude, calling on the congregation to oppose marriage equality for same-sex couples, and homosexuality in general. Castiel suddenly appears in the church, telling the preacher, the congregation, and, in effect, the viewer, "You're wrong. I am utterly indifferent to sexual orientation." Castiel then calls out the reverend for being a hypocrite, demanding that he "tell your flock where your genitals have been before you speak for me." Castiel proceeds to kill the reverend by making him choke on his own words, literally, as the reverend foams at the mouth while falling dead. The correction of an anti-gay sentiment among religious groups communicates to viewers that real Christianity does not include intolerance based on sexual orientation. Additionally, this scene references the hypocrisy of those who speak out most vehemently against homosexuality, notably, anti-gay preachers whose own homosexuality causes their downfall.[6]

The Winchesters and Uncle Bobby watch news reports about Castiel's mission of vengeance against religious leader; Castiel apparently is killing apparent hypocrites as well as members of the Vatican, along with members of hate groups such as the Ku Klux Klan. Lightning strikes and destroys the "Center for Vibrational Enlightenment," Castiel's punishment against New

Age motivational speakers. The Winchesters are surprised at this last act of vengeance, as it appears Castiel has gone a little too far in punishing those whom he believes do not fit into his version of how things should be. That motivational speakers, who may seem innocuous in comparison to the KKK, appear on Castiel's radar implies that people should listen to themselves and trust in themselves rather than seeking guidance from others (who may not really have the wisdom or intelligence to help people looking for "the answers").

Commentary on the interrelationships between conservative politics and the perverted form of Christianity espoused by conservative religious views manifests when Castiel shows up at the campaign re-election headquarters of a senator named "Michelle Walker" (a name we see as a subtle jab at Republican U.S. Representative Michelle Bachman, herself a devoutly religious politician). Walker tells a reporter that she's running again to "save my constituents from the godless policies of my opponents" (Gamble & Sgriccia, 2011). As part of his own campaign against those he deems in need of punishment, Castiel appears there and says he needs to see the senator regarding "abuse of power": "I am punishing a woman who causes poverty and despair in my name." This implies that those who forward a conservative religious agenda as the rationale for conservative policies, such as rejection of entitlements, are making things worse for humankind. Castiel then announces to the campaign workers that he is "a better God" than his father. Castiel apparently then blacks out, and wakes up to a scene of mutilated, bloodied bodies: he had murdered everyone at the campaign headquarters.[7]

Ironically, the "liberal" theology being forwarded by the new God as self-envisioned by Castiel is forcibly being enforced by a God who embodies tolerance and who does not suffer hypocrites, hate, ignorance, or disagreement. As Dean tells Sam, this God is "pissed." Dean goes on to say, "And when God gets righteous, you get the hell out of the way" (Gamble & Sgriccia, 2011). To further make his point, Dean asks Sam, "Haven't you read the Bible?" Eventually Castiel literally becomes "too big for his britches," when the power he misconstrues as divinity overtakes his human vessel—he is actually the container for the Leviathan, monsters from Purgatory—and he dies. Thus, even Castiel, who claims to be God, gets his comeuppance, much like the false prophets and hypocrites get theirs throughout the series.

Christianity and liberal theology become intertwined in "Meet the New Boss." Castiel delivers his message about intolerance and hypocrisy in a clearly Christian church. Although Christ (who preached tolerance and forgiveness) is not mentioned, the setting features a familiar church interior, with stained glass windows and a large cross on the wall. Castiel kills hundreds of religious leaders, representing a cleansing of "rotten apples" within organized religion; even the Vatican is mentioned. Similar to the story of

Christ's cleansing of the temple related in Matthew 21:12-13,[8] Castiel goes on an angry rampage to rid religion of those who have defiled the meaning of Christianity.

The lesson derived from this episode, however, extends beyond what God does or does not endorse, represent, or demand. By portraying the "tolerant" Castiel as enforcing his will through pain of death, the resulting message forwards the idea that one in reality does not need to be told what is right or wrong by a religion, a church, or even God. In essence, then, belief in God (or not believing in a higher power) does not require rules or a demand for obedience to those rules. In short, the real "God" of Christianity does not punish those who do not follow "His" rules. Further, those who claim to speak for God hold only false authority; as Castiel pointed out, no one really knows God or what God is thinking. Thus, one could view this episode that contains religious imagery and messages as actually being anti-religious, or at least anti-fundamentalist Christian.

CATHOLICISM AS "GOOD"

Beyond a Christianity-based premise regarding the "superpowers" of the earth (demons, humans, angels), *Supernatural* more specifically forwards the Catholic worldview as major and credible. "Common sense," explained Gramsci (1999), consists of "an incoherent set of generally held assumptions and beliefs common to any given society" (p. 626). A set of assumptions presented as "common sense" appears whenever the Winchesters and others use certain artifacts and rituals to confront demons from Hell. In the reality of *Supernatural*, the implicit power contained in these weapons is never questioned, even as the very existence of the God responsible for their power has not been confirmed. Thus, even with the existence of angels and demons, shown to inflict both pain and death on ordinary humans, God remains absent, and prayers made even by an angel remain unanswered.

We contend that a common sense regarding Catholicism surfaces three ways in the continuing narrative of *Supernatural*. First, the Winchesters consistently use weapons to fight demons from a God-based Hell that originate in Catholic rites, specifically those associated with exorcism. Second, in contrast to portrayals of ministers of other Christian denominations, portrayals of priests tend to be sympathetic and helpful to the Winchesters. Third, when the stakes are high, Catholic imagery becomes prominent: weapons associated with exorcism appear to hold even more power when fighting big battles, such as the closing of the gates of Hell. Finally, we offer additional observations that imply an endorsement of Catholicism over other religions.

Catholic Weapons and Artifacts

In *Sacred Terror*, Cowan (2008) observed, "Throughout Christian tradition, belief in the power of the demonic to invade our world has ebbed and flowed, but it never disappeared entirely" (p. 176). Further, he noted, "For many people, demonic possession or oppression, and either exorcism or deliverance, are predominantly Roman Catholic . . ." (p. 177). In *Supernatural*, demonic possession appears as a regular occurrence, and the most powerful and often-used weapons used by the Winchesters and other hunters come directly from the Catholic faith.

Holy water, used in the Catholic rite of exorcism as popularly depicted in films like *The Exorcist*, holds a special status in the hunter's toolbox. The Winchesters consistently rely on holy water to inflict pain on demonic entities. In "Phantom Traveler" (Episode 1.4), the brothers use holy water to fight a demon that has possessed the copilot of a passenger plane in flight. In "real life," only Catholic priests can bless water to make it holy; its potency against demons in *Supernatural* thus subtly emphasizes the power that Catholicism holds against fighting evil. In the series, however, demon hunters seem to be able to consecrate water as well, by using the proper Catholic artifacts and blessing.

The power of holy water is never questioned; indeed, holy water appears as a "go-to" weapon for hunters. For example, Dean replaces tap water with holy water at a diner as a test to see what happens when Adam Milligan (the Winchesters' half-brother) drinks it in "Jump the Shark" (Episode 4.19). Nothing happens, but it later turns out that the person posing as Adam was actually a ghoul, a creature immune to the effects of holy water and other special weapons, such as silver. In "Lazarus Rising" (Episode 4.1), Uncle Bobby splashes a resurrected Dean with holy water to see if Dean is actually a demon. Holy water also is used in sprinkler systems against demons in "No Rest for the Wicked" (Episode 3.16); its power evidently remains potent even when mixed with gallons of normal water or even toilet bowl water, as in "Jus in Bello" (Episode 3.12).

Additional Catholic-based weapons used by the Winchesters and other demon hunters include the rosary and crucifixes. For example, rosaries appear in several episodes, including "The Magnificent Seven" (Episode 3.1), "Jus in Bello" (Episode 3.12), and "No Rest for the Wicked" (Episode 3.16). The inclusion of this religious object specific to Catholicism enhances the prominence of this particular denomination in *Supernatural*; the rosary is used to create holy water in "Jus in Bello," an episode in which the Winchesters engage in an all-out battle against demons. Combined with holy water, the rosary becomes an essential part of fighting demons, who up until that time in the series posed the most dangerous threat.[9]

Latin was the original language of the Catholic Church and was used to perform Mass until Vatican II in 1962. From the very beginning of the series, Sam, Dean, and other demon hunters use Latin incantations to expel demons from possessed humans to send them back to Hell. Examples of early episodes include "Phantom Traveler" (Episode 1.4) and "Devil's Trap" (Episode 1.22). These incantations represent the power of Catholic rituals in the fight against evil, and the show consistently portrays the use of Latin, often read aloud from a prayer book of some type, as the only way to send demons back to Hell. The effectiveness of Latin as a "general-purpose" weapon against demons becomes even more prominent when Sam uses a reverse exorcism spell to keep a demon *inside* its human host in the season eight episode "What's Up, Tiger Mommy?" (Episode 8.2). In *Supernatural*, demons can expel themselves at will from their vessels in order to escape. In this episode, as one demon starts to leave the human it possesses, Sam recites Latin to keep the black smoke of its essence from escaping. When Dean asks Sam how he did it, Sam replies that he simply said the exorcism spell backward.

The repeated use of holy water, Latin, and appearance of rosaries, all decidedly Catholic in origin, furthers the effectiveness of this particular religion and its practices against the main enemies of the series' protagonists. In addition to these artifacts associated specifically with Catholicism, the Winchesters regularly use amulets, symbols, and spells in their "hunting," with antagonists such as witches and even other "Christian" foes using Coptic spells based in early Christianity. Religious historians trace the use of spells for protection and curses against one's enemies back to the early Christian/ Catholic Church, especially Coptic texts dating to early medieval Egypt (Meltzer, 1999; Meyer & Smith, 1999; Mirecki & Meyer, 2002). Saints were and still are associated with miracles. Indeed, as Loomis (1948) documented in *White Magic: An Introduction to the Folklore of Christian Legend*, "the cult of the miraculous was well established in the Christian writing of Europe by the end of the sixth century" (p. 7).

By including portrayals of effective uses of spells and rituals based in Christianity, *Supernatural* reifies the power associated with this particular religion. Even though, as Mirecki and Meyer (2002) noted, ancient Near East religions such as Judaism and early Islam also invoked aspects of "magic," the use of decidedly *Christian* rituals and spells against the major forces of evil encountered by the Winchesters further imbues what we see as the preferred religion with even more force and power.

Furthermore, one can read the use of these artifacts by non-priests as evidence of their power to combat demons despite the occupation, or ordination, of the person using them. The source for the holy water always on hand is not specific; the curious viewer might wonder if the Winchesters regularly visit churches to obtain it, or if they "make" it themselves. In one episode,

"Jus in Bello" (Episode 3.12), it appears that hunters can bless water to make it holy. If they can make holy water without being ordained, then it implies that the divine nature of the weapon comes from the power of the words in the incantation and not the inherent authority or piety of the person performing the blessing. In either case, the words associated with Catholic traditions and rites have special power in the reality of *Supernatural*.

Regardless of where it comes from, the use of holy water and Latin by "civilians" implies that these Catholic-based artifacts are imbued with so much strength that even the non-ordained can use them effectively. In that hunters, according the show, can make their own supplies for battling demons, Catholic clergy may seem superfluous. However, the Winchesters do consult priests and consider them as on the same side in the fight against evil. We see the overall depiction of Catholic priests on the show as another means by which this particular denomination becomes the main and most legitimate religion in a supernatural universe.

Depictions of Priests

Priests serve as central figures in the Catholic Church, and they appear as sympathetic characters in a handful of *Supernatural* episodes. In "Salvation" (Episode 1.21), a powerful demon known as "Meg" has entered a church and begins talking with a priest about her sins. He recognizes her as a demon and tells her she cannot be there, calling it "hallowed ground." He then runs downstairs into a bunker-like room filled with weapons, indicating that he is a demon hunter. When Meg wants to know the whereabouts of the Winchesters, the priest says she is wasting her time, telling her, "Even if I did know where they were, I'd never tell you." She replies, "I know," then slits his throat (Gamble, Tucker, & Sgriccia, 2006).

The viewer later finds out that the priest is "Pastor" Jim, a close friend of John Winchester. Based on the visual evidence in the beginning scene, we ascertained that Jim is a Catholic priest: he wears a clerical collar, and the church appears Catholic, with an altar and golden chalice similar to that used in the Eucharist. Although the title "pastor" is commonly used to denote Protestant ministers, it is used in the Catholic Church to refer to the head priest of a parish (see Papi [1911] for more information on the application of the term "pastor" within Catholicism). Although a brief scene, the depiction of Pastor Jim's resistance to the demon emphasizes the stereotype of the "good priest," one who gave his life to protect his comrades.

"Houses of the Holy" (Episode 2.13) provides an especially positive and sympathetic portrayal of priests. The spirit of Father Gregory, a parish priest gunned down on his church steps, appears as an angel to people in need of redemption and tells them that God wants them to kill those guilty of egregious sins, or who are about to commit a sin. Most of the other ghost stories in the series have no religious dimension. Father Gregory, however, is convinced he is an angel doing "God's work." Even Sam, despite being a hunter, believes he is an angel.

Sam uses a Latin séance ritual to summon Father Gregory's spirit at his crypt in the church basement. Father Reynolds, the other priest at the church, confronts the spirit and convinces him that he is not an angel but a man who needs to be at peace. Father Reynolds then performs Last Rites for Father Gregory, by invoking the Holy Spirit and the archangel Raphael, and then making the sign of the cross. Father Gregory's spirit becomes a bright light, suggesting that he moved on and found peace. In addition to showing Father Gregory as a "good" ghost who actually targets bad people, "Houses of the Holy" reinforces the power of Catholic rituals. The use of the Last Rites suggests it serves as a way for troubled souls to attain redemption and peace.

"Sin City" (Episode 3.4) involved a priest as well, although with a noticeably different take than either "Salvation" or "Houses of the Holy." In this episode, a priest at first helps the Winchester brothers as they investigate a series of suicides in a small Midwest town that has become overrun with bars, gambling, and prostitutes. The brothers find the priest drinking in a bar, appearing to have succumbed to the vice that has befallen the town. However, it later turns out that the priest has been possessed by the demon responsible for the city's downfall. This depiction implies that priests can be evil, but not by their own doing: they must be possessed by a force out of their control in order to become corrupt.

The season four finale "Lucifer Rising" depicts possession of a priest by a demon to instigate the Apocalypse. The episode opens with a scene at "St. Mary's Convent," as the dark smoke of a demon possesses a priest in the chapel. Next, the priest is performing mass for the nuns. He is reciting the Lord's Prayer when indications that something wrong become apparent: he changes the words to "blah, blah, blah." A nun looks taken aback. Next the priest locks the chapel's door and proceeds to murder the nuns. The priest had been possessed by the Winchesters' archenemy Azazel, the Yellow-Eyed Demon they have been tracking ever since he killed their mother. The depiction of a priest possessed by this demon further underscores the overarching story in which demons present the strongest power against good. Moreover, the fact that in the theology of *Supernatural* demon possession can occur against the will of the possessed further emphasizes that priests may be vulnerable because they are no match for the evil of demons, and may be in fact "easier" targets because of the inherent good that they represent.

We see a sympathetic portrayal of Catholic priests in *Supernatural* emphasized when the protagonists themselves assume this identity; the nonverbal impression of authority and goodness become underscored when the Winchesters wear the collar. For example, the connection between priests and goodness first appears in an episode in the season one episode "Nightmare" (Episode 1.14). While investigating a series of strange deaths, Sam and Dean pose as Catholic priests to gain entry into a victim's family's home. Dean introduces himself and Sam as "new junior priests over at St. Augustine's," and asks to come inside the home. Their priestly personas not only create a secure feeling that allows the family members to open up and answer their questions, but also conveys to the viewer that the brothers in essence have taken on a life similar to the priesthood, in that they deny themselves a "normal life" associated with marriage and family. Their avocation as hunters and exorcists in essence reflects the role of priests, especially if one considers their knowledge of Latin and use of Catholic-based artifacts. Indeed, the naturalness of the visual image of the brothers as priests creates the impression that the series could just as easily been about two young priests who hunt demons, ghosts, and monsters.

A similar use of the priest's uniform occurs in the season four episode "In the Beginning" (Episode 4.3). In this episode, Sam and Dean travel back in time and meet their maternal grandfather, Samuel Campbell, who turns out to be one in a long line of hunters. In addition, the brothers learn that their mother herself was a hunter who gave up her family's business when she married their father, John Winchester. When Dean and Samuel separately investigate a strange death they suspect has something to do with demons, they both pose as priests to get answers from the victim's family members. While the use of the priest's collar does not play a central role in "Nightmare" or "In the Beginning," we see the association between Catholic priests and the Winchesters as creating a sympathetic impression of Catholicism.

Catholicism as Ultimate Weapon against Hell

The use of Catholic-based artifacts in fighting demons became significant at the end of season eight; the last two episodes especially highlight the power of Catholic rites to not only fight demons, but to purify them and revert them back into humans. The purification of a demon also served as part of the story arc in season eight regarding the closing of the gates of Hell. The last of three trials as described in the demon tablet sought by the brothers in season eight required a demon to be cured; the Winchesters then capture the King of Hell, the demon Crowley. Crowley had served as one of their major adversaries, aside from the angels, since season five.

In "Clip Show" (Episode 8.22), the brothers discover an old film of two priests conducting an unusual exorcism—the priests are shown trying to purify the demon possessing a man. The priests use the usual weapons employed by the Winchesters in capturing demons. The imagery of crucifixes, rosaries, and holy water and use of Latin reaffirms these artifacts' power and origination in the Catholic religion. In addition, the priests introduce a new weapon that supposedly will cure the demon and turn it human: purified blood, which comes from one of the priests who took the Catholic sacrament of Confession just before the blood was extracted, ensuring its purity. The brothers learn from the younger priest, now an old man, that the rationale for the cleansing ritual was the older priest's belief that because demons were once human souls that became evil and twisted after their time in Hell, they could be saved and become a human soul again. One can read into this the theme of redemption forwarded in the notion that a person can be "saved" despite one's sins or past transgressions, no matter how wicked. In addition, it appears that the only way to purify one's blood—and one's soul—is through the Catholic confessional rite.

Confession, one of the seven sacraments of the Catholic Church, is officially known as Penance and Reconciliation. In order to cleanse the soul of a demon, the purified blood is then injected in the demon's vessel once an hour over the course of eight hours, after which the demon is cured. The priests' efforts resulted in one demon's escape through its human vessel, but they were successful in purifying another. At the time the brothers discovered this new ritual, Sam already succeeded in performing two of the three trials required to close the gates of Hell (killing a hellhound and rescuing Bobby's soul from Hell), and so he prepares to perform this third and final trial.

In the season eight finale, "Sacrifice" (Episode 8.23), Sam performs the purification ritual, which requires a demon, consecrated ground (a church), and purified blood. The brothers tap Crowley as the demon they plan to purify. The brothers capture Crowley and take him to an abandoned church. Dean asks Sam if he had ever done a "forgive me, Father," to which Sam replies yes, when he was a boy. This surprises even Dean, but not viewers familiar with the series; Sam has always "believed," and is known to pray to God. Sam enters the church's confessional, kneels, and begins the confession: "To anyone's who's listening . . ." (Carver & Sgriccia, 2013).

Religious imagery serves as the backdrop for the scenes in which Sam begins to save Crowley's soul—a large crucifix on the church wall and one on the altar remind the viewer of not only the religion behind, literally, the saving of a damned and wicked soul, but of the Christian messages inherent in the symbolism. As Crowley becomes infused with Sam's "holy" blood, it appears as if his soul becomes more human. Eventually, Crowley asks Sam how to begin asking for forgiveness for all the evil he has done. Sam holds up the syringe of his purified blood, which he has been injecting into Crowley's neck. In a gesture of submission, Crowley then turns his head, offering himself—as if in an act of grace—to the healing power of the blood Sam is sacrificing to save him.

In addition to the themes of forgiveness and redemption, the message of sacrifice is revealed when it is discovered that Sam will die if he completes the ritual; the angel Naomi says Sam's death was part of "God's plan"—the ultimate sacrifice. The allusion to Christ's sacrifice to save the world specifically evidences the Christianity being forwarded.[10] Additionally, these two episodes portray Catholicism as the means by which the gates of Hell can be closed as well as the way that even the most evilest of souls—including the very King of Hell—can be saved.

FURTHER OBSERVATIONS REGARDING CATHOLICISM

In our original study on the portrayal of religion in *Supernatural*, which covered the first three seasons, we concluded that Catholicism tended to hold a more prominent and sympathetic status among the religions depicted. In this chapter, we identified various ways in which Catholicism, and Catholics, continued to appear as a major, if not the major force, in combating a generalized evil and threat to the Winchesters and the world at large. In *Supernatural*, while references to Catholicism include visual imagery of Catholic rites and artifacts and portrayals of priests, it is not the religion of the Winchesters. Even though they use religious-based weapons, they do not practice a particular religion nor attend any church. Although Sam admits to believing in God and prays, Dean appears to remain skeptical of not only religion, but of God's true intent, even as he and his brother deal with the emissaries of God. Indeed, throughout the Apocalypse story arc in seasons four and five, the angels repeatedly mention how their Father is missing.

The repeated appearance of Catholicism through imagery and practice becomes especially heightened when such influence is actually *denied* by the main characters of Sam and Dean Winchester. The specific mention of Catholicism appears in the season seven episode "Defending Your Life" (Episode 7.4). The story opens with a mysterious death of a man who appeared to have been run over by a car on the tenth floor of an apartment building. Suspecting something spectral is responsible, Sam and Dean discover a sobriety coin awarded by Alcoholics Anonymous (to mark a member's progress in staying clean) in the victim's apartment. Sam tells Dean to go check out the local AA chapter to see if they can discover anything that would help solve the case. Dean replies, "I gave up AA for Lent." Sam answers, "Dean, we're not Catholic" (Glass & Singer, 2011).

Although a brief exchange, we find the denial of Catholicism notable. First, Dean's knowledge of Lent combines with a familiarity with Catholicism as demonstrated by the brothers' use of the priestly disguise and interactions with priests over the course of the series, which in turn requires at least some passing knowledge of the Church. Second, their use of Catholic artifacts, specifically holy water and Latin, conveys the impression that they *can* wield such weapons with success; even though one might guess that "civilians" could use such weapons against demons in the world of *Supernatural*, such weapons are only used by hunters. In that the Winchesters are not agents of the Church, they nevertheless must hold some kind of expertise or power to employ these artifacts in their hunting. Third, it suggests that even though Catholicism plays an integral part in their "work" as hunters, they do not adhere to the Church's practices. We read this as providing to the audience an attitude that even though one can endorse a religion, one need not actually be a devout follower of it. That is, the mythology of *Supernatural* allows the Winchesters to rely on religious artifacts imbued with power to fight evil and even to represent a religion, but they are not required to practice the faith as required by dogma. Faith, it seems, matters more than any doctrine or religious affiliation.

This denial of adherence to Catholicism combines with other observations we make about how the series treats Catholicism in particular. We have noticed, over the course of the show's eight-year run, that the character of Dean usually treats religion in general with irreverence. For example, he has referred to angels as "dicks"; this insult reflects the casting of some of the angels as agents of heaven but not protectors of humankind.[11] Dean also refers to holy water and holy oil as "Jesus juice."[12] Such references to Jesus appear occasionally throughout the series, but Christ never makes an appearance on the show (nor does God).

We see this as a means by which the show avoids appearing overtly Catholic or "preachy." Rather, the show presents a world in which the supernatural is part of reality. Thus, anything that is beyond natural explanation is plausible and tangible, regardless of its origins in a specific religion, lore, or mythology. Further, given the writers' penchant for giving Dean humorous lines and even profanity, we find it notable that the "real life" scandals in the Catholic Church remain absent from the show. Indeed, we have not detected any comments by Dean about bad priests. Perhaps in the world as portrayed in *Supernatural* all priests are good; the Catholic Church in Sam and Dean's reality might not be the same one as ours. However, given the way in which the series incorporates references to historical facts and people, we believe this observation is worth making. This adds another dimension to our reading of the program as forwarding a respectful position regarding priests, especially when they are shown battling demons or performing exorcisms. The combination of scenes and images we found in *Supernatural* offer counterevidence for Jenkins's (2003) conclusion regarding the negative portrayals of Catholicism in mass media. Rather than the "quite hostile treatment in movies and television" (p. 157), we detected an overall positive stance toward Catholicism and Catholics. Furthermore, beyond a sympathetic treatment of Catholicism, we would say that this popular television series places Catholicism at the pinnacle of religions that assist its protagonists in their battle against the ultimate evil.

With regard to hegemony theory, the prominence of Catholicism becomes notable in that, as a religious denomination under the umbrella of Christianity, it is, in reality, a minority religion. As mentioned previously in chapter 1, U.S. Census figures, Gallup polls, and the Pew Forum all show that although most respondents identify as Christian, only about 23% of them specify as being or having a preference for Catholicism (Newport, 2012; Pew Forum on Religion & Public Life, 2008; U.S. Census Bureau, 2009). The sympathetic portrayal of Catholicism as the "top" religion among those depicted in the show, we believe, illustrates how hegemony functions within civil society to endorse a way of thinking—in this case, that Catholicism is the most powerful way to fight supernatural evil. Moreover, the casting of a universal good vs. evil battle as one based in the Judeo-Christian tradition, that is, taken from the Bible, further becomes a way to demonstrate the validity of Western culture as the symbolic "center of the universe." We discuss this in more detail in chapter 5 when we address how this becomes further demarcated when considering how the Winchesters symbolize Americanism as another weapon to fight the threats to humankind in general.

SUMMARY

Plurality of religion as presented in *Supernatural* allows for the inclusion of various faiths and folklore that underlie the range of foes and combatants faced by the Winchesters, a pair of hunters of the supernatural. Simultaneously, depictions of other religions and belief systems, those that Gramsci (1999) identified as collectively surfacing under the name "folklore," become ways to reaffirm those belief systems emplaced and supported within civil society, in this case, by the media industry. Here we presented our argument that Christianity serves as the top of a hierarchal system of religions in *Supernatural*. Episodes that give viewers the stories of gods, those other than the monotheistic version presented in Judeo-Christian religious traditions, tell the story of their displacement by a new, more powerful one. The power these gods once held has waned as their believers have passed into distant memory. The new God has supplanted them, leaving them vulnerable although still able to present challenging foes to the human representatives of this new power order: the Winchesters.

Christianity thus subsumes the dominion once held by pagan theologies. However, even within the overarching faith structure of Christianity we found legitimate and non-legitimate versions, as forwarded in narratives of episodes related to how this new religions should be practiced and professed. Those who espouse a false version of Christianity, or who misuse it and instead preach distorted, hateful versions of it, usually receive some sort of comeuppance on *Supernatural*. We found a zero-tolerance policy for zealotry and hypocrisy, in particular; those who use religion for selfish ends, such as fooling people with fake "cures" or false prophecies, become examples of what Christianity is *not* about. Forwarded through the guise of a science fiction/horror series, these lessons serve to educate viewers in subtle and not-so-subtle ways about Christianity, or at least the way the writers see it. Rather than promoting or endorsing particular practices, what results is a generalized Christianity which concerns a way of treating others, rather than following "rules" that requires one to do certain tasks (such as proselytizing, "saving souls," or attending church).

Beyond Christianity, we find in *Supernatural* a subsequent hierarchy, one which places various denominations of this generalized faith in a certain order as well. Based on our analysis of the text and imagery consistently and regularly appearing in *Supernatural*, we see Catholicism placed at the top of this hierarchy. Catholicism serves as the appropriate opponent in a dichoto-my with evil, and Catholic practices and artifacts—Latin (the language of the Church), crucifixes, and holy water—serve as the most effective weapons against powerful demons. While Catholicism appears as "the" religion to fight the major enemies of the Winchesters, we do not see *Supernatural* as a religious program for Catholics by Catholics. After all, one does not have to *be* Catholic to be a demon hunter, or to enjoy *Supernatural*. Priests generally are treated sympathetically, but they are not shown physically fighting de-mons the way the Winchester brothers do. Even Jim the priest/demon hunter is called "Pastor" rather than "Father," which deflects allusions to overt Catholic favoritism.

When considering the main story of *Supernatural*, the weapons used to fight evil, such as holy water, and the depictions of priests all engender the perception that Catholicism is the main and most powerful opponent of evil. These add to what Wolff (2010) called the "mythos of 'the church'" (p. 211), in this case, the Catholic Church. Combined with other portrayals of Catholic priests in horror movies, like *The Exorcist*, for example, this evidences a popular image of priests as knowing what to do in case of a demon posses-sion (provided one believes they exist in the first place).[13]

Though not central to the narrative, the generally sympathetic treatment of Catholic priests in particular suggests that on this program rooted in the horror genre, they are also "good guys." Furthermore, Catholicism appears to sit at the top of the "food chain" with regard to religion in the show's universe. In this manner, we see Catholicism as receiving a positive treat-ment, thus supporting a Catholic-centered theme. This counters past research regarding the predominance of Protestant-themed Christianity on network entertainment programming (Clarke, 2005; Lewis, 2002; Skill et al., 1994). Our findings regarding *Supernatural*'s reliance on a particular religious doc-trine counter popular press accounts in which creator and executive producer Eric Kripke said the show is about demonology in general (Surrette, 2008).

The Winchesters readily utilize religious artifacts in their quest to destroy their archenemies. However, they are not Catholic, nor appear to actually believe in Catholic doctrines. Indeed, this denial of adherence is made explicit when Sam tells Dean, and, by extension, the viewer, that they are not Catholic ("Defending Your Life," Episode 7.4). Even though Sam goes to "Confession" in the season eight finale "Sacrifice" (Episode 8.23), he does not make his confession to a priest, but rather appears to skip the "middleman" and speak directly to God (or whoever/whatever is listening). In this manner, we see *Supernatural* as being able to forward a Catholic version of Christianity without being a Catholic show. Similarly, Primiano (2009) found that *The West Wing* presented a religious aspect without being a show about religion, even though the actor who played the President, Martin Sheen, describes himself as a "radical Catholic" (p. 104).

The careful depiction of the Winchesters as non-religious, though users of Catholic artifacts and even donning the collar as one of their investigative disguises, creates an "out" for the show so as not to appear firmly entrenched as a religious program. Episodes that allude or explicitly address religion and what it means to be a Christian manage to make their point regarding hypocrisy and the dangers of zealousness in the name of God without depicting Christ himself. In this manner, *Supernatural* relies on biblical material for narratives that surround the main story of the Winchesters as they contend with confrontations with supernatural beings.

These narratives do not serve as the focus of the program, yet nevertheless do offer lessons and elucidation about the tenets of the Christian way of life. We found several episodes that similarly use biblical references as sources for storylines. In the next chapter, we address how *Supernatural* serves a homiletic purpose by telling stories based in Scripture and making them applicable to the practice of everyday life. These stories relay lessons about the creation of human conflict, the perils of overindulgence and selfishness, and the inevitability of death construed from figures that invoke dread, awe, and the destruction of the world: the Four Horsemen of the Apocalypse.

NOTES

1. Portions of this chapter appear in "Demon Hunters and Hegemony: Portrayal of Religion on the CW's *Supernatural*" by E. Engstrom & J. M. Valenzano, III, an article whose final and definitive form, the Version of Record, has been published in the *Journal of Media and Religion*, 2010, copyright Taylor & Francis, available online at: http://www.tandfonline.com/, Article DOI: 10.1080/15348421003738785.

2. The slang term "skeevy" refers to something "unpleasant, squalid, or distasteful," according to the web site Oxford Dictionaries.com (2013; retrieved from http://oxforddictionaries.com/us/definition/american_english/skeevy).

3. According to Supernatural Wiki.com's page for the "Bad Day at Black Rock" episode, the reference to director Stanley Kubrick may allude to his direction of Dean's favorite movie, the horror film *The Shining*. (Retrieved from http://www.supernaturalwiki.com/index.php?title=3.03_Bad_Day_at_Black_Rock).

4. Pop singer Lady Gaga is a vocal and active supporter of gay rights (Zak, 2009; Zezima, 2010); she even participated in a gay pride parade in Rome, resulting in headlines like "Lady Gaga Angers the Pope" (Nadeau, 2011). Her widely publicized single, "Born This Way," a song promoting gay rights and equality, became a number-one hit just months before the airing of "Meet the New Boss." The song debuted in February, 2011 and reached number one on the Billboard pop chart on March 28, 2011 (Trust, 2011). The original airdate of the episode "Meet the New Boss" was September 23, 2011.

5. The hate-spewing Westboro Baptist Church, a subject of media attention in recent years ("Complete Coverage," 2013), blames a range of natural disasters, and even the attacks of September 11, 2001, on homosexuals. Members have gained notoriety for regularly picketing the funerals of United States servicemen and women, as well as non-religious events such as rock concerts, as a means of promoting their message of intolerance and God's hate for same-sex marriage. Vile and offensive hate speech on the Westboro "Church" web site even includes its web address, which we cannot in good conscience include here, even for reference purposes. However, one can locate it using a simple Internet search.

6. For example, in 2008, after being outed as a homosexual, antigay preacher Ted Haggard was fired from the megachurch he founded and resigned as president of the National Evangelical Association (Associated Press, 2008).

7. The intertextuality involving the political aspect of this episode becomes even more apparent later in the episode, when the Winchesters and Bobby summon Death, one of the Four Horsemen from Revelation, to help them stop Castiel. Dean had encountered Death in the previous season as part of the Apocalypse story arc. In this episode, Death, who has known God for eternity, tells Castiel, "I know God, and you, sir, are no God." One may recall the zinger from the 1988 Vice-Presidential Debate, when Democratic Senator Lloyd Bentsen told Republican Senator Dan Quayle the same thing about John Kennedy. It was Bentsen's retort after Quayle compared himself to a young John Kennedy.

8. The story of Jesus and the moneychangers relates Christ's anger at seeing what has been done to his Father's house: "And Jesus entered the temple and drove out all those who were buying and selling in the temple, and overturned the tables of the money changers and the seats of those who were selling doves" (Matthew 21:12-13, New American Standard Bible). Similarly, Castiel "cleans house" by getting rid of those who have defiled Christianity; even the Catholic Church is included, hinted at by the mention of the Vatican in the news report of Castiel's actions.

9. Holy oil, required to create holy fire, became a key artifact starting in season five. It was used to entrap angels, including the archangels Raphael in "Free to Be You and Me" (Episode 5.3), and Gabriel in "Changing Channels" (Episode 5.8). Holy oil is used for a variety of purposes in the Catholic Church (Leclercq, 1910). It symbolizes "the light of grace," according to the web page "The Holy Oils," retrieved from http://www.awakentoprayer.org/holy_oils.htm.

10. A closer reading of Sam illustrates the similarities between his character and Jesus Christ. Sam sacrificed himself at the end of season five, when he let Lucifer use him as a vessel in "Swan Song" (Episode 5.22). By doing so, he was able to overcome Lucifer and jump into "the pit" with the archangel Michael, thereby capturing him and preventing the Apocalypse. Sam was "resurrected" after going through the ordeal, an allusion to the resurrection of Christ. In "Sacrifice" (Episode 8.23), Sam is about to complete the ritual of purifying Crowley when Dean appears and stops him. Dean tells Sam he will die if he continues, to which Sam replies, "So?" Sam's willingness to rid the world of demons by closing the gates of Hell even though it means his own death reiterates the theme of sacrifice as represented by Christ. Sam's willingness to die for others further invokes *agape*, the ancient Greek concept of spiritual love inherent in altruism and self-sacrifice (Galician, 2003).

11. *Supernatural* relies on biblical versions of angels as warriors of God, as explained by Castiel in "Are You There God, It's Me, Dean Winchester" (Episode 4.2). Dean uses the term "dick" as a synonym for jerk to describe angels, who turn out to be nothing like the familiar, modern-day versions of cute cherubs or guardian angels in popular culture and figurines. Dean again uses the term "dick" to describe angels in "The Song Remains the Same" (Episode 5.13) and "Sacrifice" (Episode 8.23). The use of mild profanity serves as an aspect of Dean's

hardened-hunter persona; he uses the term "bitch" or "son of a bitch" almost as a catchphrase in several episodes. Examples include "Changing Channels" (Episode 5.8) and "Sacrifice" (Episode 8.23).

12. Dean uses the term "Jesus juice" to refer to holy water in "Jump the Shark" (Episode 4.19) and to holy oil in "Trial and Error" (Episode 8.14).

13. One may recall the last scene of the 1973 film *The Exorcist*, when the young girl Regan, no longer possessed, meets a priest and embraces him. His clerical collar triggered a memory that evoked the goodness of Father Damian, the priest who sacrificed himself to save her. Incidentally, *Supernatural* paid homage of sorts to the film and to Linda Blair, who played Regan. In the episode "The Usual Suspects" (Episode 2.7), Blair plays the role of a police detective helped by the Winchesters in solving a case.

Chapter Four

Homilies and Horsemen[1]

Religious-themed media about the end of the world offering interpretations of the Book of Revelation have become popular in recent years. The sixteen-book *Left Behind* series by Tim Lehaye and Jerry Jenkins serves as an example of the popularity of the end-times story; Hendershot (2010), in *Shaking the World for Jesus: Media and Conservative Evangelical Culture*, described the popularity of the series through book sales and related merchandise. Indeed, the familiar narrative of the "End Times" apparently has gained enough material to write about that Rehill (2010), in *The Apocalypse Is Everywhere: A Popular History of America's Favorite Nightmare*, specifically examined the end-times motif in a range of media treatments. These include Hollywood movies from the early days of cinema to hits of the recent past, television, comics and graphic novels, and music and art. The appropriation of this story for commercial enterprises shows no signs of slowing, either, as with the 2013 comedy *This Is the End*, an end-times film with a humorous twist starring actors Seth Rogen and James Franco, and a host of other Hollywood celebrities.

"Apocalyptic fiction sells, in part, because it is exciting," noted Hendershot (2010, p. 178). However, the reliance on Revelation becomes problematic, in that, as Hendershot pointed out, it is "quite simply indecipherable" (p. 178). Readers can either interpret passages as symbolic or as literal, as in the case of evangelicals. The latter approach, which emphasizes a reading without what Hendershot called "priestly intervention," has readers relying on others' interpretations of difficult verses; these others include not only pastors, but also mass media, in the form of books, television, and movies (p. 178). While offering material for exciting narratives in mass media, more "practical" purposes of the story of the Apocalypse for evangelicals include religious conversion, so as to avoid being "left behind" after the Rapture, explained Hendershot.

Cinematic versions of apocalyptic stories, whether actually depicting a cataclysmic ending of the world or offering a metaphor for it, have involved several key recurring themes, as described by Ostwalt (1995). These include the character development of strong, hero figures who vanquish the forces of evil and/or prevent the end of the world; familiar settings that have been transformed into a "terrifying Armageddon"; and a plot that emphasizes efforts to avoid the end from coming or that resolve as renewal without having to go through "cataclysmic destruction" in the first place (p. 61). Such films may or may not specifically invoke passages from the New Testament, but nevertheless rely on a story in which impending world-ending disaster is on its way.

Recent attempts on television have focused on post-apocalyptic storylines or life after a global catastrophe. For example, the Showtime cable series *Jeremiah* ran for two seasons (2002–2004), and the CBS series *Jericho* ran from 2006 to 2008, returning for an abbreviated second season after a public campaign to renew the show. Bird (2009) analyzed the failure of the 2005 miniseries *Revelations*, a treatment of the end-times theme that used quotations from the Bible to open each installment. As an indicator of the show's quality and a hint as to why it experienced a poor reception, one horror aficionado called it "Apocalyptic cheese" (p. 24).

The current eight-season run of the CW's *Supernatural* dwarfs that of these programs. Over the course of the show's first five seasons, the series' protagonists, the Winchester brothers, became central figures in a storyline featuring a fight between Heaven and Hell; in fact, they found out they were key players in both starting and preventing the Apocalypse. Sam found out he was the intended human vessel for Lucifer, while Dean spent several episodes fending off Heaven's angels, who intended him to serve as the vessel for the archangel Michael. The end-times story arc during its fourth and fifth seasons illustrates how a long-running (by Hollywood standards) network television program that did not start out with an apocalyptic theme later incorporated biblical references and text. *Supernatural*'s staying power contradicts Mitchell's (2001) observation that "the apocalyptic genre is generally not well suited to television except for tele-films and the occasional miniseries" (p. 283).

As explained in chapter 2, *Supernatural* treats gods from a variety of religious traditions and "God" as actual deities. In chapter 3, we explored the nature of the series' treatment of Christianity, and specifically, Catholicism. Here we return to the Christian-based narrative elements that undergird our argument. The Apocalypse story points to a Christian-based faith embedded in its narrative. Thus, we base the current chapter on the premise that a fictional television program can contain religious messages that connect

Scripture to contemporary concerns and issues, even if those messages appear flattened or secularized.

We explain in this chapter how television and its depictions of religion in modern American culture serve as contemporary Christian homilies. Specifically, we demonstrate that *Supernatural*'s New Testament-based stories centering on the Four Horsemen of the Apocalypse, based on Revelation 6:2-8, gave its audience messages about life grounded in biblical lessons, essentially serving the purpose of a homily that one might hear in a church on a Sunday morning. While the Four Horsemen serve as antagonists to the series' two protagonists, we argue that their symbolism became a way to convey lessons about contemporary everyday life regarding the destructiveness of war, the fear created by pestilence, famine of spirituality, and the inevitability of death. Jordan (2011) examined the Apocalypse storyline in *Supernatural* in terms of how it comments, deliberately or not, on contemporary America, and noted that clerics in the Middle Ages used Revelation to criticize the Church itself.

Here we examine this story arc in a case study of episodes from *Supernatural*'s season four to explore in depth those episodes we see as clearly offering homilies and the messages beyond the obvious Biblical interpretation inherent in them. We argue that homilies in contemporary times are not restricted to churches, but rather permeate American culture via television, and in so doing they reinforce a Christian character in American identity through the reliance on the New Testament as a source for storytelling.

MEDIATED HOMILETICS

In the Augustinian tradition, the lessons, principles, and values inherent in the Bible remain unchanged, even though they can apply to a variety of different contextual situations over time and are told through stories set in contemporary times and settings (Augustine, 1958). Howard (2006) called this the "narrative plasticity" of Christian doctrine and sacred Scripture (p. 26). Howard referred specifically to the narrative plasticity of the Book of Revelation and "End Times" discourse, but the principle of application regarding the Bible is the same. This narrative plasticity allows for a more creative construction of homilies within the Christian tradition of preaching. Authors of homilies thus seek to connect the audience with Scripture through a social commentary on their current context.

This does not imply a goal of conversion, though that may be the case, but rather an invitation to reflect on one's lived experiences through the timeless lessons of Scripture. To accomplish this, the rhetor must create messages that speak to people in a way that recognizes the audience's beliefs, attitudes, values, and experiences while helping the audience to understand scriptural lessons (Luchsinger, 1986).[2] In fact, in order to deliver a homily, one only needs to have an education in Scripture. For a message to be homiletic, then, authors must: (a) be familiar with Scripture; (b) divine the core scriptural meaning for the audience; and (c) connect that meaning to current events and issues that directly relate to the lived experiences of the audience. Non-religious television programs can contain reflections on Scripture's relationship to contemporary events and culture; writers, producers, and directors can draw on material from myriad religious sources, even though they themselves may not practice a religion or hold religious views.

We consider *Supernatural* an example of mediated homiletics, and use this approach to examine the homilies we see contained in several episodes from a specifically biblical Apocalypse storyline which ran during its fourth and fifth seasons. This decidedly Bible-based narrative was acknowledged by *Supernatural*'s creator and producer, Eric Kripke, who stated in an interview that the story arc for season five was "basically that the angels, and Lucifer and the demons are just beginning the long foretold Apocalypse from the Book of Revelation" (Rudolph, 2009a). With regard to the manifestations of the Four Horsemen of the Apocalypse in Revelation, Knight (2010a) cited executive producer Sera Gamble in the book *Supernatural: The Official Companion Season 5*:

> The things that the Horsemen represent in pestilence, famine and war are like forces of nature and are states that humans experience all the time. So it isn't as though when Lucifer comes on the scene he brings these monsters with him that are unleashed that we haven't been experiencing the effects of all throughout history. It's more that he gathers them to him. (p. 111)

Both Gamble and Kripke, as well as fellow executive producer Phil Sgriccia, pointed out that the move to a plot grounded in Christian mythology unfolded over the course of the first five seasons (Knight, 2010a). The Christian-based Apocalyptic storyline of the fifth season grew out of the story development of the first four seasons; the plot of the fifth season closely connected events in the earlier seasons to the background of the Winchester brothers, rather than a "cold" start using the Apocalypse as the main premise of the fifth season. Any other television program beginning with the events of *Supernatural*'s fifth season might have found it difficult to gain the acceptance of viewers because they would have had to "buy into" a biblical storyline from the start, whereas with the story of *Supernatural* gradually incorporated more and more Christian material after already gaining a committed audience.

In season four of *Supernatural*, viewers witnessed the first appearance of Castiel, an angel who resurrected Dean from Hell. The season four storyline focused on demonic efforts to raise Lucifer and begin the Apocalypse, while angels like Castiel seemingly tried to prevent it. Lucifer eventually escaped from his "cage" in Hell through the actions of both Winchester brothers over the course of season four. Sam and Dean also were tapped to serve as the vessels for the brother angels representing Heaven (Dean for Michael) and Hell (Sam for Lucifer) in the battle for the fate of the world.

Season five then became about the Winchesters' attempts to prevent the Apocalypse; the audience also learned that some angels actually *wanted* to start the Apocalypse, which would result in the end of humankind. Additionally, God apparently went missing, and the elements of the Bible's Book of Revelation began to manifest on Earth, thus signaling the "End Times." Several episodes throughout season five focused on narratives drawn directly from the Book of Revelation, adding to the Christian "flavor" of the series as we described in chapter 3.

To examine the use of homiletics in this television series, we used textual analysis to examine story scripts and visual images in three episodes from season five, aired from 2009 to 2010. These offer detailed and specific depictions directly taken from Revelation: "Good God, Y'All!," "My Bloody Valentine" and "Two Minutes to Midnight."[3] In particular, we looked for: (a) any direct references to Revelation in the form of quoted Scripture; (b) visual images of the Four Horsemen, especially any symbols and metaphors embodied in their physical appearance; and (c) text we considered as serving as homily-related messages that connected the Four Horsemen and their underlying abstractions (such as "war" and "death") to specific contemporary issues and events.

REVELATION AS NARRATIVE

The Book of Revelation, the last book of the New Testament, contains a prophecy of the End Times attributed to Saint John of Patmos, who wrote it during the reign of the Roman emperor Domitian (AD 81–96). Scholars acknowledge Revelation as both a response by John to contextual political issues, including his banishment to the island of Patmos and the Roman persecution of Christians (Farrer, 1988; Friesen, 2001; Jordan, 2011; Torrey, 1958), and a timeless piece of Apocalyptic discourse (O'Leary, 1997, 1994; Snyder, 2000). "The Book of Revelation remained a contentious text throughout the early development of the Christian canon. At once canonical and apocryphal, the Church Fathers argued both for and against its inclusion, and attempted to formulate an official stance on the text that rendered it ideologically and institutionally 'safe,'" noted Jordan (2011, pp. 3–4).

Despite its timelessness, popular misconceptions about the contents of this prophetic book from the Bible have surfaced throughout history. The Four Horsemen serve as one aspect of Revelation that readers have often

confused with other elements of the book. Scripture labels the Four Horsemen as Conquest, War, Famine, and Death. However, popular culture accounts often replace Conquest with Pestilence, with the order of the Horsemen's appearance as follows: War, Famine, Pestilence, and Death.

This misunderstanding of the text of Revelation in popular culture portrayals actually may result from a compression of Revelation 6:2-8, as it
appears in the New American Bible (NAB) and New Jerusalem Bible (NJB).
These two versions, and the more common King James, all contain essentially the same text, including the proper labeling of the Four Horsemen. However, the last line of the passage differs between the editions. The King James
Version reads: "And power was given unto them over the fourth part of the
earth, to kill with sword, and with hunger, and with *death*, and with the
beasts of the earth." The NAB and NJB both change the word "death" in this
line to "plague," quite possibly to clarify the redundancy of the King James
Version, which essentially says "kill with death."

The popular version of the Four Horsemen seen in movies and other
media, then, represents an amalgamation of the entire passage, rather than a
specific reference to the exact Four Horsemen in the Book of Revelation.
Popular media versions of the Four Horsemen from film and print illustrate
this interchangeability. For example, in the 1921 film *The Four Horsemen of
the Apocalypse*, Conquest is replaced by Pestilence when the Horsemen are
referenced (Rehill, 2010). More recently, Marvel Comics' *The X-Men* comic
book rendition of the Four Horsemen includes Pestilence instead of Conquest. In Gaiman and Pratchett's 1990 novel *Good Omens: The Nice and
Accurate Prophecies of Agnes Nutter, Witch,* Pestilence is one of the Four
Horsemen, but is said to have "retired" with the advent of penicillin and is
replaced by Pollution. The 2009 crime movie *Horsemen* (released by Lionsgate) also depicts Pestilence while leaving out Conquest. [4]

In *Supernatural,* this blended version of the Four Horsemen appears in
specific episodes during the Apocalypse story arc in season five, and, as an
extrapolation, presents within their subtext a homily about contemporary
American culture via their fictional representation on screen. We see the
subtext of these stories as doing more than simply relaying biblical myths
and narratives to the audience. Specifically, we contend that these episodes
not only give viewers recognizable and intelligible versions of the Four
Horsemen of the Apocalypse informed by Scripture, but also provide a secular homiletic experience in the form of commentaries on current prescient
cultural issues. By providing an indirect and entertaining turn on the homily,
Supernatural uses the modern medium of television as a "cultural storyteller"
(Hoover, 1988, p. 241) and substitute Bible for its audience.

"GOOD GOD Y'ALL!"—WAR

"Good God Y'All!" (Episode 5.2) aired on September 17, 2009.[5] The episode opens with Sam and Dean traveling to River Pass, Colorado, after a fellow hunter, Rufus Turner, contacts them requesting immediate assistance in ridding the town of an apparent demon infestation. The town seemingly has been overrun by demons when the brothers arrive; they find a group of townspeople holed up in a church basement protected by longtime Winchester friend and fellow hunter Ellen Harvelle, who reports she cannot find her daughter, Jo. Sam and Dean then search for Jo and encounter a pair of demons, whose eyes manifest their true identity: completely black eyes mark demons in *Supernatural*, who possess humans and appear in human form. The brothers become puzzled when the demons do not succumb to the traditional anti-demon weapons of salt and holy water. Not until after Dean consults a Bible and finds a verse that connects recent events in the town to signs of "end times" and the demons capture Sam do Dean and Ellen finally realize that the town is not infested with demons, but has been occupied by War, the first Horseman. War has used the power of illusion to turn people against each other, making them see each other as demons.

Rufus and Jo capture Sam, tying him to a chair and leaving him in a room in the house where they wage their own fight against the townspeople/"demons." While Sam sits there helplessly, "Roger," a 30-something businessperson nondescript from the rest of the townspeople, walks into the room. He reveals to Sam his true identity: War. While pretending to be Roger, War was in fact manipulating the townspeople into conflict with each other. War tells Sam that he is looking for his fellow Horsemen so they can bring about the end of the world by releasing Lucifer from Hell. Sam manages to escape, and joins Dean, Ellen, and Jo in ending War's illusions and saving what remains of the town. Sam and Dean then confront the Horseman and cut off his ring, stripping him of his power.

The scriptural basis for "Good God Y'All!" comes from Revelation 6:4: "And there went out another horse that was red: and power was given to him that sat thereon to take peace from the earth, and that they should kill one another: and there was given unto him a great sword." In this episode, War's "horse" appears as a red Mustang convertible. In *Supernatural*'s version of this Horseman and his destructive power, the anthropomorphized character of War took peace from the town of River Pass by inducing people to kill one another, thus creating a battleground where people fought based on perceived difference. The delusion cast by War almost resulted in all-out battle fought among humans against each other, rather than one caused by or won by a supernatural entity.

Contemporary Context: World at War

The context in which this episode was written, developed, and eventually aired establishes the homiletic quality of the episode. During this time, the United States was still engaged in conflicts in Afghanistan and Iraq, as well as focused on the larger fight in the War on Terror. In Afghanistan and Iraq, the U.S. military had recently undertaken a strategy whereby the indigenous population was trained to root out and fight insurgents in their own midst.[6] Speech during war, including the War on Terror, seeks to demonize the enemy (Ivie, 1974, 1980). These events and rhetorical devices provide a context for this particular episode and the way in which War "takes peace from the earth" by creating the rhetorical and literal demonization of the enemy. In *Supernatural,* War the Horseman embodies the destructive power of conflict resulting from the demonization of an enemy.

"Good God Y'All!" sets the story of War in a small town of "ordinary folks," where the fighting is house to house. One can view this setting as similar to the urban warfare and counterinsurgency techniques used in the cities and towns of Iraq, and, indeed, modern war in general. In this episode, the aftermath of skirmishes between the residents of River Pass reveals over-turned cars, houses secured from demon incursion, and people scavenging for supplies. When the demon hunter Rufus first contacts the brothers for help, he performs first aid on a townsperson while under fire, much like a soldier conducting triage and radioing for support during a firefight. The hunters Sam, Dean, Rufus, Jo, and Ellen all train the local people to fight each other and teach them how to distinguish demons from humans, similar to the training of local militias by military personnel. Additionally, one of the people in the town reveals he had served two tours "in Fallujah." This reference to the U.S. military involvement in Iraq further connects the storyline to real-world events. It also offers a version of war "closer to home," literally and figuratively, by showing how war today, especially in terms of the action in Iraq and Afghanistan, is fought within the civilian arena where soldiers cannot easily discern "friendlies" from insurgents; soldiers in such situations must fight in and around people's homes. Furthermore, War's mental "occu-pation" of the people of River Pass reifies the destruction borne out of the rhetorical demonization of an enemy.

The homiletic message of this episode becomes even more apparent when one consideres the title itself, taken from lyrics of the popular rock song "War" recorded by Edwin Starr and released in 1970. "War" the song served as a blatant anti-Vietnam War protest message. The phrase "Good God, Y'All!" comes from the song's refrain, and follows the lyrics, "War! Huh! What is it good for? Absolutely nothing!" (Whitfield & Strong, 1970). We see the connection between "War" the song and contemporary conflicts as being even more salient given the many editorials from major news outlets, notably *Newsweek* and CNN, that made comparisons between the Vietnam War and the prolonged engagements in Afghanistan and Iraq (Barry, 2009; Hornick, 2009; Tran, 2006). Just as "War" the song forwards the message that war is good for "absolutely nothing," the connection between the dramatic material in the episode to the contemporary events it reflects forwards a similar message about the destruction and damage caused by war. By appropriating a war protest song and using its lyrics as the title for the episode, the homily forwarded by the producers of the show points to the very nature and effects of war: nobody really "wins," as everyone and everything in its wake is destroyed in some way.

Literal Demonization: Creating the Enemy "Other"

The connection between War, a biblical character, and the human experience becomes explicit when his personification "Roger" holds his conversation with Sam near the end of the episode. When Sam asks him to tell him who he really is, War responds: "Here's a hint. I was in Germany [pause], then in Germany, then in the Middle East. I was in Darfur when my beeper went off" (Gamble & Sgriccia, 2009). In revealing himself as War the Horseman, his response referred to World War I, World War II, the Israeli-Palestinian conflict, and the genocide in Darfur, Sudan. This list implies War has always been here, rather than a new arrival. War then confirms to Sam that there never were any demons in town; rather, the so-called demons were "just frightened people, ripping each other's throats out. Frankly, you're really vicious little animals, Sam." War further explains: "People don't need a reason to kill each other. I mean, you've seen the Irish? They're all *Irish*," an allusion to the conflict between Catholics and Protestants in Northern Ireland. Essentially, War makes the point that when we demonize each other, we invite ourselves to commit acts of violence upon each other despite the fact we are not very different from each other.

Similar to the portrayal of the devil as being present during times of turmoil in the Rolling Stones' song "Sympathy for the Devil," illustrated by the lyrics, "I stuck around St. Petersburg when I saw it was time for a change," and "it was you and me" who killed the Kennedys (Jagger & Richards, 1968), War in this episode of *Supernatural* appears as an ordinary guy, someone just like "you and me." He serves as a metaphor for the destructive potential within "regular" people when they see each other as "the enemy." Dean summarizes this process when he and Ellen finally realize what is happening to them. "They think we're demons; we think they're demons," Dean says (Gamble & Sgriccia, 2009). In fact, nobody is a demon, but War's spell creates an illusion of difference, much the way war rhetoric does. Human conflict, then, originates in fear, self-interest, and misattribution, all weaknesses to which human beings fall prey too often.

War's comments to Sam argue that war itself is not caused by some supernatural effect or design, but rather flows from the reactions of frightened people who do not realize what they are doing to each other, and by extension, all humankind. In short, this episode illustrates the power of the binary casting of the self against the "Other," what Hall (1997) termed the "symbolic frontier" created by stereotyping and the notion of "normal" versus "deviant," wherein the Other becomes a site for aggression and hostility (p. 258). The success of perceiving a different people, culture, or group as an Other that threatens our existence emanates from the uncritical acceptance of war rhetoric based on self-interest and fear. In this episode, War does not have to do much to create this illusion, demonstrating how quickly and easily people fall prey to their own suspicions and fears.

This fear leads to a dehumanizing of the Other, and drives the fighting in the town throughout the episode. When people are demonized, they lose their humanity, thus making them easier to kill. This demonization has become a familiar device in various forms of war rhetoric to help make killing other people palatable (see Uribe, 2004). In "Good God, Y'All" the townspeople *literally* see each other as demons, as inhuman. Rather than taking part in the killing himself, War essentially stands back and watches as people succumb to the illusion he created: they do not question what they see, thus allowing fear and dehumanization of the opponent to make it easier to fight and kill their fellow townspeople. The war in the town ends and the killing stops only after Sam and Dean convince the townspeople that the "demons" they perceive are actually humans and break War's "spell" by cutting off the ring that gives him power. As a secularized homily on the pointless, destructive power of war, *Supernatural* utilizes biblical passages and references to contemporary wars to inform our understanding of how war results from the demonization of the Other. We can only stop killing each other when we cast off that illusion and see that we are *all* human, just as Sam and Dean were able to do at the end of the episode.

"MY BLOODY VALENTINE"—FAMINE

The Horseman Famine makes his appearance in "My Bloody Valentine" (Episode 5.14), which aired on February 11, 2010. The episode opens with an apparent Valentine's Day theme revolving around love: a man and woman start aggressively kissing each other after their first date. They literally eat each other to death, consumed by their passion. Sam and Dean arrive in town and learn about other recent deaths involving couples that killed each other in expressions of mania, the term by which the ancient Greeks named clingy, obsessive love (Galician, 2003, p. 18). The angel Castiel appears, and assists the brothers in their investigation. Castiel suggests Cupid is the villain. However, after he and the brothers locate Cupid, depicted in this episode as a cherub taking the form of an overweight, baby-faced man dressed in a diaper, they soon realize he is not to blame. Seemingly stumped, the brothers and Castiel soon determine the culprit is actually Famine. This Horseman activated a literal famine via a hunger in the townspeople that they can neither control nor satiate.

In the *Supernatural* version of Famine, he appears as a pale, thin, sickly old man in a motorized wheelchair who relies on oxygen and appears on the verge of dying. Famine's power is so strong that it even affects Castiel the angel, who constantly eats red meat as a result of a craving of his human host "Jimmy." Dean, however, seems unaffected, despite his well-known enjoyment of drinking and womanizing. The brothers finally confront and stop Famine, but not before he delivers a message that contains a criticism of consumerism and consumption specifically related to contemporary American life.

The passage found in Revelation 6:5-6 informs the anthropomorphized Famine in "My Bloody Valentine":

> And when he had opened the third seal, I heard the third beast say, Come and see. And I beheld, and lo a black horse; and he that sat on him had a pair of balances in his hand. And I heard a voice in the midst of the four beasts say, A measure of wheat for a penny, and three measures of barley for a penny; and see thou hurt not the oil and the wine. (King James Version)

Like War in "Good God, Y'All," an automobile symbolizes Famine's horse: he rides into town in a black Cadillac Escalade. This fuel-inefficient status symbol denotes luxury and excess, standing in complete juxtaposition to the notion of "famine" as starvation, dearth, and scarcity.

Contemporary Context: America's Addiction Epidemic

"My Bloody Valentine" addresses several familiar "lifestyle" issues related to modern life in the United States. For instance, obesity, a public health concern for many years, came into sharper focus in 2009 and 2010 as First Lady Michelle Obama named fighting childhood obesity as one of her major initiatives. Coincidentally, during the week that "My Bloody Valentine" aired, the First Lady rolled out the official tenets of her initiative, called "Let's Move" (Sweet, 2010). Accusations of greed also still abounded in the news media in the wake of the economic collapse of late 2008; Wall Street became the poster child for greed and excess, and President Obama and Congress sought to overhaul financial regulations governing investment firms throughout the first two years of his presidency (Hulse, 2009).

This episode also addresses real-world social and public health issues such as alcoholism, drug abuse, and efforts to combat these social illnesses, such as the so-called "war on drugs" (Cardona, 2010; "Obama Rebalances U.S. Drug Policy," 2009). Allusions to a culture of addiction appear not only in the depictions of excess in the episode, as described below, but by the subplot concerning the angel Castiel. As an angel, Castiel does not eat. However, Famine causes his human host "Jimmy" to activate his own hunger for red meat. Castiel succumbs to this addiction by eating hamburgers one after the other. He even gorges on raw hamburger like an animal. Castiel invokes the cliché associated with denial of one's addiction when he states, "I'm an angel. I can stop anytime I want" (Edlund & Rohl, 2010). The irony of an *angel* having no control and denying his problem underscores the illusory notion that one can "stop anytime" and regain control without help. These contextual factors allow for an interpretation of Revelation that becomes prescient for the viewers of *Supernatural* in that they have become familiar, high-profile, and relatable issues that in some way affect everyday life.

Emptiness in the Land of Plenty

In the Book of Revelation, God bestowed upon War the power to make men fight each other. In the passage quoted previously, God appears to give Famine the power to control commerce and ration food. The character of Famine in *Supernatural* wields power over people's self-control, rather than explicit control over a market of goods and food. This power manifests itself as an insatiable hunger for food, sex, drugs, alcohol, and even attention so the people can get *all* they want, which, ironically, is never enough. In this episode, as people's cravings grow, their lack of self-control leads them to kill themselves in pursuit of that which they crave: the first daters at the beginning of the episode eat each other's flesh; lovers complete a suicide pact; the town's alcoholic coroner drinks himself to death; and a man with a gastric band gorges on so many Twinkies that his stomach bursts. Even Famine in this episode has a craving: he hungers for human souls, and the more people who die, the more souls he consumes.

Hunger, in its various forms, serves as one of the primary themes in the depiction of Famine in *Supernatural*. First, Castiel identifies Famine as the source of the problems in the town. Sam begins the discussion by saying, "I thought famine meant starvation, like as in, you know, food." Castiel responds, "Yes, absolutely. But not just food. Everyone seems to be starving for something: sex, attention, drugs, love" (Edlund & Rohl, 2010). Though the Bible does not explicitly describe Famine the Horseman as a manifestation of hunger, he becomes synonymous with hunger in this episode when Castiel declares, "And great will be the horseman's hunger, for he is hunger." Castiel's description of Famine as hunger serves as a voice-over for the scene in which Famine arrives at a local diner where a neon sign reading "All You

Can Eat" flashes over a gruesome "orgy" of customers and employees eating everything, swallowing entire bottles of pills, and drinking mass quantities of liquor. The cook even dives into a deep fryer headfirst to get at French fries.

The homily reflected by this episode centers on hunger and want. Castiel explains famine as starvation for something, the intense desire that we all have as we look to fill an emptiness in our being. Because an angel of the Lord delivers this message, and those who seek to fill their emptiness with material desires lose their souls to the Horseman, one can interpret emptiness, or "drought," as a lack of spirituality and faith that people unsuccessfully try to fill with the "wrong" things. The disturbing images of diner customers and employees literally consuming themselves with their wants illustrate the power of our cravings when we lose self-control. Rather than depicted as lack of sustenance, the interpretation of Famine originates in the notion of people's spiritual emptiness; they focus on obtaining an excess of material things, such as food, sex, or property, to their detriment. Famine, then, can and does lead to our end just as he serves as a sign of the End Times in the Book of Revelation.

Toward the end of the episode, the exposition of this message of spiritual want becomes even more apparent, as Famine directs his lesson at American society specifically. Sam and Dean finally confront Famine at the diner, where Famine first addresses Dean, who seemingly appears unaffected by this Horseman. Famine tells Dean he can see inside him and cannot affect him "because inside you are already dead." Dean has stopped even trying to fill his own emptiness, and therefore has no needs or cravings. This aspect of Famine's lesson relates to the establishment of the characters in the series' previous seasons and overall narrative, as viewers familiar with Dean and his personal story arc understand how he has become this way. It illustrates how the writers were able to fold the Apocalypse story into season five by tying specific characters and their histories into the episodes featuring the Horsemen, thus weaving a homiletic message into the story of the Winchesters, rather than presenting an obviously religious story.

Against the backdrop of the "All You Can Eat" sign, Dean mocks Famine, saying, "So this is your big trick, huh? Making people cuckoo for Cocoa Puffs?" Famine then responds:

> Doesn't take much. Hardly a push. Oh, America: All you can eat, all of the time. Consume, consume. A swarm of locusts in stretch pants and yet you are all starving. Because hunger doesn't come from the body. It also comes from the soul. (Edlund & Rohl, 2010)

Famine's characterization of Americans as a "swarm of locusts in stretch pants" refers to the obesity epidemic in this land of plenty and his conversation reinforces the idea that hunger does not come from our need for food or other sustenance, but from the emptiness within ourselves created by selfishness and moral relativism. Pope John Paul II (1995) expressed this same concern about moral emptiness when he referred to the detrimental effects of capitalism in several encyclicals issued during his papacy. The story of Famine as told by *Supernatural* teaches us that people today, specifically Americans, hunger for something spiritual, yet try to fill that void with material things. Only through their own willpower do the Winchesters overcome Famine by cutting off his ring and his power. By extension, only through self-control and spiritual realization can people combat the emptiness within; without such control, their own end times will fast approach.

"TWO MINUTES TO MIDNIGHT" — PESTILENCE AND DEATH

The final two Horsemen, Pestilence and Death, make their appearance in "Two Minutes to Midnight" (Episode 5.21), the penultimate episode of season five which aired on May 6, 2010. Pestilence actually made a brief appearance in "Hammer of the Gods" (Episode 5.19); he drives a dilapidated green car to a convenience store, where he sneezes and contaminates it. Visual effects underscore the manifestations of disease, as Pestilence literally spews his greenish-yellow vile on the humans he encounters.

Pestilence again only briefly appears in "Two Minutes to Midnight"; most of this episode centers on Death. At the beginning of the episode, the Winchester brothers hunt down Pestilence at a convalescent home where they suspect he is a patient. It turns out he is actually a doctor, infecting patients with combinations of rare deadly diseases, while also orchestrating the worldwide distribution of a "vaccine" for the swine flu through a demon-fronted pharmaceutical firm. The vaccine, in fact, will infect the population with a demon-created virus that will lead to the end of humankind. The brothers and Castiel successfully defeat Pestilence, when Castiel comes to the brothers' aid and cuts off Pestilence's ring in much the same fashion as the brothers did with War and Famine.

After vanquishing Pestilence, Dean hunts down Death, who is about to release a weather-related catastrophe on the city of Chicago. Death has been bound to Lucifer. Death explains that Dean can release him from that tether and prevent the Apocalypse so long as Dean is willing to allow Sam to die as Lucifer's vessel. In return for Dean's promise to allow Sam to die, Death freely gives his ring to Dean. The visual imagery and dialogue between Dean and the Horseman Death in this episode represents the final component of the overall homiletic message drawn from Revelation in *Supernatural.*

Contemporary Context: Natural Disasters, Disease, and Doom

Just as with the previous Horsemen episodes featuring War and Famine, understanding the context within which these episodes were filmed and delivered helps to explain the homiletic nature of *Supernatural*'s interpretation of the passage from Revelation. At the time these episodes were produced and aired, the H1N1 swine flu epidemic gripped the world. This strand of the flu contained several different variants of influenza, including the traditional pig flu and Eurasian pig flu resulting in its *nom de guerre* (Szabo, 2009). The pandemic slowed by November, 2009, and was officially declared over by the World Health Organization in August, 2010, with fewer recorded deaths than expected in a worst-case scenario ("Swine Flu Pandemic Over," 2010).

Larger, more calamitous natural disasters occurred around the time "Two Minutes to Midnight" was filmed and broadcast. On January 12, 2010, a massive earthquake in Haiti killed more than 200,000 people (Romero & Lacey, 2010). Over the next four months there were two more major earthquakes, one in Chile and another in China (Boyle & Shapiro, 2010; Jacobs, 2010). Although it did not occur at the time of filming, Hurricane Katrina also remained a part of the public consciousness (Bowman & Bowman, 2010). Indeed, in this episode Death specifically mentions hurricanes as being a sign of his presence and power. The outbreak of the H1N1 virus, earthquakes, and the lingering memory of Hurricane Katrina all enhance the historical context in which the rendering of the Revelation passage becomes homiletic in "Two Minutes to Midnight."

Revelation 6:8 serves as the passage from the Book of Revelation that informs the characters of Pestilence and Death in *Supernatural*:

> And I looked, and behold a pale horse: and his name that sat on him was Death, and Hell followed with him. And power was given unto them over the fourth part of the earth, to kill with sword, and with hunger, and with death [plague], and with the beasts of the earth. (King James Version)

As mentioned previously, both the NAB and NJB versions of Revelation replace the word "death" with "plague." Whereas War and Famine each have an episode dedicated to their individual characters, one can view the appearance of both Pestilence and Death in the same episode as illustrating the confusion and yet close connection between Pestilence and Death in this biblical passage. In this sense, Revelation 6:8 indicates that Death can use any of the powers of the other Horsemen. So, too, does "Two Minutes to Midnight" depict Death's vast power by combining his appearance with that of Pestilence.

In this episode, the real-world threat, and subsequent fear, of swine flu figures prominently in the plans for the coming Armageddon. In fact, after Sam and Dean defeat Pestilence, the demon named Crowley shows them a headline that reads, "Swine Flu Vaccine to Stem Tide of Unprecedented Outbreak." In the storyline, demonic elements plan to use swine flu vaccine to bring about the end of the world; this correlates to the part of the biblical passage in the NAB and NJB that references death will come by plague. However, one could view the relative ease with which Sam, Dean, and Castiel dispatch Pestilence at the beginning of this episode as a metaphor for the way in which modern medicine has the potential to eradicate disease, and the relative lack of power of Pestilence as opposed to War, Famine, and Death. We find the way in which Death himself provides a big-picture explanation of his purpose, and the inevitability of death for not only humankind, but even God, even more relevant to the homiletic nature of this episode and its companion stories during season five.

Death: The Final Reaper

In "Two Minutes to Midnight," Death reveals himself as a gaunt, older man dressed in a black suit and carrying a walking stick. When he first appears onscreen, a remake of the traditional funeral dirge "O' Death" plays in the background as he exits his "horse," a white 1950s Cadillac, to walk along a Chicago street. Shot in slow motion, the scene shows Death moving among the people on the sidewalk. The ominous strains of the song "O Death" give an almost magisterial tone to a scene of everyday life, implying that death is both awesome and, literally, pedestrian. "O Death" tells the story of a man begging Death to let him live another year, appropriate for the *Supernatural* story arc in which the brothers try to stave off Armageddon. Singer Jennifer Titus performs the song, her lilting voice adding an additional dimension of sweetness to the prospect of dying.[7] The closing lyrics convey the theme for this episode and the significance of Death's appearance in Revelation: "My name is Death and the end is here."

The depiction of Death in this episode emphasizes the indiscriminant aspect of death in the human experience. In his first scene, Death brushes by a man who is walking along the street while texting on his cell phone. The man rudely responds to the contact, then drops dead; the camera makes it seem as though Death killed the man for his rude transgression. Death later meets with Dean in a pizzeria where all the customers and employees are dead, apparently having died at Death's casual hand. Indeed, Death enjoys his pizza without any concern for what he has done.

The main reason for Death's arrival in Chicago is that he is about to strike it with a weather-related catastrophe, but Dean makes a deal with Death in which he will remove Lucifer's hold over him. When Dean asks what will happen to Chicago, Death replies, "I suppose it can stay. I like the pizza" (Gamble & Sgriccia, 2010b). Death's nonchalance regarding the fate of millions of people demonstrates that he needs no reason to kill or to spare people. His previous encounter with the texting man on the sidewalk further illustrates how he can touch anyone at any moment.

Throughout the conversation with Dean, Death's power becomes even more apparent. Their exchange also offers a philosophically and theologically-based perspective of death's role in the world and in the universe. Death explains to Dean: "I'm more powerful than you can process." He goes on: " . . . as old as God, maybe older. Neither one of us can remember. In the end, I'll reap him, too" (Gamble & Sgriccia, 2010b). These statements show both the obvious, that death is something humans cannot comprehend or counter, and the abstruse, in that it has power over time and space. Death's claim that he also will "reap" God subtly argues that Death itself is the only constant. Death reminds us of his place in the cosmos while reflecting the central premise of the passage from Revelation: He is the final Horseman, the ultimate reaper.

Death also comments on Dean's sense of self-importance as a human being. As Dean represents humankind in this episode, Death comments on how humans perceive their own importance: Death sees humans the way humans view bacteria, and refers to earth as "one little planet in an insignificant solar system, in a galaxy barely out of its diapers" (Gamble & Sgriccia, 2010b). This assertion runs counter to the way humans, and in particular those in individualistic cultures such as the United States, understand their existence by portraying humanity as small and insignificant.

After Dean agrees to free Death from Lucifer's hold in exchange for his brother Sam's life, Death reminds him, "You know, you can't cheat Death" (Gamble & Sgriccia, 2010b). This adage becomes more relevant due to the fact that later in the episode Dean reveals he intends to try. Further, Death's warning symbolizes the futility of trying to prolong life and avoid death. The interpretation of Revelation 6:8 in this episode illustrates that death comes to all of us in many different forms and at any given time; we cannot escape it nor comprehend its power. In essence, death itself is the "end times" for each of us.

REVEALING REVELATION'S RELEVANCE IN THE "NEW CHURCH"

Homilies require three characteristics: the author must (a) have knowledge of Scripture, (b) be able to divine its core spiritual meaning for the audience, and (c) connect that meaning to the audience's lived experience. The three episodes of *Supernatural* analyzed here fulfill these three requirements. Each appropriated a verse from the Book of Revelation (Knight, 2010b), then constructed a story from a core message that related to contemporary concerns and events, demonstrating its epic and timeless quality. The first,

"Good God Y'All," introduced War, the first of the Four Horsemen of the Apocalypse, by melding characteristics from contemporary conflicts to make the point that in war, people lose their humanity rhetorically and in practice. If people do not recognize the damage that division and suspicion can do, then they will become the instruments of their own destruction, making war on each other. In "My Bloody Valentine," we found an anthropomorphized Famine destroying people by inducing overindulgence. Broadcast in the shadow of a public campaign against obesity and drugs, this episode calls America to task for its lack of self-control and desire for excess. Finally, in "Two Minutes to Midnight," Pestilence shows the potential destruction and fear created by an epidemic like the swine flu. In the same episode, Death arrives and emphasizes the insignificance of humankind, while also showing how indiscriminate and inescapable it is, despite all human efforts to "cheat death." Of the Four Horsemen depicted in *Supernatural*, Death actually is the only Horseman the Winchester brothers, and, through them, humanity, cannot overcome or defeat.

Whereas John of Patmos offered a very dramatic, symbolic, fantastical, and non-literal description of the End Times, *Supernatural* took that story and made a case about everyday life. *Supernatural* reified the story of the Book of Revelation by depicting the Four Horsemen without extravagant special effects. Despite their more global goals, they appeared as ordinary humans in street clothes instead of in visually spectacular costumes, makeup, or computer-generated graphics. Indeed, this rather un-supernatural approach mirrors the human depictions of demons and angels within the series. For example, the angel Castiel appears as a man in need of a shave dressed in a shabby suit and overcoat; viewers only get a hint of his true nature as an "angel of the Lord" when his wings appear as shadows. Demons also appear as regular people, with only the occasional flicker of their all-black eyes revealing their identities. These portrayals run counter to traditional and familiar depictions of demons as pitchfork-wielding, brimstone-spewing, fire-breathing beasts, and of winged, haloed angels. Instead, such characters literally appear "down to earth."

In turn, we see the homilies contained in each of the Horsemen episodes as even more effective because they represent common and familiar aspects of human life: conflict, hunger, disease, and death. Thematically, the end of the world represents the ultimate war between Heaven and Hell. However, *Supernatural*'s telling of this timeless motif made the Apocalypse much more personal than any visually spectacular war by focusing on the Winchester brothers and consistently utilizing commonplace, non-dramatic settings for their encounters with the Horsemen: a small town (War), a small town diner (Famine), a nursing home (Pestilence), and a pizza parlor in Chicago (Death). Thus, the biblical component of the program's storyline becomes even easier for a secular audience to accept by grounding the Four Horsemen as existing in "normal" life where we all hold the potential for war and conflict, we all hunger for more than food, we are all vulnerable to disease, and ultimately we will all die.

More pointedly, one can interpret the low-key way in which this particular television series depicts demons, angels, and the Four Horsemen as implying that evil, good, war, famine, pestilence, and death surround us every day, illustrating that the power to be destructive or constructive lies within *us* and the choices we make. In this sense, the Apocalypse as the end of the world may not result from a spectacular all-out war, but rather through individual actions that eventually lead to humankind's downfall.

In keeping with Ostwalt's (1995) listing of Apocalyptic plotline elements commonly found in filmic depictions of the end times, Dean and Sam do manage to prevent the end of the world in the season five finale, "Swan Song" (Episode 5.22).[8] The locale of the anticlimactic final battle that will determine the fate of the world appears as a grassy field adjacent Stull Cemetery in Lawrence, Kansas, the Winchesters' hometown. Sam had agreed to serve as Lucifer's human vessel. As Lucifer, Sam has a showdown with the archangel Michael (whose human vessel turned out not to be Dean, but the third Winchester brother, Adam Milligan). Dean arrives on the scene, followed by Castiel and Bobby, both of whom are killed by Sam/Lucifer, but not before Castiel temporarily vanquishes Michael. Sam/Lucifer then turns on Dean, beating him to a bloody pulp before Sam is able to take momentary control of Lucifer, grab a returned Michael, and jump into the pit created by a spell using the Four Horsemen's rings.[9] Further adding to the "smallness" of *Supernatural*'s version of Armageddon/the Apocalypse, Castiel is resurrected; he proceeds to resurrect Bobby and heal Dean, making it appear as if the whole thing never happened. The only indication that the end of the world almost happened is the absence of Sam, who literally saved the world from its foretold destruction.

The depiction of "Armageddon" as occurring in the American countryside between two "ordinary" humans further underscored *Supernatural*'s imagining of heavenly and hellish forces as occurring in an ordinary setting. In this way, the writers' vision, translated through the lens of everyday life, creates a more palatable version of the Book of Revelation for a secularized audience. In this manner, this group of episodes simultaneously makes religious principles, practices, and parables easy to digest for that audience while not appearing to proselytize. The storyline of the Apocalypse might come directly from the New Testament, and the Bible may serve as a source for material, but *Supernatural* manages to avoid an overtly religious tone that may alienate viewers.

SUMMARY

Originally a story told for contemporaries of John of Patmos, storytellers have used Revelation time and again in different contexts. *Supernatural* gave a modern venue for telling that story, and through its focus on one passage provided a homily that comments on the lifestyles and world events encountered by its audience. *Supernatural* connected Scripture to contemporary concerns and issues, and did so thanks to writers and producers who crafted the story of the Four Horsemen in an entertaining and creative way. The series' protagonists, Dean and Sam Winchester, essentially "fought" each of the Four Horsemen—War, Famine, Pestilence, and Death—all of whom appeared in human form. By portraying these larger-than-life entities as persons walking the earth, the program not only visually "grounded" them to everyday life, but further utilized the concepts they symbolize to convey life lessons regarding war, disease, spiritual emptiness, and death.

Taken as a whole, the episodes featuring the Horsemen provided not only a way of approaching these concepts in a non-threatening way, but also, we contend, provided an overall lesson that points to how human beings need to overcome prejudice, fight diseases, and fill inner emptiness. The one thing that we cannot defeat is death. In this manner, the message became that of human power vanquishing the ills presented by conflict, diseases, and lack of self-control. By presenting Death as an almost calming presence, one that has existed as long as God, the lesson ultimately concludes with the message that nothing and no one can avoid "the end."

The use of the Bible to tell a story in a fictional setting is akin to allegory and parable, two tools often employed by priests and ministers when constructing homilies. Audiences who would normally bristle at overt evangelism might find that this particular method of appropriating elements of the Bible results in a secularized homily, which perhaps they find more acceptable. Thus, one could view the manner in which *Supernatural* takes Scripture and puts a secular spin on it as an even more effective way of communicating homiletic messages, especially when it comes to taking the Bible and making it relevant to a particular audience that is traditionally apprehensive about receiving overt theological lessons through media.

We see *Supernatural* as an example of Clark's (2003) "dark side of evangelicalism," which essentially creates a universe in which "good" characters can, and do, fight demons and other evil creatures. The use of the horror genre, which allows fantastical visual depictions of sacred stories, events, and figures, becomes a way to reach an audience that otherwise might reject religious characters, or characters who clearly practice or preach certain religions. The producers of *Supernatural* may not have had evangelical intent in their telling of the Apocalypse as based in Revelation, but they still told a story grounded in religion.

We find *Supernatural*'s approach to telling a story grounded in a biblical Apocalypse exceptional in view of the absence of a central figure in the New Testament and Book of Revelation. Jesus Christ, the Lamb of God in Revelation and a central figure in the Apocalypse, does not appear in these episodes at all, something made possible by only focusing on a small excerpt of Revelation that does not mention the Lamb. Even though *Supernatural* as a series relies on religious material for its storylines, Christ does not play any central role, even though God, angels (such as Michael), and Lucifer all do. [10] This approach avoids the kind of controversy experienced by the short-lived network series *Book of Daniel*, which became a lightning rod for criticism because of its depiction of Christ as a character in that program (Bird, 2009).

The explicitly biblical nature of Revelation served as the storyline for other television series without much success, but *Supernatural* has escaped the kind of criticism aimed at those other efforts. The reliance on Revelation makes the three Horsemen episodes, and perhaps the entire fifth season, a cleverly packaged exposition on Christianity that ties morality rooted in this religious tradition to contemporary events. The Winchesters pretty much defeated any and all enemies they were up against, until Lucifer, that is. While contending with Lucifer and the power of the host of Heaven, the Winchesters also had to combat their Horsemen adversaries, defeating all but Death (whom no one can defeat).

In this chapter, we unpacked the homilies offered through the Horsemen episodes, tying the everyday lessons associated to the figures of Pestilence, War, Famine, and Death. Through the story arc of the Apocalypse, we also find another lesson regarding the will and determination of two brothers from Kansas—two brothers who thwart the plans of the ultimate representation of evil within the ultimate religion in the hierarchy of *Supernatural*'s belief systems.

In the next chapter, we explore what the Winchesters represent in terms of an American belief system, one that casts America as much of a powerful force as the host of Heaven, and of Hell. This notion serves as the foundation for the belief that America, like the Winchesters, holds a divinely appointed place in the world, one that bestows upon it the responsibility for saving people and hunting the things that threaten their *modus vivendi*, what we call the American way of life. We further explain how the religious role that hunters play becomes a way to exert a divine authority. This authority for the Winchesters comes from a divine origin, and becomes secularized through their version of righteousness and justice. These they mete out as they encounter the many foes that challenge the American identity and threaten the innocents placed under their charge.

NOTES

1. Portions of this chapter appear in "Horsemen and Homilies: Revelation in the CW's *Supernatural*" by J. M. Valenzano, III, and E. Engstrom, in *Journal of Communication and Religion*, 2013, Vol. 36, Issue 1, pp. 50-72), Religious Communication Association.

2. One also can consult the training programs in seminaries across the globe that instruct nascent preachers on how to construct an effective homily or sermon.

3. Episode titles and original airdates: "Good God, Y'All!," September 17, 2009; "My Bloody Valentine," February 11, 2010; "Two Minutes to Midnight," May 6, 2010.

4. The narrative replacement of Conquest with Pestilence in popular culture also occurred in the Fox network's *Sleepy Hollow*, which debuted in 2013. At the beginning of the series' second episode, "Blood Moon," which aired on September 23, 2013, the Four Horsemen are explicitly listed as War, Famine, Conquest, and Death. In the episode "John Doe," which aired October 14, 2013, Conquest appears, and described by main character Ichabod Crane as also being called Pestilence.

5. Whether its airdate was simply coincidental or deliberate, we see the chronological proximity to the date September 11 as enhancing its storyline regarding war and conflict.

6. U.S. Army General David Petraeus outlined the principles of his counterinsurgency strategy in a speech at Kansas State University, among other venues (Baker, III, 2009). In fact, this strategy, developed by General Petraeus in Iraq, proved so successful that when President Obama removed General Stanley McChrystal from his post as commander of Afghanistan military operations, Obama appointed Petraeus in charge there to implement a similar strategy.

7. The 2000 movie *O Brother, Where Art Thou?* featured a version by bluegrass artist Ralph Stanley.

8. "Swan Song" originally aired on May 13, 2010.

9. Although the use of Revelation clearly invokes a degree of religiosity, the absence of more overtly Christian figures, notably Jesus Christ, as we note, prevents an evangelical purpose of conversion to Christianity. The viewer/critic familiar with religious-based films, however, can read allusions to Christ in the text of "Swan Song." To wit, even after being pummeled by Sam/Lucifer, Dean tells him, "It's okay. It's okay. I'm here. I'm here. I'm not going to leave you" (Kripke & Boyum, 2010). This scene mirrors a similar one in the 2004 Mel Gibson-directed film *The Passion of the Christ*, when Mary the Mother of Jesus, anguished by what is happening, finally goes to her beaten and bloodied Son as He carries the cross through the streets of Jerusalem.

10. *Supernatural*'s writers also circumvent mention of another key figure from Revelation, the Antichrist. This character instead becomes a little boy with supernatural powers named "Jesse." In the season five episode "I Believe the Children Are Our Future" (Episode 5.6), Castiel explains that the notion of an "Antichrist" actually refers to "demon spawn." Jesse is the product of a demon that possesses a woman to give birth to its offspring. Jesse's powers are similar to those portrayed in the classic 1961 *Twilight Zone* episode "It's a Good Life" about a little boy whose powers to banish people to a dreaded cornfield frighten those around him to acquiesce to his every wish.

Chapter Five

A Divinely Ordained Civil Religion

In *Monsters in America*, Poole (2011) explained that monsters bring a nation's collective fears to life through narratives that embody cultural conflicts, moral dilemmas, and questions about identity in different periods of history. The generalized fear of the dark and unknown becomes manifest in these monsters; outside threats become reified in the form of strange and monstrous beasts and creatures. *Supernatural* serves up these myths, urban legends, monsters, and stories based in religious material. Though depicted in fantastical ways, they nevertheless illustrate certain fears and beliefs regarding everyday life—lessons that warn against moral emptiness, destruction resulting from demonizing the "Other," and the futility of trying to avoid the inevitable.

Sometimes involving the intervention of divine beings, the origin myth serves as one of the more powerful and culturally resonant myths perpetuated through storytelling; one can view these myths as reaffirming hegemony, in a sense conveying and re-conveying commonly held beliefs that bind societal members together. These stories identify a group of people, or beings, who emerge from a chaotic universe to establish a community that serves as the ancestral relation to the audience's own society (Leeming 1990). Such origin myths are found throughout history in different cultures. For example, the Romans had Romulus and Remus, the Mesopotamians had Gilgamesh, and, of course, the Judeo-Christian tradition has the story of Adam and Eve. Americans are no strangers to origin tales, despite the relative youth of their country.

In the previous chapter, we illustrated how *Supernatural* functions as a pseudo-religious medium through which it delivers secular homilies, providing its audience interpretations of biblical passages through the lens of contemporary events in interesting, poignant, and captivating tales. But homilies are not the only messages we see conveyed through those interesting tales. In addition to giving life to the allegories presented in the Book of Revelation, we contend that *Supernatural*'s overarching narrative also serves as a vehicle by which institutions within the civil realm convey an American civil religion, a hegemony of identity that relies on a mythos that tells the story of what this country stands for and what it means to be an "American."

In this chapter, we continue our inquiry of *Supernatural* and its homiletic qualities to explicate how the show tells the story of America and brings into the narrative a kind of replacement for a strict sense of a god/God-based religion—one that suggests there is something equal to or even more powerful than God.[1] Popular culture in particular serves as a source of hegemony, so it makes sense that secular homilies transmitted through television narratives simultaneously can reify and at times reinterpret civil religion and central elements of American identity. As Forgacs (in Gramsci, 2000) pointed out, Gramsci expanded on the notion of the "ethico-political sphere" which consists of ideological, moral, and cultural "cements" that bind a society together (p. 190). In that civil society provides a conduit for indirect hegemony, it must be noted that it also remains open to counterhegemony and the communication of ideas that go against prevailing common sense. Thus, even as *Supernatural* may include reinforcement of religious ideologies, it also has the potential to present ideas that counter commonly held or accepted notions regarding God, gods, and religion.

Here we explore the underlying mythos of America—one which venerates "America" and Americanism in a similar way in which religion worships a deity—that consists of (a) the myth of American Exceptionalism, which claims the superiority of the American experience and design, and (b) the Frontier Myth, which glorifies American westward expansion and the individuals who explore new frontiers. These serve as the core tenets of an American civil religion, an idea first advanced by Bellah (1967), and establish the parameters of the origin myth for Americans.

We offer our reading of how *Supernatural* transmits a story of a prototypical American family that simultaneously promotes two fundamental components of civil religion as embodied in a mythos communicated through its small-screen storytelling. We argue here that the depiction of the main characters in *Supernatural* also embodies principles related to the reaffirmation of a hegemonic American identity. Through their actions, which we see as operating at personal and societal levels, the religious and secular-based tenets of American Exceptionalism and the Frontier Myth become folded into a larger story of the hegemony of Christianity, and the perpetuation of the Judeo-Christian tradition within a national identity.

Using this perspective, we see the Winchesters and their fellow hunters as serving a religious role in which their representative character reinforces the ideals associated with American Exceptionalism, the characteristics associated with figures symbolic of the Frontier Myth, and the status of Christianity within the hierarchy of religious traditions depicted on the show. Thus, we view both the characters and the plotlines of *Supernatural* as offering logical points of discovery for how this show about ghosts, monsters, and gods tells a familiar story—one that finds its roots in the Christian-based founding of America. As we deconstruct these portrayals, we also demonstrate that these characters, namely, the Winchesters and their most trusted hunter allies, serve in essence as priests who reinforce civil religion in much the same way presidents do.

THE MYTHS OF AMERICA

An entire area of rhetorical criticism centers on the way in which presidential speeches convey an American identity; examinations of such texts reveal the persuasive techniques and strategies that presidents use to bolster arguments for going to war (Butler; 2002; Ivie, 1979, 1980, 1989, 2005; Medhurst, Ivie, Wander, & Scott, 1990; Murphy, 2003), for example, and those that reaffirm the characteristics of "Americans" (Beasley, 2004, 2006; Stuckey, 2004). As described in chapter 1, the myth of American Exceptionalism finds its roots in a religious foundation, one that existed even before the birth of the nation. The sermon titled "A Model of Christian Charity," communicated by John Winthrop in 1630, reveals these religious origins. The "model" for the new nation is one of courageous individuals unafraid to start a new life that were divinely chosen to serve as an example for the rest of the world, a "shining" city above all other people and nations. The notion of "America's" cultural identity thus inherently involves Christianity as part of a national identity.

Three tenets mark American Exceptionalism; these inform the use of this rhetorical strategy by politicians who invoke it as part of rationalization for foreign policy action. First, America (the United States) is divinely appointed with a special future (McKrisken, 2003). This special quality often manifests itself in religious fashion; this divine national mission in turn reinforces the goodness of the American people. Herman Melville (2006, originally published in 1850) even referred to America as "the Israel of our time" (p. 189). As Edwards (2008) noted, this divine appointment "helps America sincerely maintain that its intentions are pure and that its spirit will be emulated by other states and peoples" (p. 6). Bercovitch (1978) also characterized the settlement of America as a religious quest, lending credence to the idea that God ordained the United States as a mission as well as a country. This ecclesiastical origin serves as the source of that "shining" city on the hill metaphor proclaimed by Winthrop, and later by President Ronald Reagan (Reagan, 1989).

The second tenet posits that the United States is qualitatively different from the Old World of Europe, and not simply because of divine decree (McKrisken, 2003). Another important element of the United States that makes it different from Europe is its founding documents, which supposedly eliminated the corruption inherent in Europe while maintaining the nation's ability to always move forward. This is not to say the United States is flawless, but rather, as McKrisken put it, "Americans regard themselves as being uniquely able, given time, to overcome the imperfections of their society" (p. 184). Thus, cultural adaptation and inherent goodness become core aspects of American identity as understood through this myth.

The third tenet of the myth of American Exceptionalism says that America will succeed when other nations have not because God made it special and because the America people are always trying to better themselves. Madsen (1998) explained that American Exceptionalism provides "a mythological refuge from the chaos of history and the uncertainty of life" (p. 166). In effect, it reinforces the idea of the nation's status in world history for its people. The United States will *always* overcome tough times, according to the myth. Thus resilience and perseverance also play central roles in conceptions of American identity.

The notion of an exceptional America articulates the idea of a nation as unique and holding a special place on the world stage. This viewpoint plays an important part in the psyche of the American polity. For an American to question America's exceptionalism leaves one open to criticism, especially when done in public. In 2009, for example, President Barack Obama came under fire from numerous Republican critics for equating the idea of American Exceptionalism with British and Greek exceptionalism, rendering it not exceptional at all. Shortly after taking office, Obama was asked about what he thought of American Exceptionalism. He responded,

> I believe in American Exceptionalism, just as I suspect that the Brits believe in British exceptionalism and the Greeks believe in Greek exceptionalism. I'm enormously proud of my country and its role and history in the world. . . . I see no contradiction between believing that America has a continued extraordinary role in leading the world towards peace and prosperity and recognizing that that leadership is incumbent, depends on, our ability to create partnerships because we create partnerships because we can't solve these problems alone. (Obama, 2009)

In equating American Exceptionalism to the nationalism of other countries, Obama came under fire from Republican pundits and started a debate over the specialness of the United States (Krauthammer, 2009). This later became magnified during the 2012 presidential campaign ("Condoleezza Rice RNC Speech," 2012; "McCain: Obama Doesn't Believe," 2012).

Thus, American Exceptionalism manifests itself most often in political rhetoric, particularly messages regarding foreign policy, the result of which offers two different interpretations that prescribe mutually exclusive policy options. On the one hand, exemplarists hold that the United States should serve as a model for the world, but not actively intervene to shape it in its own image. McCartney (2004) articulated this view succinctly when he contended that America works best "standing apart from the world and serving merely as a model of social and political possibility" (p. 401). Exemplarists believe that serving as the best possible model of freedom for the rest of the world requires complete focus and effort, and therefore the country should not actively build other nations as such efforts would be detrimental to them as well as to the United States.

Those who subscribe to the interventionist mission disagree with the notion that modeling democracy and good behavior is enough to fulfill the responsibilities of an exceptional nation such as the United States. Bostdorff (1994) noted that interventionists see America as the world's leader: this role has become the true burden of the divine mission given to the United States. We see the mission of intervention informing the depiction of the Winchesters on *Supernatural*, especially when combined with the hegemony of religion that becomes forwarded in the overall narrative.

The Frontier Myth holds an equally important role in the formation of the American identity. The Frontier Myth performs the duties of an origin myth by combining many of America's "stories, norms, explanations, icons, justifications and sustaining myths" (Hartnett, 2002, p. 2) into a thematic representation of where the country and its people came from, what they value, how they should behave, and the overarching significance of their existence. The frontier, as embodied by the West, is "so often declared as the most American part of America" (Wrobel, 2008, p. 77).

Just as the myth of American Exceptionalism comes from the early Puritans in America, Bercovitch (1978, 1993) also traced the root of the Frontier Myth to the Puritans in New England. The popular story of the Puritans tells a tale of a group that came to the New World in the hopes of creating a community that respected freedom of religion. Thus, the story goes, they sought to establish a "New Israel" in the wilderness of a New World. As Bercovitch (1993) pointed out, this story creates justifications for a set of behaviors and beliefs that guide and govern society in such a way that they seem both proper and just.

The perception that this persecuted group sought refuge in the wilderness and was rewarded by God with a new land to freely practice its faith neglects to account for the fact that the Puritans provided freedom to like-minded individuals alone, often hanging Quakers, outlawing Baptists, and executing witches (Seiple, 2012). Nevertheless, this experience provided the basis for the myth of the American experience in the frontier, where citizens sought to explore and develop the wilderness. America, the protagonist in the Frontier Myth, had a divine calling to conquer and develop the chaotic wilderness. That calling inherently involves the use of violence. In fact, a cursory examination of the Western storytelling tradition in American popular culture reveals a tendency for the heroes in its drama to use guns, knives, and other forms of weaponry to achieve their noble intentions. "Horse operas" allowed for cowboy characters to fire an infinite supply of bullets with accuracy against any antagonist in their pursuit of truth and justice. In the 1950s and 1960s, Hollywood produced cinematic Western after cinematic Western in which John Wayne and other actors portrayed macho cowboys who shot up bad guys threatening innocent pioneers. In fact, the science fiction genre often employs elements of the Western archetype and Frontier Myth in its stories, as evidenced in the historically popular *Star Wars* and *Star Trek* franchises (Brode & Deyneka, 2012), and the short-lived Fox television series *Firefly* (Rabb & Richardson, 2008). The early Puritans' "hunting" of the "Other" (especially witches) and the Western cowboys' conflicts with Native Americans and bandits on the frontier become transformed and reified via the horror genre as the Winchesters' hunting of witches and monsters that represent the frontier "Other." In this way, we view *Supernatural* as offering another text to explore the notion of familiar threats to normalcy and the need to root out what is considered evil.

THE WINCHESTERS: AN AMERICAN IDENTITY

We see the myths of America applicable to *Supernatural* in several salient ways. One of these lies in the archetypal figures that serve as elemental in these narratives. As the most notable of these figures, the American cowboy plays the central character in the story of the Frontier Myth (Bellesiles, 2000; Billington, 1981; Slatta, 2010). The Winchesters perform this role on television in a supernatural American frontier. Indeed, *Supernatural*'s creator, Eric Kripke, envisioned them as cowboys put into the middle of an epic battle (Knight, 2010a).

In the story of *Supernatural*, the Winchesters' hometown of Lawrence, Kansas, places them squarely in the heart of America.[2] Indeed, the acknowledged geographic center of the continental United States is near the town of Lebanon, Kansas (Fastenberg, 2010). The all-American character of the Winchesters further becomes underscored by Dean and Sam's parents' names: John and Mary Winchester (Winchester invokes the name of the historic American gun manufacturer as well). Further adding to the all-American, working-class nature of the Winchester family, John had served as a United States Marine during the Vietnam War and worked as a auto mechanic prior to becoming a hunter (as detailed in "The Song Remains the

Same," Episode 5.13). Both of these identities embodied in the character of John Winchester—the enlisted soldier and the blue-collar worker—represent occupations central to the "average American" experience.

The Frontier Myth forwards the idea of eliminating those who do not fit into the normal way of life. It also endorses notions of America's victory over the wild frontier, the idea of personal aggression in order to protect the community, and constant movement—against the frontier and to conquer the wild (Stuckey, 2011). Conquering a wilderness that is a physical manifestation of all we fear, hate, and consider "not us" (Rushing & Frentz, 1995) serves as an analogy for positive movement toward perfecting the imperfect.

In *Supernatural*, the Winchester brothers constantly move along a frontier between darkness and light, taming a wilderness full of monsters and creatures from "foreign" lore, as we outlined in chapters 2 and 3, and bringing order back to the community. They then began to tackle the forces of the Judeo-Christian version of Heaven and Hell as an equal participant when they became entangled in the Apocalypse storyline during seasons four and five. In the following pages, we deconstruct several episodic examples of how *Supernatural* consciously reifies American Exceptionalism and its traditional Frontier Myth heroes just as the series' creator, Eric Kripke, has overtly admitted, and as we find evidenced in the program's text.

Even after Kripke's departure as showrunner at the end of season five, the Winchesters continued to demonstrate their identity as cowboys; Kripke's vision of the "stubborn and cocky" American cowboy (Knight, 2010a, p. 9) actually became the basis for the season seven episode aptly titled "Frontierland" (Episode 6.18). Having averted the world's end at the conclusion of season five, by the show's seventh season the brothers faced a new, powerful enemy: "Eve," the mother of all monsters. In "Frontierland," Sam and Dean actually go back in time to 1861 and meet Samuel Colt, the maker of a magical gun that can kill anything, including demons from Hell. We find notable that the most powerful weapon in the *Supernatural* universe happens to be a made-in-the-U.S.A. firearm.

To underscore the "American-ness" of *Supernatural*, this episode shows Dean as holding a long-time "fetish" with the Wild West (and Clint Eastwood, star of numerous Western films); in preparing for the task, he is shown enjoying having to dress in Western clothing to blend in with the local townsfolk. Indeed, Dean actually becomes sheriff of the town where the episode takes place, Sunrise, Wyoming. In this episode, the brothers go back in time to the actual American frontier in order to protect the world from the destructive force of "Eve" by obtaining the only thing that will kill her, the "ashes of a Phoenix." The brothers do manage to accomplish their mission, and, with the help of Samuel Colt, eventually defeat Eve, just as American Exceptionalism has America always overcoming the challenges it faces.

In the seventh season episode "Time After Time After Time" (Episode 7.12), Dean again travels back in American history, this time to the 1930s. In this episode, Dean partners with contemporary "cowboy" and lawman Eliot Ness. The real Eliot Ness was largely responsible for bringing infamous mobster Al Capone to justice thanks to his group of "Untouchables." As one may recall, the story of good guy Ness and his anti-gangster squad already has a place in the collective television and movie memory of the nation, in the 1959-1963 television series *The Untouchables* and the 1987 film of the same title.

In the world of *Supernatural*, it turns out the iconic lawman is himself a hunter like the Winchesters. The appropriation of a historical figure like Ness not only shows a contemporary "heroic" cowboy such as Ness performing what the Winchesters themselves do, but also creates a connection between the legal wing of the United States and the divine mission to defeat demons and gods of "lesser" religions. To reify this intertextuality of American legend in the show, as well as the interconnectedness between real law and order and mythical law and order, Ness and Dean work together to destroy Chronos, the ancient Greek Titan and god of time.

In the frontier tradition of the Wild West, cowboys ride horses as their primary mode of transportation. These horses often have names and serve as much a part of the cowboy's persona as the cowboy character himself. *Supernatural* has updated the representation of the cowboy to reflect contemporary life, and in so doing the horse has become a car, a black 1967 Chevrolet Impala that belonged to John Winchester. Dean has restored it several times and considers it a prize possession. Indeed, the brothers have few belongings, which further enhances the car's value to Dean. He actually refers to the car by the name "Baby" and has a clear attachment to the vehicle, much like a cowboy does to his horse. This exchange in the season two episode "Bloodlust" (Episode 2.3) illustrates the importance of "Baby" to Dean (and thus the viewer):

> Dean: Woah! Listen to her purr! Have you ever heard anything so sweet?
>
> Sam: You know, if you two want to get a room, just let me know, Dean.
>
> Dean: Don't listen to him, Baby. He doesn't understand us. (Gamble & Singer, 2006)

The importance of Baby became clear in "Swan Song" (Episode 5.22), when Armageddon was about to commence in a field near the boys' hometown of Lawrence, Kansas. Just as Sam was about to lose the battle to Michael, the car itself triggered long-held childhood memories: Sam was able to remember all the adventures he had with Dean, evoking a strong emotional reaction that made it possible for Sam to resist Lucifer's possession long enough to leap back into the devil's cage in Hell, thus averting the end of the world.

The brothers use all manner of weapons to defeat various monsters: silver daggers against shape-shifters, holy water against demons, and lots of guns that fire rock salt against ghosts and vengeful spirits. The brothers store modified shotguns and pistols in the trunk of the Impala, fitted with a hidden weapons compartment. This serves as the primary storage facility for all manner of demon-and-monster-fighting apparatuses the brothers use while on the road. It also serves as storage for their disguises and fake forms of identification which they use when investigating occurrences in new towns. The Impala, much like a saddled horse, thus serves as a key element of the cowboy archetype. The Impala, an *American* "muscle car," thus imbues the show with a key component of the Frontier Myth, the cowboy and his trusty horse.

Cowboys, however, are more than their horses or, in this case, cars; they are also brave characters who seek to protect communities of people from bad elements that threaten their peaceful way of life. In virtually every episode of *Supernatural* the brothers travel to small towns, suburbs, and even big cities to fight monsters or demons who threaten the lives of innocent citizens. The people under attack most often do not even know the nature of what is happening, but the brothers do and also know how to vanquish the foe through research into the lore regarding the monster. In the first season episode "Wendigo" (Episode 1.2), for example, the Winchesters hunt and eventually kill the mythical beast that lives off the flesh of the living whom it hunts in a forest. The *wendigo* had been terrorizing campers, but the Winchesters were able to defeat it thanks to their father's journal notes on the creature's weaknesses.

Once they complete a job in a particular town and feel they have made it safe and secure, the brothers board the Impala and ride on down the road until they hear about another creature or mysterious event to investigate. Rather than waiting for "fate" to come to them, the Winchesters—ever on the move through space and time—reify the cowboy archetype: they seek out that which threatens to do harm to the people they protect. In this manner, they intervene on behalf of the innocent. When considered as a composite, their surname of Winchester (the name of a famous American gun manufacturer), their use of Dean's car as similar to the cowboy's trusty horse, and their movement along the wild frontier, the brothers become reifications of Eric Kripke's vision to have them serve as American cowboys: sensible, mission-driven, and American to the core. The Winchesters and their mission of perpetual protection along the supernatural frontier—hunting threats and eliminating them so that ordinary, unknowing people can live in peace—in turn serve as a composite representation of an American identity grounded in the interventionist interpretation of American Exceptionalism.

FRONTIER JUSTICE, INTERVENTIONIST STYLE

As discussed in detail in chapters 2 and 3, episodes in which the Winchester brothers defeat evil creatures serve to confirm the superiority of the Winchesters' (and by extension America's) judgment regarding the need to destroy them. The elimination (with extreme prejudice, that is, death) of creatures and pagan gods from the Old World largely represents "cut and dry" incidents in which the brothers discover a threat or mysterious deaths of humans, find out what the culprit is, then find and destroy it. This interventionist system of justice exemplifies the brothers' self-appointed mission of surveillance and elimination of an "Other" that threatens the peace. In a way, the Winchesters serve as sheriff, judge, jury, and executioner, and dispatch villains and lawbreakers with well-honed efficiency.

However, some stories illustrate scenarios where even the brothers disagree on how to proceed when dealing with an "Other" and its past crimes or potential threat. For instance, in "The Girl Next Door" (Episode 7.3), Sam and Dean encounter a *kitsune*, a creature from Japanese myth that eats the pituitary glands of its victims to survive. The backstory of the *kitsune* had Sam befriending her years earlier when he was just a boy; she saved him from her own mother. Although already a hunter at the time, Sam actually saved this *kitsune*'s life, and allowed her to live. When they run into the creature again years later, she has become a parent, and was killing people in order to save the life of her own son, who needed their pituitary glands or else he would die. Unfortunately, because she has killed humans, Dean cannot forgive her for this offense, despite the need to do so to save her child. Despite promises to Sam that he would not kill her, Dean does so anyway, and in right in front of her child. However, he lets the child live because the boy has not harmed a human—yet.

Here, not only did Dean, the militant brother, administer swift and violent justice, but he did so while lying to Sam about it. This created a rift between the brothers that, although eventually healed, lasted quite some time. As representations of America, this speaks to the swift justice promoted by the "cowboy" culture and attitude attributed to the Bush administration during its prosecution of the War on Terror. However, if one views each of the Winchesters as opposing sides in the debate concerning interventionism (Dean) versus exemplarism (Sam), their short-lived quarrel also reflects the ability of Americans who similarly hold opposing views regarding American Exceptionalism, or other policies for that matter, to bridge their differences of opinion given time. In effect, they exemplify the notion that Americans can adapt to and overcome the differences and challenges they face.

We offered several examples previously discussed in chapter 3 that involved either perverted or imperfect versions of Christianity. Those episodes involved erroneous or misguided ideas about justice and meting out punishment among "sinners." In such episodes as "Faith," "Hook Man," and "99 Problems," the brothers ensure that perversions of others' justice are righted. Similar to how they deal with monsters that prey upon the innocent, they also take on those who claim to work for a higher power and reaffirm an interventionist version of America, which seeks justice and will right wrongs where it sees them.

This sense of justice extends beyond monsters and pagan gods to include the Judeo-Christian theology that began to take a more prominent place in *Supernatural*'s season arcs beginning in season four with the arrival of an angel of the Lord. As discussed in chapter 3, the angel Castiel attempts to claim the vacuum of power in Heaven left by God's absence at the end of season six. In the season-ending episode "The Man Who Knew Too Much" (Episode 6.22), Castiel unlocks Purgatory, absorbs the souls languishing there, and immediately disintegrates the archangel Raphael. Upon this action, he turns to the Winchesters and their surrogate father, Uncle Bobby, proclaims himself God, and demands they kneel to worship and love him.

As the follow-up to "The Man Who Knew Too Much," the season-seven opener "Meet the New Boss" (Episode 7.1) shows the brothers refusing to submit to Castiel/"God"; they plead with their former friend to stop what he is doing, essentially decreeing that he cannot be God. Castiel abruptly leaves and proceeds to kill angels who defy him and eradicate humans he deems as religious hypocrites. In Castiel's storyline in which he appoints himself God, the Winchesters take the stance that not only is Castiel wrong and not doing God's work, but they know what God is—and Castiel is *not* God. Furthermore, Castiel's taking on of the divine mantle becomes a bit too much for the brothers to take, just as too much explicit religion by leaders is not acceptable to most Americans. In rejecting Castiel, the Winchesters similarly claim a supremacy over those who claim to hold the position of God—and thus become wielders of justice by intervening on behalf of humankind. In this manner, the Winchesters assume the role of protectors of humanity, intervening on behalf of those who seemingly cannot stand up to the power of a god, those who think they have the power of a god, or even "the" God.

The idea that "swift justice" is itself justified when applied by those in the right and who fight on the behalf of the innocent becomes evident even for minor characters in the myth-based world of *Supernatural*. Those who implicate themselves as harming or murdering innocent others become vulnerable to the hunters' code of justice. Although not central to the plot, an example of swift justice, sans judge and jury, presents itself in the season eight episode "What's Up, Tiger Mommy?" (Episode 8.2), when the Winchesters attend an auction of supernatural artifacts held by Plutus, the Roman god of greed. At the beginning of the episode, an elderly gentleman, named "Mr. Vili" collects objects from an old safe deposit box at a bank, assisted by a young female bank employee; from the number assigned to the box (labeled "1"), it becomes apparent that the man is much older than he looks. The old man's bespectacled, almost-feeble appearance belies his evil intent, however. After retrieving the item in the box (a large, desiccated animal appendage of some sort), he tell the young woman he needs to make a "withdrawal." He looks at her slyly. The viewer then sees blood splattering on the wall of safe deposit boxes, implying he killed her.

At the auction, Vili bids on Thor's hammer, offering the finger bone of Ymir, the Norse frost giant, which turns out to be the item he retrieved from the bank. The inquisitive viewer might conduct a few minutes' worth of research and discover that "Vili" is the name of one of the two brothers of the Norse god Odin; the three had slain Ymir (Ashliman, 1997-2010); hence, how the bone in the safe deposit box came into the old man's possession. The finger bone isn't enough to secure the hammer, so Vili offers up "five-eighths of a virgin," presumably the bank employee contained in the bloody brown paper grocery bag he holds up. The viewer is left wondering what happened to the other three-eighths. Vili wins the hammer, as Sam looks on with a quizzical look on his face.

Later in the episode, Sam uses Thor's hammer to kill Plutus's assistant, after which Vili demands Sam give him back his hammer. Sam replies, "Where'd you get five-eighths of a virgin?" (Dabb, Loflin, & Showalter, 2012). Before Vili can answer, Sam swings the hammer, killing him. Vili's execution at the hand of Sam, wielding Thor's hammer no less, provides a sense of justice for the murder of the young bank employee. Sam literally "puts the hammer down" on Vili, thus avenging the young woman's death. Serving as judge, jury, and executioner, Sam's actions symbolize the notion of vigilante justice as carried out via an active sense of righteousness. Simultaneously, he vanquishes a pagan deity, thereby reaffirming the lowered status of "Other" mythologies. This scene provides an example of a two-pronged efficiency by which the Winchesters avenge the death of an innocent while at the same time enforcing the hierarchy of religions in which the "old" gods remain obsolete.

As described in chapter 3, a hierarchy of religious traditions in which Christianity holds a higher rank than all "Others" emerges even though we found a plurality of religions that become reified on *Supernatural*. We see this as applicable to the notion of an exceptional America that displaced the Old World, just like the Olympic gods and Titans of Greek myth pose no match for the power of the Winchesters/America: the Fate Atropos, god of time Chronos, goddess of the hunt Artemis, and even the god of gods Zeus all fall before Sam and Dean. The brothers likewise vanquish Egyptian and Roman gods and goddesses, leave them powerless, or otherwise dispatch them. By defeating the gods drawn from non-American religions, the Winchesters' cleansing of American towns of these invaders demonstrates America's ability to eradicate the Old World, which we contend presents a twist on the interventionist strand of American Exceptionalism.

EVOLUTION OF EXCEPTIONALISM

The true lineage of the Winchesters and their connection to the very founding of the nation commonly called "America"—which secures their place not only as Americans, but descendants of the Pilgrims—becomes even more emphasized in "Exile on Main St." (Episode 6.1). The boys' maternal grandfather, Samuel Campbell, returns from the dead (thanks to the power of a demon) and is now hunting with a resurrected, but soulless, Sam. Samuel tells Dean that his Campbell family ancestors were "hacking heads off vampires on the *Mayflower*" (Gamble & Sgriccia, 2010a). Not only this, but the Winchester brothers can trace their paternal family line to a divine origin all the way back to the Book of Genesis, as they learned in "The Song Remains the Same" (Episode 5.13).

Their paternal family line of divine origin thus becomes amplified when it is revealed that their maternal family line has always been hunting. This becomes symbolic of how American Exceptionalism invokes destiny and fate, thereby tying the brothers explicitly to the origin of the country. Thus, the brothers descend both from a lineage rooted in the very origins of humankind as told in the Bible *and* from a family of hunters traced back to the first Pilgrims of the New World. It appears that the brothers' very blood contains, ostensibly, an innate genetic disposition for hunting evil creatures.

As hunters and protectors, the Winchesters' mission to shield humanity from the evil embodied in the Old World through pagan deities has begun to extend beyond the realm of those pre-Christian and non-Christian beings. This foreshadowing of where the Winchesters' path might lead began even before season seven, when the brothers had to intervene against the angel Castiel, himself deluded by the righteousness associated with the Judeo-Christian God. Indeed, during the series' fourth season, they fought against the very agents of "the" God established as the presumably most powerful in the deity hierarchy of *Supernatural*.

Additionally, that God does not answer the prayers of Castiel in the season six episode "The Man Who Would Be King" (Episode 6.20). In this episode, Castiel pleads for the Judeo-Christian God to show him a sign to tell him what to do. Castiel essentially begs his absent Father to return and help the angels sort out Heaven in the wake of the averted Apocalypse. Castiel's prayer is met with silence. God remains mute and gives no indication either of what Castiel should do, nor that He even exists anymore. The "mysterious" ways in which He acts, it appears, indicates that He takes no official sides in the battle between Heaven and Hell. As Jordan (2011) similarly observed regarding this storyline and episode, the abandonment of God on *Supernatural* leaves a vacuum regarding hegemonic power. We see the numerous interventions to save Sam and Dean from certain death, which they learned about in the episode "Dark Side of the Moon" (Episode 5.16), as implying God has a "soft spot" for the Winchesters (America). Not only can we infer sympathy for America, but as the show continues through its seasons, it appears that the Winchesters increasingly take on the divine burden vacated by God.

When viewing the Winchesters-as-America metaphor as an overarching narrative in *Supernatural*, one can apply the Winchester brothers' acceptance and well-honed abilities as monster hunters to the way in which "America" came to realize its divine appointment and special place on earth. One finds historical similarities between the destiny of the Winchesters, all-American boys from Kansas, and the isolationist policies of a "young" America coming of age in the early twentieth century. The acceptance of the "city on a hill" mantle became a rhetorical touchstone used by Ronald Reagan. It has become even more strongly applied during the time post 9/11, when George W. Bush reminded Americans of their place in the world. When taken together, the examples of the Winchesters as carrying out their divine fate to save others mirrors the way in which America does so on the world stage, as Kagan (2012) noted in the CNN opinion article "America Has Made the World Freer, Safer and Wealthier."

THE BURDEN OF AN EXCEPTIONAL IDENTITY

The Winchesters work *pro bono*, as it were, to keep innocent people safe. They do not seek monetary reward, nor any of what Maslow (1943) famously termed "esteem" needs; Sam and Dean require no recognition for their work. However, as they endeavor to intervene on the behalf of others, their own dreams for a normal life become unattainable. As hunters, they get no reprieve nor any kind of "vacation" from the job—indeed, it has cost them dearly. As Elliott (2013), in her examination of the dark side of the Winchesters' occupation noted, "Sam and Dean must compromise much of what makes them human through the function that they serve to 'protect' humanity" (p. 7). In order to destroy monsters, they risk losing their own humanity, in a sense becoming like monsters themselves. The show constantly depicts the brothers as "miserable, isolated, and constantly in loss," further noted Elliott, as they witness their family and friends die and as their minds "are compromised by memories of torture or trauma in unearthly planes . . ." (p. 7).

As noted by Garvey (2009), the heroes of *Supernatural*, the entire Winchester family, embody the theme of sacrifice. As hunters, Sam and Dean can never attain the "good life" promised in the myth of the American dream—a family and a home. Indeed, this literally serves as a dream for Dean in "What Is and What Should Never Be" (Episode 2.20), when he finds himself living a "normal" life in Lawrence, complete with a live-in girlfriend and a normal job as an auto mechanic, echoing his father's occupation prior to his becoming a demon hunter. In the episode, Dean's apparent joy becomes evident when he grins broadly while mowing his mother's lawn and waving to a neighbor. This scene conveys the deepest wish of the brothers: to live a "normal life," just like the one enjoyed by the people they protect. Dean's almost-comical delight at eating a sandwich made by his mother reinforces the happiness of simple pleasures. As it turned out, it was all just a dream: Dean had been poisoned by a *djinn*, a creature from Islamic myth that feasts on its drugged victims (the "genie" who can grant wishes). Dean had been hallucinating that he had a normal life during his capture. In reality, his mother had been dead for years, he had no girlfriend, and he was not a simple mechanic. While basking in the happiness he was experiencing, he almost died. He would have perished in his perfect dream if Sam did not come to his rescue at the last minute.

Although Dean "awoke" from the perfect dream life created by the *djinn* in season two, he had the American dream almost in his grasp again for real at the beginning of season six. After successfully ensuring the Apocalypse did not come to pass, and seeing Sam become Lucifer's vessel and disappear into the abyss while fighting the archangel Michael (in the form of his half-brother Adam), Dean buries his grief and allows himself to live a suburban life with his girlfriend Lisa and her young son, Ben.

Alas, the dangers of hunting come back to haunt Dean, when the offspring of the same *djinn* the brothers defeated in "What Is and What Should Never Be" return to seek their revenge in "Exile on Main St." (Episode 6.1). Eventually, the normal life so fervently desired by this young hunter comes to a final and permanent end in "Let It Bleed" (Episode 6.21), when Dean lets Castiel erase Lisa and Ben's memories of Dean forever. Thus, Dean leaves his new family to resume hunting with his brother, just as it *should* be. Additionally, the theme of personal sacrifice in *Supernatural* becomes reified in depictions of the hunting life and in the way Sam in particular consistently shows courage and willingness to give his life to save the world, literally. He did so in "Swan Song" (Episode 5.22) and again in "Sacrifice" (Episode 8.23).

This notion of sacrifice permeates the narratives of American soldiers; its essentialism in the story of the hero has become a familiar theme of tales of those who have fallen in order that others may live. Headlines such as "Soldier Sacrificed His Life for Others" (Somashekhar, 2007) reaffirm the requirements and burden of protectors, tying the notion of altruism to heroism. The myths of America thus invoke this notion as well; an exceptional and interventionist people will put themselves in harm's way to protect its citizens, and the cowboy of Frontier Myth willingly patrols the border of the wilderness to make the area safe for current and future citizens. The Winchesters willingly have sacrificed themselves as well: their selfless actions not only ensure the protection of the nation's citizens from creatures and monsters, but the continuation of the entire world.

AN EXCEPTIONAL AMERICA, BEYOND RELIGION

The evil from which the Winchesters protect people is embodied in an Other that includes a multitude of actualized threats and shadows drawn from human lore and experience. The portrayal of these things and the traditions they represent as evil and destructive illustrate how American adults should see symbolic shadows in the form of Others that seek to harm the American way of life in the "real" world. Furthermore, *Supernatural*'s treatment of pagan gods and even angels, agents of "the" God, endorses the perspective that gods—of any kind—are *not* good, but are self-interested and exploit humanity, so any religious messages need to be questioned.

Beyond serving as a mode of confirming a core American mythos, we see *Supernatural* as actually promoting the religious dimensions of American national identity. In short, we believe the show serves as a text that does more than reify the myth of American Exceptionalism: it also provides a reinterpretation of what it means to be an American in today's world through a recasting of foundational myths tied to the American core identity. This happens in much the same way that the show functions as a secular homily by "preaching" timeless religious lessons in a more contemporary vein. The homilies of the Four Horsemen, examined in the previous chapter, present evergreen moral lessons within the context of the twenty-first century in a particular setting—the United States. The grounding of mythic characters from the Bible in contemporary American society further underscores that this country is exceptional—the Four Horsemen choose to make themselves known *in America*.

In addition to forwarding an explicit "American-ness" of the Winchesters and their ancestors, the writers and producers of *Supernatural* simultaneously further complicate these concepts throughout the show's eight-season run. The resulting narrative both reinforces and recasts the idea that God appointed America to serve as the world's shining light. The ability of the Winchesters to fight angels, who pose an even more powerful adversary than demons, and *defeat* them reflects a morphing of an identity of a special nation into the notion of an America as fulfilling a good, even divine, mission.

It also bears noting that the role religion plays in American life also is reflected in this narrative and transmitted to a younger generation. In *Supernatural*, God remains absent, leaving the angels to figure out what to do, and what to do with the Winchesters/America. God, it appears, at a minimum no longer cares about His people—and at worst does not exist. This fundamentally changes the divine nature of American Exceptionalism: God can disappear and America will be "OK" because America has always been divine.

It also echoes what recent surveys have found about the views Americans have regarding religion, God, and the role of religion in society. In October, 2012, The Pew Forum on Religion in Public Life found that one in five Americans claimed no religious affiliation, the highest percentage in their history of collecting this data (Pew Research Center, 2012). Gallup, while finding a similar rise of non-religious individuals in the United States, also found that 75% of Americans felt more religion would be better for society ("Americans Say," 2013). These data illustrate that Americans hold less faith in God than before, more faith in themselves, and yet feel religious belief needs to be rekindled. It is important, however, to remember the God indicated here belongs primarily in the Abrahamic tradition, as gods of other faiths are viewed as strange and even evil through the prism of *Supernatural*. Not only does this God and His/Its accompanying religious tradition serve as the top of the hierarchy of world religions, lore, and practices encountered by the Winchesters in their adventures, but even this version of "religion" takes on a secondary status when one considers the brothers' role as divine *American* cowboys who stare down the forces of Heaven and Hell.

"AMERICANISM" AS CIVIL RELIGION

In 1967, Bellah revitalized the term "civil religion," referring to the "certain common elements of religious orientation that the great majority of Americans share" (p. 42). He believed these religious tenets "played a crucial role in American institutions and still provide a religious dimension for the whole fabric of American life, including the political sphere" (p. 42). Bellah drew the term from Chapter 8, Book 4 of Rousseau's *The Social Contract* wherein the French political philosopher outlined some core aspects of what a civil religion would embody, such as an acknowledgment of the existence of God and the afterlife, the reward of virtuous behavior, the punishment of personal and social vices, and religious tolerance.

Bellah (1967) traced public discourse from the American Revolution to President John F. Kennedy's inaugural to drive home his point that the expression of religion in a civil and political sphere in the contemporary United States is not unlike that which is uttered and professed in houses of worship. Further, he demonstrated that American civil religion, although drawing much from Christianity, is not itself solely Christian. In short, Bellah saw America as not especially or specifically a Christian nation. To underscore his observation, he pointed out that although every president mentions God in his inaugural address, none actually uses the word "Christ."

"God" in America does not necessarily mean the Christian God, though it could. Instead, as Bellah put it, the God associated with American identity looks more "Unitarian" and austere, seeking to uphold ideas of law and order rather than profess salvation and love. This God especially concerns Himself/ Itself with America and actively intervenes on behalf of the nation, creating the impression of the United States as holding a kind of favored-son status. This perception by Americans of a generic God that looks favorably on this particular nation among all others becomes incorporated into a version of God in *Supernatural*, one who seems through His mysterious actions to both favor the Winchesters (American) and their mission of law and order—a mission that does not have them proselytize or profess a specific religious faith.

Even though God and civil religion in America do not mean "Christian" specifically, they also do not mean to serve as some sort of generic religious catchall either. Instead, civil religion specifically has to do with America itself as a singular entity and with a monotheistic Abrahamic deity that saves it from "empty formalism," thus serving as a "genuine vehicle for national religious self-understanding" (Bellah, 1967, p. 46). Indeed, according to Bellah, one readily can find this understanding throughout U.S. history. In reading the history of the nation, even prior to its founding, the thirteen colonies fighting off British rule becomes a metaphor for the Jewish Exodus from Egypt during the time of Moses. Even Abraham Lincoln, in this narrative, becomes a civil religion version of the Christ, dying by the hands of his own countrymen in order that the nation be reborn. These historical analogies drawn by Bellah illustrate how politics, history, and the nation's own identity have become wrapped in a cloak of religiosity seemingly unrelated to religion. In effect, one can view these historical events as secularized Bible stories.

Others have since critiqued and attempted to reconfigure Bellah's definition of civil religion, most notably Hart (1977), who argued that a more apt moniker for civil religion would be "civic piety," and offered an alternative model for interpreting the same behaviors noted earlier by Bellah (1967): "Civic piety, in America at least, emerges not so much from blind momentary passion, but from a knowing, practiced thoroughly pragmatic understanding of the suasory arabesques demanded when God and country kick up their heels rhetorically" (Hart, 1977, p. 45). Both Hart's (1977) and Bellah's (1967) assertions regarding the fusion of religion and political life have come under even more scrutiny, but the idea of civil religion has been affirmed by a plethora of other scholars (Erickson, 1980; Goldzwig, 1987; Kaylor, 2011).

As Kaylor (2011) noted, presidential rhetoric scholars have posed the question as to whether or not civil religion still exists, while others even question whether or not it ever actually existed. Further, Friedenberg (2002) argued that despite the concept of separation of church and state, in the United States the invocation of religion and religious principles by governmental leaders during times of crisis when "they have attempted to rally the nation" likely will continue (p. 35). Friedenberg concluded that the principles of civil religion, notably those described by Hart (1977), "will largely hold true for the foreseeable future" (p. 46).

It bears noting that numerous other scholars have used civil religion and civic piety to explore the growing trend of the importance placed on the particular practiced religion of candidates for public office, despite the U.S. Constitution's admonition and prohibition against a religious test for office. In fact, Kaylor (2011), in *Presidential Campaign Rhetoric in an Age of Confessional Politics*, argued that a new framework for understanding the relationship between religion and politics in public discourse might be worth considering. Reflective of this growing connection between practiced religion and politics, *Supernatural* provides a popular culture tableau upon which we can examine the depiction of the relationship between these two powerful prominent public institutions, and how it serves as a representative anecdote for a current depiction of the parameters of civil religion in popular culture.

Popular culture remains an unexplored text in terms of its contributions to the promulgation of civil religious practices and beliefs in society. That said, scholars have identified political practices and objects imbued with a religious definition by Americans. Kao and Copulsky (2007) pointed out that the on-again, off-again debate over the inclusion of "God" in the Pledge of Allegiance concerns itself more with the proper role of civil religion in public life than a debate over the existence of an Almighty. Similarly, Cloud (2004) examined the long-held tension between a need for national unity and the desire to express religious beliefs in the taking of public oaths. Regarding the American flag itself, a tangible symbol of national identity, Gamoran (1990) argued that when schoolchildren learn patriotic songs and stories in school, the educational system reaffirms civil religious practices and symbols for them, enshrining those beliefs for the next generation of citizens. In a sense, then, the citizenry learns this civil religion much in the way children learn religious doctrine in Sunday school or catechism; *Supernatural* in a similar fashion can transmit core elements of American identity to its audience.

Albeit less overt, television, and fictional television such as *Supernatural*, also plays a role, however small, in advancing the religious dimensions of American identity in the same way as songs, stories, and politicians do. Just as expressions of religion and politics become acceptable because they do not explicitly tie political life to a specific denomination, we contend that *Super-*

natural provides entertainment shrouded in Judeo-Christian myth, doctrine, and messages. In previous chapters, we described how the narrative of *Supernatural* offers a palatable, even enjoyable way for its audience to consume hegemonic views of religion, and how it adds to a mythos of the Catholic Church. We see this television show as a storytelling vehicle that similarly relates the core mythos of American identity embodied by American Exceptionalism and the Frontier Myth.

"PREACHING" THE MYTHIC WORD OF CIVIL RELIGION

In *Defining Americans: The Presidency and National Identity*, Stuckey (2004) noted that presidents have always played a role in advancing American national identity. She argued they define who Americans are, sometimes by establishing clear parameters regarding who they are not. Stuckey focused on terms of inclusion and exclusion expressed by presidents to articulate who fits in the American identity and why. This work contains mythic characteristics as noted by Dorsey and Harlow (2003) regarding the messages of President Theodore Roosevelt. However, presidents do not serve as the only promulgators of creating, maintaining, and adjusting definitions of "Americans" and "others." Television plays a key role in this process as well. Although Stuckey (1991) declared presidents serve as "interpreters-in-chief," they definitely serve more as interpreters of the meaning that the myths regarding American identity contain for the American public. If one can apply the analogy that the president is the pope of civil religion, then one can see the priest role played by others within civil society, such as institutions that support hegemonic thinking, including mass media.

In the world of *Supernatural*, we see the priest role of promoting American civil religious faith, played by the Winchester brothers and, at times, their surrogate father, Uncle Bobby. If one reads these characters as representing a sort of priesthood, conveying in essence homilies regarding a civil religion centering on America as something to be worshipped, then these characters function as priests of the American civil religious faith. Based on this reading, then, we see these characters as conveying the doctrine of American civil religion several ways. First, like actual priests, they engage in missionary work throughout the United States: they travel across the land trying to literally save people and raise their awareness for a supernatural world and life outside their daily, mundane existence. In addition, they have given up the hope of attaining their own families; marriage is not an option, given the hunters' way of life. Even though the brothers do experience romantic relationships, they do not last, but always give way to the larger mission. In this way, their calling, as it were, compares to that of priests sacrificing a family life in favor of serving a higher power. Additionally, as discussed in chapter 3, the Winchesters actually don the collar of priests, which not only implicitly associates them with Catholicism, making it a "good" religion, but also gives a visual image of them as priests as well. Only here we read their actions as hunters as symbolizing the actions of priests of a civil religion.

The Winchesters also appear as the authority on who can become a "priest" like them, and, by extension, what the American identity does *not* mean. In several episodes over the course of seasons two and three, they encounter a fellow hunter, the fanatical Gordon Walker.[3] As mentioned in chapter 3, Walker seeks to wipe out anything that isn't human—including Sam Winchester, whom he saw as evil. Walker's extremism symbolizes an excess regarding the hunter's mission to eliminate non-humans. The Winchesters, though committed to protecting humans, elect to spare some supernatural entities who do not kill humans. For example, in "Bloodlust" (Episode 2.3), the Winchesters encounter a group of vampires who have vowed not to kill humans, and so spare them. Walker sees no difference between the benign vampires and those who harm humans, and kills those spared by the Winchesters.

Eventually, in "Fresh Blood" (Episode 3.7), Walker receives his comeuppance, a sort of punishment for his errant version of hunting: he himself becomes a vampire, and Sam kills him. Prior to this turn of events, a homily of sorts regarding the civil religion of Americanism becomes played out in the narrative of Gordon Walker and his dealings with the Winchesters. This homily tells viewers that Americanism rejects hate and prejudice, while it values fairness, justice, and the principle that someone (or something in this case) is innocent until proven guilty. The subtext of the narrative of Gordon Walker involves the rejection of this mindset in that the brothers make it clear they do not wish to work with him. Thus, because he is not a hunter like them, his character becomes a representation of what Americans are not (prejudiced and hateful). In this manner, the Winchesters in essence preach the message of Americanism, and ensure that not only errant Christianity is kept in check, but that a real hunter/American does not espouse the views embodied in the Walker character.

During *Supernatural*'s sixth season, the Winchester brothers develop an awkward relationship with their own grandfather, Samuel Campbell, and their Campbell cousins, the descendants of a long line of hunters as described earlier in this chapter. Sam, who has been rescued from Hell, has returned, although his soul is missing. The soulless Sam actually becomes an even greater hunter, apparently because he lacks any empathy. Sam has teamed up with the Campbells, hunting monsters with great efficiency. However, Sam and Dean soon learn that their familial counterparts are actually working with the demon Crowley to capture monsters in an effort to help Crowley find Purgatory. Thus, rather than pursuing the true mission of hunters to save people, the Campbells instead now have a different purpose, one that has strayed from the "priesthood." Dean, ever the skeptic, had distrusted his grandfather Samuel all along, pointing to the difference between "real" hunters and those who are not; this becomes apparent in the episode "Family Matters" (Episode 6.7). Later, Dean learns that Samuel, who had long been dead but was resurrected by and agreed to work for Crowley, was promised that he would see his daughter Mary (Sam and Dean's dead mother) again; the misguided motive of working with the devil, so to speak, in order to have a dead loved one reappear thus clearly is not acceptable.

Sam and Dean eventually turn on their familial but errant cohorts, declaring them unfit to be hunters. Dean kills their cousin, the ironically named Christian, in the process; Christian turns out to have been possessed by a demon ("Caged Heat," Episode 6.10). This further denotes the good hunter from the bad: the Campbells have lost their way, and the Winchesters further differentiate themselves from "bad" hunters by rejecting them and their motives. These examples, of the zealous Walker and the misguided Campbell family, illustrate how the brothers serve as symbolic priests who excommunicate, in essence, others from the priesthood of hunting.

The brothers also decide to "permit" certain hunters to continue hunting as well, as in the season eight episode "Freaks and Geeks" (Episode 8.18). In this episode featuring young hunters-in-training, the Winchesters encounter a group of teenagers, including the daughter of a hunter they met previously, who are working to kill vampires at the behest of an adoptive "father" who is also a former hunter. After assisting them in the hunt, the brothers discover that the young hunters have been duped into killing an innocent vampire, one who had not fully become one. The father figure the young hunters had trusted actually deceived them not only about the vampires who killed their parents, but had them kill a vampire who had not harmed a human. As mentioned previously, the Winchesters' philosophy dictates that innocents, even monsters, should not be punished. After the teenagers' "father" kills himself, which again presents to viewers a comeuppance for the errant hunter, the brothers allow the teenagers to continue hunting, but only in their locality. This episode reiterates the correct version of the hunter, showing the demarcation between the Winchesters and those who rely on perverse versions of hunting. In this manner, we see the difference between right and wrong versions of Americanism as civil religion—and the consequences of following the wrong path.

Another example of the errant, misguided hunter appears in the episode "Citizen Fang" (Episode 8.9). Dean had befriended a vampire who helped him escape from Purgatory, Benny Lafitte. For Dean, Benny initially complicated the hunter's idea of a good vampire, but Dean had come to regard him as an ally, even a brother figure (hence, the title of an earlier episode featuring Dean and Benny, "Blood Brother"). In this episode, a former hunter named Martin, whom the brothers helped in the episode "Sam, Interrupted" (Episode 5.11), has returned to hunting and is stalking Benny at the behest of Sam, who did not trust Benny. Although Benny has sworn off killing humans for their blood, and thus has become one of the "good" vampires, Martin still comes to believe Benny needs to die. At the end of the episode, Benny offers himself to be killed by Martin, who has kidnapped Benny's granddaughter and tortured her. At the last moment, just as it appears Martin is about to kill Benny, Benny attacks him. When Dean reports Martin's death to Sam, Dean tells his brother, "He had it coming" (Loflin & Copus, 2012). Martin's demise echoes the lesson of what happens to hunters who go astray and disregard any sense of morality.

As discussed in chapter 3, Sam, Dean, and their Uncle Bobby also act as priests by performing rituals, notably ones specifically tied to Catholicism, in their line of work. They bless their own holy water, use Latin in exorcisms, and carry crucifixes and rosaries as part of their arsenal. Although they do not practice Catholicism, attend church services, take communion, or otherwise follow any other religious practices personally, their hunting methods nonetheless invoke a religious nature.

Hunters, too, have their own rituals that imbue a sense of religiosity, especially when marking the death of a fellow hunter. For example, in the season six episode ". . . And Then There Were None" (Episode 6.16), their ally Rufus Turner died at the hands of Bobby, who was possessed by the power of Eve, "mother of all monsters," as mentioned in chapter 2. At the end of the episode, Bobby oversees Rufus's burial at the Jewish cemetery. Normally, a funeral pyre serves as the ritual for hunters, ostensibly to ensure that their bodies cannot be resurrected and possessed (by demons or other creatures). After reminiscing about Rufus and how he helped Bobby over the years, Bobby drops a shot of Johnny Walker Blue on Rufus's grave, then takes a drink of it himself. In the next season, when Bobby himself perishes, the brothers burn his body according to the hunters' funeral ritual.[4] Although specific to the world of hunters, both funeral proceedings present the main characters as taking on a pseudo-religious role, similar to what a priest or religious authority would do regarding ceremonies marking the death of a loved one, albeit the Winchesters do so without the collar, crucifix, or holy water.

These examples suggest that, in much the same way presidents and other politicians serve as the priests-in-chief of American civil religion, so, too, do the righteous Winchester brothers play a similar metaphoric role in their universe. In their fictional world, they both embody *and* promote myths regarding Americanism—the very same myths politicians rely on in their speeches—and in doing so emphasize core dimensions of American identity. These notions regarding Americans, such as the correct behavior of a true American as portrayed in the good hunter persona on *Supernatural*, thus become a more palatable, creative, and subtle way to complete what Stuart Hall (1973) termed the "circuit of culture," as discussed previously in chapter 1. The beliefs of a culture become inculcated in its stories, thus reconfirming hegemonic, commonly held, and accepted notions regarding a cultural/national identity. Garbed in the shadow of civil religion, the stories of *Supernatural* serve a political function within American culture by reinforcing religious aspects of American national identity—specifically those characteristics that support the origin myths of exceptionalism and the frontier.

SUMMARY

As we described here, we see the premise, storylines, and characters of *Supernatural* as embodying the notion of a country and culture chosen by God to literally and metaphorically serve as the world's protectors against evil. The inherent superiority of America unfolds throughout *Supernatural* in the adventures of the Winchesters as they vanquish the gods and mythic creatures of the "Old World." Eventually they take on even the host of Heaven, the top of the religious hierarchy as depicted in the show. In this manner, the Winchesters as America symbolize how the nation's exceptionalism has evolved from a feeling of being better than other people and cultures to being divine.

Further it points to a hegemony regarding America's status as a world power: the implicit acceptance of America as a global force responsible for intervening in the affairs of other nations. Thus, it has become intertwined with what America stands for and its identity on the world stage. The "dream" of these hunters is to live a normal life, the familiar yet mythic American dream. In a sense, the Frontier Myth and the myth of American Exceptionalism forward the same simple, idealized goal, albeit set against the backdrop of contemporary world events.

The Winchester brothers, in their early twenties when the series began, over the course of the series have come to accept their destiny and responsibility as hunters and protectors of not only a people (Americans), but of the world. Their hero's journey reflects how a young America has matured and developed into the world power it is today, similarly accepting its role as protector. In this manner, we see it providing an appropriate example of American Exceptionalism and its burden to its audience, no matter what age. Through its depiction of a family whose "business" involves hunting monsters, demons, ghosts, and other dark forces that threaten the American way of life, *Supernatural* relies on a familiar theme of accepting one's responsibility, even though it means one must also sacrifice something—no matter what it is.

In addition, the Winchesters do not profess or advocate the Christian faith, or any other religion or religious tradition. That they are able to succeed *despite* this suggests their power lies in being humans, without innate divine or superhero powers. That is, they might have help from the angel Castiel, and even assistance from an interventionist God, but they are still human. Their exceptionalist status thus derives from their humanness. This humanness and ability to reconsider the hunting doctrine to kill all monsters, no matter what, has developed to include a gray area that has forced the Winchesters to make decisions regarding sparing creatures that do not harm humans. In contrast, those hunters who aim to wipe out all monsters meet gruesome ends—at the hands of those they seek to destroy. This becomes a homily mirroring the verses in Matthew 22:52-54, in which Christ admonishes that "those who take up the sword shall perish by the sword." Thus, hunters whose sole purpose is to kill monsters can expect to meet their end in the same manner in which they live.

Homiletic undertones of the episodes described in this chapter present an interweaving of religious—yet non-religious and ethical—philosophies and codes of conduct. However, even as we detect and explain how religion appears, both overtly and covertly in *Supernatural*, we also can view its narrative as moving beyond "traditional" notions of religion. The religion the Winchesters do profess, through their actions and through the show's depictions of the demise of hunters who forget or forgo their creed by destroying innocent creatures, aligns more closely to a civil religion that, like American civil religion, contains elements of Christianity, but is not explicitly or specifically Christian. They also are able to be seen as a civil religious priests or messengers because, like politicians in the "real world" they do not advocate for a particular religion. We see them as becoming warrior priests, as it were, who patrol not only the supernatural frontier, but the hunting profession as well. Thus, the Winchester brothers' mission to hunt monsters and save people has evolved into a sense of justice regarding the enforcement of a civil religion, which we view as representative of an ideal American identity.

Regarding the evolution of the American identity as reflected over the course of *Supernatural*'s run thus far, we see the Winchesters as essentially moving beyond the divinely appointed protectors fulfilling their destiny as agents of God. Their role in the Apocalypse, or more aptly, its prevention, points to their ability not only to face up to the powerful forces of the Judeo-Christian God, but to defeat even that power. Combined with their successful victories over pagan gods positioned on lower scales of the religious hierarchy we examined in chapter 3, their "victory" at averting the end of the world becomes a way to frame them as equal to even the angels. In this sense, we see a connection between them and America: the divine appointment has given way to equality with the forces that hold the most sway in the world of gods, God, angels, and demons. In essence, they have exceeded the dream, as it were, of a God that saw them as special. Now they have become as God—invoking their own power in the matters of the world, supernatural or not.

NOTES

1. We acknowledge the complications that arise from using "America" as a generic, hegemonic term that refers to the United States of America, as it subsumes the identity of other nations and cultures that exist geographically on the continents of North and South America. For purposes of our discussion, we use "America" to refer to the United States and "Americans" for those who identify as citizens and residents of the country known as the United States of America. Rather than an indicator of citizenship, our use of "American" denotes a cultural membership that coincides with a national identity.

2. Recall also that Kansas is the home state of the heroine Dorothy Gale in L. Frank Baum's *The Wizard of Oz* series of books. Dorothy similarly encountered supernatural creatures and even destroyed an evil witch. Given the way in which the witch dies, one could even say Dorothy used "holy" water—in that it burned the witch much like the holy water used by the Winchesters against demons in *Supernatural*.

3. The Gordon Walker character, played by actor Sterling K. Brown, appeared in "Hunted" (Episode 2.10), "Bloodlust" (Episode 2.3), "Bad Day at Black Rock" (Episode 3.3), and "Fresh Blood" (Episode 3.7). Walker's number-one monster enemy was vampires; he was out for revenge after his sister was turned into one. This all-consuming hate for vampires led Walker to disregard whether they were good or evil—he wanted to kill them all, and his character serves as the opposite of the Winchesters' persona as hunters.

4. Bobby had died in the season seven episode "Death's Door" (Episode 7.10). His funeral pyre is not shown, but Sam alludes to the brothers' having burned Bobby's body in a later episode ("The Slice Girls," Episode 7.13). However, Bobby had refused to move on to the afterlife after his death, instead choosing to remain on earth and becoming a ghost. Eventually, Bobby becomes a vengeful spirit, exhibiting the same destructive behaviors as other ghosts the Winchesters have encountered and destroyed. His soul had possessed his whiskey flask, which the brothers eventually burned as well in order to ensure his soul would not remain on earth. In the season eight episode "Taxi Driver" (Episode 8.19), Bobby's soul is released from Hell by Sam, and his spirit finally ascends to Heaven thanks to the intervention of the angel Naomi. The final scene of Bobby's spirit indicates he belonged in Paradise, befitting his good works as a hunter and as a human.

Chapter Six

Conclusion

In this book, we examined the text of the CW television network series *Supernatural* (2005-), a program based in the horror genre that offers viewers myriad religious-based antagonists, through the portrayals of monsters which its two main characters "hunt" and destroy, as well as storylines based in the Bible. The series' producers claim a non-religious perspective, as reported by Bellefonte (2011) in a *New York Times* article on the show; indeed, Bellafonte quoted then-showrunner Sera Gamble as saying, "We consider ourselves a mishmash of all kinds of lore." However, even as Gamble noted that the show wants to avoid offending people, "we've heard that some priests really love it." We find this comment unsurprising, given our contention that story arcs and outcomes of episodes actually forward a hegemonic portrayal of Christianity, and Catholicism in particular, that includes a good-versus-evil motif regarding the superiority of Christianity. Moreover, we contend the show forwards a pro-American perspective regarding a more generalized fight against evil in contemporary times.

Using hegemony theory, homiletics, and mythic criticism as theoretical approaches, we centered our analyses of this cult "fan favorite" (Rudolph, 2010) around the argument that network fictional television forwards a certain hegemonic viewpoint regarding religion and identity. We found that, in addition to providing enjoyable and imaginative stories about two brothers from Kansas, *Supernatural* forwards a theology in which the Judeo-Christian and Catholic traditions sit atop a hierarchy of religions. We found that of 172 episodes, 38 episodes had aspects associated with non-Catholic, Christian-related religiosity or religious text or imagery, and 52 included text or imagery specifically associated with Catholicism. Further, we found a sympathetic treatment of Catholicism, based on the usage of Catholic-related artifacts and depiction of Catholic clergy, namely, priests.

We approached our examination of this television horror series using hegemony theory to explain the presence, or absence, of certain religions, with the perspective that despite a plurality of religious traditions, there would emerge a preference or favorable treatment of some more than others. An essential version of hegemony theory would predict a dominant world-view presented by those who create media products. We did find evidence of this when we identified episodes as depicting a generalized impression of Christianity, such as the reliance on Scripture from the New Testament.

Beyond a proportion of religion-inspired episodes, we determined that Catholicism tended to be associated with artifacts that the Winchesters relied upon to combat a formidable adversary, demons from Hell assumed to project a Christian version of the supernatural world. In *Supernatural*, holy water has detrimental physical effects on the human vessels used by demons as hosts, and Latin used in exorcism is used to expel demons from those vessels. Moreover, the portrayal of Catholic priests as "experts" in exorcism, and, indeed, even pioneers in dealing with demons as depicted in the season eight episodes "Clip Show" and "Sacrifice," adds to a Catholic mythos in popular media. In this way, we see *Supernatural* as part of the continuum of texts reflective of the "fantastic": fantasy, horror, and science fiction. This treatment thus adds to what Hansen (2011) in *Roman Catholicism in Fantastic Film* called "the fascination with the way in which the stuff of Catholicism—its supernatural claims, its rituals and artifacts, its moral exigencies and contradictions—have appealed and continue to appeal to filmmakers in the fantastic genres" (p. 1). Furthermore, while the concept of "magic" may hold a negative valence as compared to "religion," as Meltzer (1999) explained, when magical items associated with "good" religions or intent are used by "good" characters, the line between what is magic and what is legitimate religion becomes further blurred. Indeed, one can go so far as to say that *Supernatural* naturalizes religion as magical. In this way, *Supernatural* adds to a historical continuum of religions that tie the spiritual to the physical.

Not only does magic deal with the physical aspects of religion, as Mirecki and Meyer (2002) noted, but spells and amulets in early Christianity were used for practical purposes. Spells to drive out demons, to heal a range of ailments, as protection from evil spirits, and even protection against "headless powers" invoked the power of God and Jesus Christ (Meyer & Smith, 1999, p. 47). The invocation of the divine even in the absence of a divine presence in the series implicitly endorses a certain viewpoint, one that reaffirms the place of Christianity within the milieu of contemporary and ancient religions.

When combined with the imagery and tactile depictions of the Winchester brothers using specific, Catholic-associated weapons against their enemies—notably those from non-Western religions—it further demarcates Catholicism as the most powerful religion. We believe the emergence of Catholicism as hegemonic in *Supernatural* is not really reflecting things as they are, but as depicting a struggle between Catholicism and other faiths that casts other religions—and even other versions of Christianity—as evil. In that Catholicism actually is a minority denomination in the United States, the reaffirmation of its power in a physical way (the use of holy water and Latin) presents Catholicism as the original form of Christianity, and thus invokes a sort of authenticity regarding the presumed and assumed existence of *one* "good" religion. In this manner, not only do we see *Supernatural* as supporting Beal's (2002) conclusions that monsters, both beastly and human, from "Other," non-Western religions confirm the "rightness" of Western culture/society, but as taking this notion to the next step: Catholicism becomes distinguished from "Other" Christian denominations as the true and best form of Christianity.

This does not in any way diminish the way in which *Supernatural* simultaneously offers a plurality of religious traditions. In that its narratives rely on myths, legends, and fables rooted in belief systems from around the world and historical eras, one can see it as offering viewers a "religion of the week" as well as a "monster of the week." The Winchesters must do physical battle with these entities, which in and of itself conveys the notion that these "obsolete" beings from past civilizations still exist in some form. Those mythologies, once practiced religions just like those we consider real today, incorporated into the adventures of Sam and Dean evidence a staying power that allows for the application of ages-old themes to the present day. Rather than conjuring up imagined realities based on "fictional" mythology, such as in the alternate dimensions portrayed in the WB network series *Angel*, this series relies on real tales of the weird and fantastic. Just as another WB network series, *Charmed*, associated Wiccan with its protagonists, sisters who used magic for good in their battle against evil (Meyer, 2007), *Supernatural* relies on actual religions and practices in its storylines in a similar manner. Curious viewers of *Supernatural* thus may find they want to learn more about the gods and creatures they see onscreen. Further, they could find out about the religions behind those same monsters, as Meyer found with fans of *Charmed* who admitted to wanting to learn more about Wiccan.

In addition to depictions of Christianity and Catholicism, we see *Supernatural* as offering commentary on the way in which these particular belief systems should be practiced and expressed. While the "flattening" of religion in television texts in general may protect against negative feedback by some audience members, there seems to be room nonetheless for a framing of religion as positive. That is, rather than watering down religious tenets, television narratives set within an un-realistic or fantastical setting appear to allow for more valence regarding religions than those that overtly claim or depict religious contexts.

In *Supernatural*, any preaching or teaching is not really performed by characters representing clergy, but by mythical figures. The episode "Meet the New Boss" (Episode 7.1) provides such an example, when the angel Castiel rebukes a representative of "God"—a preacher invoking righteousness as he tells his congregation to essentially hate others—for justifying un-Christian behavior. Even as Castiel believes he is doing God's work, he ironically does the same thing against those he believes are not. Castiel gets his comeuppance by the episode's conclusion, when God's true equal (Death) tells him he is "no God." In essence, the episode taken as a whole forwards the message of "judge not lest ye be judged," a tenet of Christianity that extends beyond this particular faith. Indeed, this most religious-based of messages in reality knows no one religion, but may be taken as an ethical guidepost applicable to all. In a sense, then, one might take *Supernatural* as utilizing religion to forward a message *against* religion: those who claim to be Christian do not necessarily follow Christ, nor understand the philosophy it, as a religion and belief system, conveys. Indeed the "golden rule" becomes more of a directive here than any doctrine, commandment, or Scriptural crutch used to justify bigotry and hate.

Starting in its fourth season, *Supernatural* began introducing characters based in Judeo-Christian theology, notably, angels from Heaven, including archangels actually mentioned in Old and New Testament Scripture (Wimmler & Kienzel, 2011). The angel Castiel, in "Lazarus Rising" (Episode 4.1), identifies himself as an "angel of the Lord." Acknowledgment of the Judeo-Christian Apocalypse in "Hammer of the Gods" (Episode 5.19) and eventual demise of the non-Christian gods at the hands of Lucifer firmly placed non-Christian gods in a lowered status to the Heaven-and-Hell structure that would be responsible for the destruction of the entire world and all the gods in it. However, even as the very term "Judeo-Christian" is uttered by the Norse god Balder, we find the absence of Jesus Christ in the series (so far) warrantable of extended discussion.

Indeed, even though imagery of Jesus appears, and the name of "Jesus" is invoked—and therefore acknowledged as equally as real as other deities—Christ does not appear as a character in storylines. We commented on this in chapter 4, when we analyzed the homiletic aspects of the Four Horsemen episodes. The absence of Christ conveys that while Christianity holds what appears to be a superior status among all the religions and mythologies in *Supernatural*, it is not a show about Christianity. Though the Winchester brothers readily utilize and rely on Christian artifacts—those that specifically represent Catholicism and, hence, *the* Church from whence Christianity originated—they do not practice or adhere to any particular faith. One can argue that this allows viewers who do not belong to or identify with Christianity per se to nevertheless identify with the show's two main characters.

By having Dean and Sam not say they are Christians, not attend church (of any kind), and even to specifically say they are *not* Catholic leaves open the possibility that their experiences will bolster them against having a religious conversion. On the other hand, the depiction of Sam as holding some belief in God and the power of prayer, and even in faith healing (as in the season one episode "Faith") may prove correct. Either way, the generalized and nebulous belief Sam has in God lets *Supernatural* exhibit a tendency toward believing in something—but that something does not include organized religion, nor its assumed opposite, spiritualism.

Beyond depictions in the series itself, the Winchesters' beliefs have become a topic of non-scholarly discussion in organized events related to the show's fandom. For example, a session titled "Angels, Demons and Creatures" appeared on the schedule at the 2013 fan convention known as "Salute to *Supernatural*." Fans learned, or, more correctly, got confirmation that Dean is "not a believer," while Sam believes and prays. Even the brothers' mother, Mary Winchester, is described as a believer. [1]

In *Supernatural*, the character of Dean Winchester, always the skeptic, represents a somewhat agnostic viewpoint. In "Are You There, God, It's Me, Dean Winchester" (Episode 4.2) he asks an age-old question, "Where is God? If bad things happen to good people, why doesn't He help?" Dean then questions the existence and motives of a personal God, if one exists: "If there's a God out there, why would He care about me? I'm just a regular guy" (Gamble & Sgriccia, 2008). The openness that results when Dean gets no answer, coupled with the silence Castiel receives when even he, an angel, asks God for a sign in "The Man Who Would Be King" (Episode 6.20), serves as another lesson in faith: does one continue believing even when no concrete answers are given?

Gramsci's theory of hegemony, which seeks to explain how we come to believe what we believe and how "common sense" becomes what Landy (1994) called "a collage of opinions and beliefs that fails to be not only coherent but also critical" (p. 29). In *Supernatural* we see religion as contributing to a common sense—in Gramsci's words *senso comune*—that presents the existence of gods, and the presumed existence of an absent Judeo-Christian God. In short, while evidence of angels and demons is quite concrete, in that the Winchester brothers fight these entities consistently, no such evidence is given to assure the Winchesters, or the viewer, that there is a God in the first place—it is taken, and presented, as a matter of faith. Further complicating this openness regarding the existence of God, in *Supernatural* human souls do exist as actual things; souls are depicted as orbs of light and even have been depicted as going to Heaven. [2] Here, then, we see a common sense regarding the existence—and value—of human souls, whose depiction on the show adds to an inherent presumption that there is an afterlife, which in turn presumes life does not end with death.

When taken together, then, one can argue that *Supernatural* serves as a conduit for presenting religion as a collage of inconsistent beliefs. Attempts at avoiding the "religious show" label result in the flattening of that collage in order to retain viewers. Further, its fantastical portrayal of the world allows the audience to uncritically enjoy the equally, if not more, fantastical tales about things called "angels," "demons," and "God." Not only this, but we found a consistent presence of religious artifacts that hold paranormal powers associated with a particular collage of beliefs. These artifacts in turn are unquestioned by the characters who wield them, and, in turn, viewers who see their use depicted on the screen.

Supernatural thus perpetuates certain fragmentary ideas regarding faith in the unseen and unknown (evidence in "real life" of human souls has no basis in science, for example) and the use and effectiveness of religious artifacts whose powers have no rational explanation. Furthermore, it has found a way to present these in a way so as not to offend viewers, which serves as a critical point of hegemony theory: by consistently depicting these beliefs—related to already familiar portrayals in other media—*Supernatural* helps to perpetuate a certain worldview even of the "imaginary." In this way, we see this program as exhibiting indirect power, through its narratives, that adds to "the habituation of loyalty in maintaining traditional associations" (Landy, 1994, p. 29). These associations in turn help in maintaining the mythos of the Catholic Church, and, by extension, in religion in general. Despite the producers' insistence that the show is not about religion, it nevertheless is: by depicting the already familiar, the already familiar remains familiar and becomes indirectly reinforced for the next generation, thus perpetuating its power.

When considered within the context of the culture in which *Supernatural* is produced, a Christian but mostly Protestant one, the sympathetic presentation of Catholicism illustrates the influence of institutions based in civil society (mass media) to perpetuate hegemony, in this case, the idea that Catholicism outranks other Christian denominations in the world of the supernatural. That is, if a an un-natural, spiritual dimension exists, then Catholicism is the "best bet" in fighting the most fearsome of malevolent forces—demons, which also find their origins in that tradition. Hence, hegemony operates via even the most innocuous means: a fanciful television show about two boys who meet ghosts, gods, and angels.

Television functions as "as an instrument for continuity as well as change, a communication system devoted most of the time to entertaining as many of us as possible with stories and fables that earlier media and story systems had told before" (Thorburn, 1987, p. 167). As an institution of "myth making and popular narrative," it has taken its place within a continuum of storytelling conduits "that extend back into Western history to at least the time of Homer," added Thorburn (p. 167). We find Thorburn's observations completely apropos for *Supernatural*, in that several episodes actually find their origins in Homer. Creatures like the siren and the Olympic gods from ancient Greek myth maintain a presence on earth, even millennia later. Gods from Greek, Norse, and other mythologies, and past and current religions have some origin in the ancient, attesting to their appeal even in the present.

As we articulated in chapter 3, the supplanting of these gods in favor of the "new" Judeo-Christian God and theology, which includes the hierarchy of angels from the Bible and other sources points to a progression of myth-making, one in which there seems to be an evolution of sorts from darkness to light. The analogy of this progression, as presented in the story of Prometheus related in "Remember the Titans" (Episode 8.16), has humankind escaping from the power of the gods, thanks to Prometheus's gift of fire/light.

In Norse mythology, a similar transition from dark to light occurs when the old gods, the Aesir, are replaced with a new one. After a great battle, which marked the end of the Aesir, the dawn of a new day saw the last remnants of humankind, a man and woman named Lif and Lifthrasir, emerge from a secret grove of trees; their descendants would populate the new earth. The pagan gods then faded into memory: "Lif and Lifthrasir did not lift their heads and hands in prayer to the Aesir gods. They prayed to God Almighty, who had stepped out from above to rule all the worlds in eternity" (D'Aulaire & D'Aulaire, 1967, p. 152).

As we explained, the supplanting of pagan gods reinforces the common sense, implicit understanding among viewers that in the *Supernatural* universe it is "God Almighty" whose proxy is held by the Judeo-Christian mythology as depicted in the show, and it is He that holds the alpha-god status. However, even the presumed "good" forces in this mythology, the angels of Heaven, are vulnerable to displacement and corruption. The story arcs of the past four seasons have the angels actually working against human beings, those they were obligated to protect. The Winchesters, two humans, have found a way to defeat even the angels. In their successful struggle to subvert the angels' plan to bring on the Apocalypse, the Winchesters symbolize that humans can defeat almost anything, including War, Pestilence, and Famine. The composite homily offered by the Four Horsemen episodes during season five tells us that humanity can overcome hate, disease, and emptiness of spirit. The only thing humans cannot defeat or overcome is Death, something that the God of Judeo-Christian myth cannot do either.

In a *TV Guide* article previewing *Supernatural*'s fifth season, series creator Eric Kripke hinted that the Winchesters would be able to overcome whatever challenges, however supernaturally great, they faced: "Our attitude is that humans, with all their imperfections, are the heroic ones, and everyone else is just messing with them" (Rudolph, 2009b, p. 32). Through the lens of American Exceptionalism and the perspective of the Frontier Myth, we see Kripke's allusion to the Winchesters' placement within a larger power struggle as representative of the United States' position in the world itself. More than simply fictional characters combating urban legends in a science fiction/ horror TV show, the Winchesters as America provides a way of interpreting this particular televisual text in terms of a political discourse. That discourse addresses the United States' national identity and an approach to dealing with others who similarly seek to "mess with" it. When combined with the explicit way in which series creator Eric Kripke saw the brothers facing down Armageddon and putting an "American cowboy" in the middle of an epic struggle between good and evil, we view *Supernatural*'s story of two boys fighting ghosts, demons, and monsters as a narrative field for telling the story of America. This nation, too, was young once, faced incredible obstacles, yet emerged strong, courageous, and determined to serve as a force for good in a world that needs its protection from radical, non-supernatural Others.

Supernatural's transmission of a consensus narrative that (re)defines national identity and cultural values—embodied in the Frontier Myth and American Exceptionalism—becomes significant when considering its younger demographic, a segment of the population becoming more apt to participate in national affairs (Conley, 2012). Just as media narratives in the form of teen dramas can provide young people information about what it means to be an adult (Meyer, 2009), we see *Supernatural* as having the potential to serve a similar function regarding what it means to be an American. The official civil religious practices which convey the ideals associated with the American identity become enforced as well. In this manner, its text—the story of two American brothers who sacrifice the American dream to protect Americans and the world itself—provides what Thorburn (1987) called a "consensus narrative" that tells viewers that real Americans do the same: make sacrifices to protect people from evil because that's what America does.

Combined with how *Supernatural* relays a stance regarding a hierarchy of religion traditions, it relays a stance regarding a hierarchy of nations. The additional "divinity" associated with an exceptional nation completes the circuit between national identity, religious beliefs, and the resulting hegemony that incurs an implicit, tacit approval regarding what this nation is and what it believes—and believes in. The American Exceptionalism that underlies the story of the Winchesters' battle against enemies on a biblical scale— literally—extends Beal's (2002) assertion that religion serves as a source for the demarcation of cultural Others in order to justify Western colonialism. "Oriental" religions thus become the demonized Other. "At the same time, this colonial discourse identifies the colonizers with the holy armies of God and the forces of light, enlightenment and cosmic redemption, fighting a chaos battle of apocalyptic proportions," wrote Beal (p. 116). In the case of *Supernatural*, "America" replaces Western colonialism, and its mission to enlighten and bring order to the chaos of the world is mirrored in the Winchesters' mission to save people *and* the world.

Supernatural offers a rich text for examining how national discourse permeates all levels and genres of cultural work. In this manner, hegemony theory becomes even more applicable, as the subtext of the story of the Winchesters illustrates how "common sense is a multifaceted representation of social life under determinate conditions," as explained by Landy (1994, p. 78). Here we see how storytelling serves as a means by which Gramsci's theory of hegemony operates in the realm of civil society, wherein indirect power presented as entertainment promulgates and enforces a socially created mutual understanding of who we are, what we represent, and how we should behave. The circuit of culture thus becomes complete, as the storytellers incorporate the already-functioning belief system into the narrative disseminated to their audience.

CARRY ON, WAYWARD SONS

At the close of *Supernatural*'s eighth season, its staying power in a post-network viewing environment was evidenced in an article on the 2012-2013 television season. Vulture.com, the entertainment web site for *New York* magazine, reported that the big four broadcast networks—ABC, CBS, NBC, and Fox—"bled viewers," losing a collective 10% of the under-50 viewing audience, based on Nielsen ratings: "The vast majority of the nearly 90 series that had their second or higher season on ABC, CBS, NBC, Fox, and the CW lost ground among adults under 50" (Adalian & Woocher, 2013). However, when compared to the 2011-2012 season, the percentage change in the increase in the number of adults between 18 and 49 during the 2012-2013 season experienced by *Supernatural* had it at the top of all five networks. With a 22% increase in viewers in this demographic, *Supernatural*'s ratings outpaced those for ABC's *Shark Tank* (with a 17% increase) and the CW's *Vampire Diaries* (with a 15% increase). Coupled with the series' renewal for an "impressive" ninth season (Harnick, 2013), wins as Favorite Sci-Fi/Fantasy TV Show and for its fan following at the People's Choice Awards in 2013 ("And the Nominees Are," 2013), and even a course for college students on the series' multiple levels of meaning, *Supernatural* evidently holds an appeal beyond the cosmetic.[3] In October of 2013, the premiere episode of the ninth season saw a 50% increase in ratings over the eighth season's opening episode, with 2.5 million viewers in the 18 to 49 age range tuning in (Hibberd, 2013). Though partially explained as a result of the show's lead-in (a new series about a family of vampires titled *The Originals*), the show saw an increase in ratings for a premiere episode despite a change in time slot.

We examined here episodes of *Supernatural* from its first through its latest completed season. "Sacrifice" (Episode 8.23), the final episode of season eight, ends with an almost-cataclysmic scene typical of a classic television cliffhanger. Just as Sam is about to complete the final step in the demon-cleansing ritual that will close of the gates of Hell, his big brother stops him. As Dean and Sam watch, the night sky becomes lit by what appears to be shooting stars—angels falling from heaven, their wings catching fire as they lose their divine power. The power of the angels, it seems, has left them, leaving the Winchesters to face the "killer" angels—who seek their revenge on the brothers. As of this writing, the ninth season of *Supernatural* continues the fallen-angel storyline, with the Winchesters' ally Castiel dealing with the everyday privations of being an ordinary human, and Dean making a deal with an angel named Ezekiel to possess Sam.

The religious themes that have marked the series over its near-decade-long run continue as well during the first few episodes of the ninth season: the struggle between agnosticism and religious practice—particularly Catholicism—appeared in the episode "I'm No Angel" (Episode 9.3), which aired October 22, 2013. Castiel, now homeless and penniless, wanders into a Catholic church, indicated by the statuary reliefs of the Stations of the Cross, stained glass windows (including one depicting Jesus and a dove) statues of angels, votive prayer candles, a statue of Christ on the cross, and a hint of a statue of the Virgin Mary in the background during a scene between Castiel and a woman he encounters there. He listens to the woman praying a few pews away; she holds a rosary and makes the Sign of the Cross. As she leaves the church, he poses the question of whether or not God can hear her prayers. "What if you were to find out that no one is listening? That God pretty much left. That heaven had gone out of business. What would you do"? She replies that those things are not possible, that she has faith. Pointedly, she tells him: "Your lack of faith doesn't cancel what I believe" (Buckner, Ross-Leming, & Hooks, 2013).

Castiel's query, informed by his knowledge as a former angel that God apparently remains absent in the *Supernatural* narrative, reflects the dichotomy that the show presents: the questionable existence of a higher power and a legitimate and serious depiction of religious belief. This particular episode also relies on other religious images and depictions that juxtapose "false" and authentic versions of Christianity: a comically depicted televangelist is used by the angels to recruit their human hosts (humans must give consent to allow angels to possess them) and his naïve, "true believer" followers who watch his broadcasts invite the angels to possess them. This is in contrast to two Catholic priests depicted in the same episode who run a homeless shelter and are brutally tortured and killed by angels seeking Castiel. Again, based on our analyses presented in this book, we find a sympathetic and benevolent portrayal of Catholicism over other forms of Christianity.

The revelations regarding the true nature of angels and the continued absence of their "Father" suggest an eventual denouement for the series that has the supernatural forces of Heaven and Hell no longer holding sway on the earth. Just as the old worlds based in myth were replaced, perhaps *Supernatural*'s series arc will lead to a renewed world in which the destiny of humanity depends on personal decisions based on rationality and reason rather than any interference by the gods, God, angels, or demons.

Whatever the course of the series, the fate of the Winchesters likely will reflect the lyrics of the show's theme song by the rock group Kansas, an anthem of sorts for the hunters and protectors of the real and *Supernatural* world: "Carry On, Wayward Son" promises "peace when you are done" (Livgren, 1976). These words offer if not the promise of an afterlife in paradise, but some sense of comfort and ease, which is, after all, what true faith offers those who do believe.

NOTES

1. One of the authors attended the "Salute to *Supernatural* Convention" operated by the corporation Creation Entertainment and held in Las Vegas in March of 2013. Consisting of a series of presentations held in an auditorium/convention hall at a large hotel, augmented by private photo opportunities with the series' actors available to attendees (mostly female) for a fee, the event also includes a vendors' room. Fans can purchase photos for actors to sign, as well as souvenir items such as t-shirts and coffee mugs. The most-attended convention session, unsurprisingly, was the appearance of the two stars of the series, Jensen Ackles and Jared Padelecki (fans refer to the two actors as one unit named J2). Conducted in a question-and-answer format, during the convention described here questions to the actors centered on inquiries regarding the actors' personal lives and favorite episodes or aspects regarding working on the series. The "Angels, Demons and Creatures" session appeared to serve as a more of a "filler" between guest appearance by other actors on the series rather than a resemblance to those at an educational or research conference.

2. In "Taxi Driver" (Episode 8.19), Sam completed the second trial required to close the gates of Hell when he rescues the soul of Uncle Bobby, wrongly kept in Hell. When Bobby's soul is released, it appears as an orb of light ascending upward, toward Heaven. As described in chapter 3, in "Houses of the Holy" (Episode 2.13), the soul of Father Gregory is depicted as a bright light when he is released from earthly existence through the power of the Last Rites.

3. In spring 2013, DeCal, the student-run democratic education program at the University of California, Berkeley, offered "The Mythology of *Supernatural*." According to the course description, attendees critically analyze the series using film analysis. Topics include the mythological creatures portrayed on the show, as well as recurring themes that include "morality, the importance of family, good vs. evil, and fate" (Freeman & Duhovny, 2013).

Bibliography

Abbott, S. (2011). Introduction: Then: The road so far. In S. Abbott & D. Lavery (Eds.), *TV goes to hell: An unofficial road map of* Supernatural (pp. ix-xvi). Toronto, Canada: ECW Press.

Abbott, S., & Lavery, D. (Eds.). (2011). *TV goes to hell: An unofficial road map of* Supernatural. Toronto, Canada: ECW Press.

Adalian, J., & Woocher, M. (2013, May 28). The 2012-13 TV season in one really depressing chart. *Vulture.com* [Web site]. Retrieved from http://www.vulture.com/2013/05/201213-tv-season-in-one-depressing-chart.hmtl

Americans say more religion in U.S. would be positive. (June 3, 2013). *Gallup* [Web site]. Retrieved from http://www.gallup.com/video/162860/americans-say-religion-ositive.aspx

And the nominees are. (2013). *People's Choice.com* [Web site]. Retrieved from http://www.peopleschoice.com/pca/awards/nominees/

Ashliman, D. L. (1997-2010). *The Norse creation myth.* Retrieved from http://www.pitt.edu/~dash/creation.html

Associated Press. (2008, November 5). Haggard admits 'sexual immorality,' apologizes. *NBC News.com* [Web site]. Retrieved from http://www.nbcnews.com/id/15536263/ns/us_news-life/t/haggard-admits-sexual-immorality-apologizes/

Augustine. (1958). *On Christian doctrine.* (D. W. Robertson, Jr., Trans.). New York, NY: Macmillan.

Awards for *Supernatural.* (2012). *IMDb (Internet Movie Database)* [Web site]. Retrieved from http://www.imdb.com/title/tt0460681/awards

Baker, III, F. W. (2009, April 28). Petreus parallels Iraq, Afghanistan strategies. Retrieved from http://www.defense.gov/news/newsarticle.aspx?id=54107.

Barry, J. (2009, January 31). Obama's Vietnam. *Newsweek.* Retrieved from http://www.newsweek.com/2009/01/30/obama-s-vietnam.html.

Beal, T. (2002). *Religion and its monsters.* New York, NY: Routledge.

Beasley, V. (2004). *You the people: American national identity in presidential rhetoric.* College Station, TX: Texas A & M Press.

Beasley, V. (Ed.) (2006). *Who belongs in America? Presidents, rhetoric, and immigration.* College Station, TX: Texas A & M Press

Bellafonte, G. (2011, February 27). Heaven, hell, brothers and an Impala. *The New York Times.* Retrieved from http://www.nytimes.com/2011/02/27/arts/television/27supernatural.html.

Bellah, R. N. (1967). Civil religion in America. *Daedalus, 134*(4), 40-55.

Beeler, K., & Beeler, S. (2007). Introduction. In K. Beeler & S. Beeler (Eds.), *Investigating* Charmed: *The magic power of TV* (pp. 1-6). New York, NY: I. B. Tauris.

137

Bellesiles, M. A. (2000). Guns don't kill, movies kill: The media's promotion of frontier violence. *Western Historical Quarterly, 31*, 284-290.

Bercovitch, S. (1978). *The American Jeremiad.* Madison, WI: University of Wisconsin Press.

Bercovitch, S. (1993). *The rites of assent: Transformations in the symbolic construction of America.* New York, NY: Routledge.

Bible verses about Leviathan. (n.d.). *The official King James Bible online.* Retrieved from http://www.kingjamesbibleonline.org/Bible-Verses-About-Leviathan/

Billington, R.A. (1981). *Land of savagery, land of promise: The European image of the American frontier in the nineteenth century.* Norman, OK: University of Oklahoma Press.

Bird, S. E. (2009). True believers and atheists need not apply: Faith and mainstream television drama. In D. Winston (Ed.), *Small screen, big picture: Television and lived religion* (pp. 17-41). Waco, TX: Baylor University Press.

Bostdorff, D. M. (1994). *The presidency and the rhetoric of foreign crisis.* Columbia, SC: University of South Carolina Press.

Bowman, M. S., & Bowman, R. L. (2010). Telling Katrina stories: Problems and opportunities in engaging disaster. *Quarterly Journal of Speech, 96,* 455-461.

Boyle, C., & Shapiro, R. (2010, 28 February). Massive temblor devastates Chile: 8.8 magnitude quake kills scores, sparks tsunami fear. *New York Daily News,* p. 9.

Brode, D., & Deyneka, L. (2012). *Myth, media and culture in* Star Wars: *An anthology.* Lanham, MD: Rowman & Littlefield.

Brown, N. (2011). *The mythology of* Supernatural: *The signs and symbols behind the popular TV show.* New York, NY: Berkeley Boulevard Books.

Buckner, B., & Ross-Leming, E. (Writers), & Ackes, J. (Director) (2012). Heartache. In E. Kripke (Creator),*Supernatural.* Los Angeles: CW Network.

Buckner, B., & Ross-Leming, E. (Writers), & Hooks, R. (Director) (2013). I'm no angel. In E. Kripke (Creator), *Supernatural.* Los Angeles: CW Network.

Bullock, J. (1994). Augustinian innovation: A spokesperson for a post classical age. *Journal of Communication and Religion, 20,* 5-13.

Butler, J. R. (2002). The imperial savage and the continuities of war. *Western Journal of Communication, 66,* 1-24.

Cardona, J. (2010, February 11). Mexico's Calderon pledges aid in drug war. Retrieved from http://www.reuters.com/article/idUSTRE61B05R20100212

Carey, J. (1989). *Communication as culture.* Boston, MA: Unwin Hyman.

Carver, J. (Writer), & Sgriccia, P. (Director). (2010). The point of no return. [Television series episode]. In E. Kripke (Creator), *Supernatural.* Los Angeles: CW Network.

Carver, J. (Writer), & Sgriccia, P. (Director). (2013). Sacrifice. [Television series episode]. In E. Kripke (Creator), *Supernatural.* Los Angeles: CW Network.

Carver, J. (Writer), & Tobin, J. M. (Director). (2007). A very supernatural Christmas.[Television series episode]. In E. Kripke (Creator), *Supernatural.* Los Angeles: CW Network.

Category: Writer. (2013, June 11). *Supernatural Wiki* [Web site]. Retrieved from http://www.supernaturalwiki.com/index.php?title=Category:Writer

Chesterton, G. K. (2009). *What I saw in America* (Reprint). London, England: Anthem Press. (Original work published 1922)

Clark, L. S. (2003). *From angels to aliens: Teenagers, the media, and the supernatural.* New York, NY: Oxford University Press.

Clarke, S. (2005). Created in whose image? Religious characters on network television. *Journal of Media and Religion, 4,* 137–153.

Cloud, M. (2004). 'One nation, under God': Tolerable acknowledgement of religion or unconstitutional Cold War propaganda cloaked in American civil religion? *Journal of Church and State, 46,* 311-340.

Complete coverage on Westboro Baptist Church. (2013). *CNN.com* [Web site]. Retrieved from http://topics.cnn.com/topics/westboro_baptist_church

Condoleezza Rice RNC speech. (2012, August 29; updated September 4). *Politico.com* [Web site]. Retrieved from http://www.politico.com/news/stories/0812/80402.html

Conley, R. (2012, November 8). Young voter turnout increases from 2008 to 2012. Retrieved from http://redallterpolitics.com/2012/11/08/young-voter-turnout-increases-from-2008-to-2012/

Cowan, D. E. (2008). *Sacred terror: Religion and horror on the silver screen*. Waco, TX: Baylor University Press.

Cowan, D. E (2010). *Sacred space: The quest for transcendence in science fiction film and television*. Waco, TX: Baylor University Press.

Dabb, A., & Loflin, D. (Writers), & Bota, R. (Director). (2010). Hammer of the gods. [Television series episode]. In E. Kripke (Creator), *Supernatural*. Los Angeles: CW Network.

Dabb, A., & Loflin, D. (Writers), & Woolnough, J. (Director). (2010). Dark side of the moon. [Television series episode]. In E. Kripke (Creator), *Supernatural*. Los Angeles: CW Network.

Dabb, A., & Loflin, D. (Writers), & Showalter, J. (Director). (2012). What's up, tiger mommy? [Television series episode]. In E. Kripke (Creator), *Supernatural*. Los Angeles: CW Network.

D'Aulaire, I., & D'Aulaire, E. P. (1967). *D'Aulaire's book of Norse myths*. New York, NY: The New York Review of Books.

DeCandido, K. (2009). Not just a pretty face (or two). In Supernatural.TV (Ed.), *In the hunt: Unauthorized essays on* Supernatural (pp. ix-xii). Dallas, TX: Benbella Books.

Dorsey L. G., & Harlow, R. M. (2003). 'We want Americans pure and simple': Theodore Roosevelt and the myth of Americanism. *Rhetoric and Public Affairs, 6*, 55-78.

Dow, B. (1990). Hegemony, feminist critique and *The Mary Tyler Moore Show*. *Critical Studies in Mass Communication, 7*, 261–274.

Ebert, R. (2002, April 12). *Frailty* [Review]. *Chicago Sun-Times*. Retrieved from http://www.rogerebert.com/reviews/frailty-2002

Edlund, B. (Writer & Director). (2011). The man who would be king. [Television series episode]. In E. Kripke (Creator), *Supernatural*. Los Angeles: CW Network.

Edlund, B. (Writer), & Boyum, S. (Director). (2009). The end. [Television series episode]. In E. Kripke (Creator), *Supernatural*. Los Angeles: CW Network.

Edlund, B. (Writer), & Rohl, M. (Director). (2009). On the head of a pin. [Television series episode]. In E. Kripke (Creator), *Supernatural*. Los Angeles: CW Network.

Edlund, B. (Writer), & Rohl, M. (Director). (2010). My bloody valentine. [Television series episode]. In E. Kipke (Creator), *Supernatural*. Los Angeles: CW Network.

Edlund, B. (Writer), & Sgriccia, P. (Director). (2013). Everybody hates Hitler. [Television series episode]. In E. Kripke (Creator), *Supernatural*. Los Angeles: CW Network.

Edwards, J. A. (2008). *Navigating the post-Cold War world: President Clinton's foreign policy rhetoric*. Lanham, MD: Lexington Books.

Edwards, J. A., & Weiss, D. (2011). *The rhetoric of American exceptionalism: Critical essays*. Jefferson, NC: McFarland.

Edwards, N. (2009a, June/July). Welcome! *Supernatural Magazine*, p. 3.

Edwards, N. (2009b, February/March). Myths and legends: Angels. *Supernatural Magazine, 8*, 28–30.

Elliott, J. (2013, February). *Saving people, hunting things:* Supernatural *and the posthuman*. Paper presented at the Far West Popular and American Culture Associations annual meeting, Las Vegas, NV.

Engstrom, E., & Semic, B. (2003). Portrayal of religion in reality TV programming: Hegemony and the contemporary American wedding. *Journal of Media and Religion, 2*, 145–163.

Engstrom, E., & Valenzano, III, J. M. (2010). Demon hunters and hegemony: Portrayal of religion on the CW's *Supernatural*. *Journal of Media and Religion, 9*, 67-83.

Erickson, K. V. (1980). Jimmy Carter: The rhetoric of private and civic piety. *Western Journal of Speech Communication, 44*, 221-235.

Farrer, A. (1988). A rebirth of images: The kingdom of darkness. In H. Bloom (Ed.), *Modern critical interpretations: The Revelation of St. John the Divine*, (pp. 55-68). New York, NY: Chelsea House Publishers.

Fastenberg, D. (2010, July 28). Geographic center of the US: Lebanon, Kans. *Time*. Retrieved from   http://www.time.com/time/specials/packages/article/ 0,28804,2006404_2006095_2006115,00.html

Femia, J. (1981). *Gramsci's political thought: Hegemony, consciousness, and the revolutionary process*. Oxford, England: Clarendon Press.

Fiorenza, F. S. (2003). The conflict of hermeneutical traditions and Christian theology. *Journal of Chinese Philosophy, 27*(1), 3-31.

Freeman, S., & Duhovny, G. (2013). The mythology of *Supernatural* [Course syllabus]. Retrieved from http://www.decal.org/courses/2553

Friedenberg, R. V. (2002). Rhetoric, religion and government at the turn of the 21st century. *Journal of Communication and Religion, 25*, 34-48.

Friesen, S. J. (2001). *Imperial cults and the Apocalypse of John: Reading Revelation in the ruins*. New York, NY: Oxford University Press.

Gaiman, N., & Pratchett, T. (1990). *Good omens: The nice and accurate prophecies of Agnes Nutter, witch*. New York, NY: Harper Torch.

Galician, M-L. (2003). *Sex, love, and romance in the mass media*. Mahwah, NJ: Lawrence Erlbaum.

Gamble, S. (Writer), & Sgriccia, P. (Director). (2008). Are you there, God? It's me, Dean Winchester. [Television series episode]. In E. Kripke (Creator), *Supernatural*. Los Angeles: CW Network.

Gamble, S. (Writer), & Sgriccia, P. (Director). (2009). Good God y'all! [Television series episode]. In E. Kripke (Creator), *Supernatural*. Los Angeles: CW Network.

Gamble, S. (Writer), & Sgriccia, P. (Director). (2010a). Exile on Main St. [Television series episode]. In E. Kripke (Creator), *Supernatural*. Los Angeles: CW Network.

Gamble, S. (Writer), & Sgriccia, P. (Director). (2010b). Two minutes to midnight [Television series episode]. In E. Kipke (Creator), *Supernatural*. Los Angeles, CA: CW Network.

Gamble, S. (Writer), & Sgriccia, P. (Director). (2011). Meet the new boss. [Television series episode]. In E. Kripke (Creator), *Supernatural*. Los Angeles: CW Network.

Gamble, S., (Writer), & Singer, R. (Director). (2006). Bloodlust. [Television series episode]. In E. Kripke (Creator), *Supernatural*. Los Angeles: CW Network.

Gamble, S., & Singer, R. (Writers), & Rohl, M. (Director). (2010). Appointment in Samarra. In E. Kripke (Creator), *Supernatural*. Los Angeles: CW Network.

Gamble, S., & Tucker, R. (Writers), & Kroeker, A. (Director). (2006). Faith. [Television series episode]. In E. Kripke (Creator), *Supernatural*. Los Angeles: CW Network.

Gamble, S., & Tucker, R. (Writers), & Singer, R. (Director). (2006). Salvation. [Television series episode]. In E. Kripke (Creator), *Supernatural*. Los Angeles: CW Network.

Gamoran, A. (1990). Civil religion in American schools. *SA: Sociological Analysis, 51*, 235-256.

Garvey, A. (2009). 'We've got work to do': Sacrifice, heroism, and Sam and Dean Winchester. In Supernatural.TV (Ed.), *In the hunt: Unauthorized essays on* Supernatural (pp. 87-96). Dallas, TX: Benbella Books.

Giannini, E. (2011). 'There's nothing more dangerous than some a-hole who thinks he is on a holy mission': Using and (dis)-abusing religious and economic authority on *Supernatural*. In S. Abbott & D. Lavery (Eds.), *TV goes to hell: An unofficial road map to* Supernatural (pp. 163-175). Toronto, Canada: ECW Press.

Glass, A. (Writer), & Singer, R. (Director). (2011). Defending your life. [Television series episode]. In E. Kripke (Creator), *Supernatural*. Los Angeles: CW Network.

Goldzwig, S. (1987). A rhetoric of public theology: The religious rhetor and public policy. *Southern Speech Communication Journal, 52*, 128-150.

Gramsci, A. (1999). *Selections from the prison notebooks of Antonio Gramsci*. (Q. Hoare & G. N. Smith, Trans. & Eds.). London, England: Electric Book.

Gramsci, A. (2000). *The Antonio Gramsci reader: Selected writings, 1916–1935*. (D. Forgacs, Ed.). New York, NY: New York University Press.

Grigg, R. (2007). Vanquishing evil without the help of God: *The Man from U.N.C.L.E.* and a world come of age. *Journal of Communication and Religion, 30*, 308–339.

Hall, S. (1973). *Encoding and decoding the television discourse*. Birmingham, England: University of Birmingham.

Hall, S. (1977). Culture, the media, and the 'ideological effect.' In J. Curran, M. Gurevitch, & J. Woollacott (Eds.), *Mass communication and society* (pp. 315–348). Beverly Hills, CA: Sage.

Hall, S. (1997). *Representation: Cultural representation and signifying practices*. Thousand Oaks, CA: Sage.

Hansen, R. (Ed.). (2011). *Roman Catholicism in fantastic film: Essays on belief, spectacle, ritual, and imagery*. Jefferson, NC: McFarland.

Harnick, C. (2013, February 11). *Arrow* renewed: *The Vampire Diaries*, *Supernatural* also returning for 2013-2014 season. *The Huffington Post* [Web site]. Retrieved from http://www.huffingtonpost.com/2013/02/11/arrow-renewed-the-vampire-diaries-supernatural-the-cw_n_2663614.html

Hart, R. P. (1977). *The political pulpit*. Purdue, IN: Purdue University Press.

Hartnett, S. J. (2002). *Democratic dissent and the cultural fictions of antebellum America*. Urbana, IL: University of Illinois Press.

Hendershot, H. (2010). *Shaking the world for Jesus: Media and conservative evangelical culture*. Chicago, IL: University of Chicago Press.

Hibberd, J. (2013, October 9). *Supernatural* season 9 premiere ratings biggest in years. *Entertainment Weekly*. Retrieved from http://insidetv.ew.com/2013/10/09/supernatural-season-9-ratings/

Hill, A. (2011). *Paranormal media: Audiences, spirits, and magic in popular culture*. New York, NY: Routledge.

Hills, M. (2005). *The pleasures of horror*. New York: Continuum.

Hodgson, G. (2009). *The myth of American Exceptionalism*. New Haven, CT: Yale University Press.

Hoover, S. M. (1996). Mass media and religious pluralism. In P. Lee (Ed.). *The democratization of communication*. Cardiff, Wales: University of Wales Press.

Hoover, S. M. (1988). *Mass media religion: The social sources of the electronic church*. Newbury Park, CA: Sage.

Hoover, S. M. (2002). Introduction: The cultural construction of religion in the media age. In S. M. Hoover & L. Clark (Eds.), *Practicing religion in the age of the media* (pp. 1–6). New York, NY: Columbia University Press.

Hornick, E. (2009, December 9). Will Obama's war become his Vietnam? *CNN.com* [Web site]. Retrieved from http://articles.cnn.com/2009-12-1/politics/afghanistan.vietnam_1_south-vietnam-afghanistan-coalition-forces?_s=PM:POLITICS

Howard, R. G. (2006). Sustainability and narrative plasticity in online Apocalyptic discourse after September 11, 2001. *Journal of Media and Religion, 5*, 25-47.

Hulse, C. (2009, December 11). Democrats defend bill to rein in Wall Street. *The New York Times*, p. B1.

Hunter, J. D. (1983). *American evangelicism: Conservative religion and the quandary of modernity*. New Brunswick, NJ: Rutgers University Press.

Irvine, A. (2007). *The* Supernatural *book of monsters, spirits, demons, and ghouls*. New York, NY: Harper Collins.

Ivie, R. (1974). Presidential motives for war. *Quarterly Journal of Speech, 3*, 337-345.

Ivie, R. (1979). Progressive form and Mexican culpability in Polk's justification for war. *Central States Speech Journal, 30*, pp. 311-320.

Ivie, R. (1980). Images of savagery in American justifications of war. *Communication Monographs, 47*, 279-294.

Ivie, R. (1989). Metaphor and motive in the Johnson Administration's Vietnam War rhetoric. In M. Leff & F. Kauffeld (Eds.), *Texts in context: Critical dialogues on significant episodes in American political rhetoric* (pp. 121-141). Davis, CA: Hermagoras Press.

Ivie, R. (2005). *Democracy and America's war on terror*. Tuscaloosa, AL: University of Alabama Press.

Jacobs, A. (2010, April 14). Large earthquake strikes China's northwest region. *The New York Times*, p. A12.

Jagger, M., & Richards, K. (1968). Sympathy for the devil. *Beggars Banquet* [album]. London, England: Decca.

Jastrow, Jr., M., McCurdy, J., Kohler, K., Jastrow, M., & Husik, I. (2009). Azazel. *JewishEncyclopedia.com*. Retrieved from http://www.jewishencyclopedia.com/view.jsp?artidD2203&letterDA&searchDdemon

Jenkins, P. (2003). *The new anti-Catholicism: The last acceptable prejudice*. New York, NY: Oxford University Press.

John Paul II. (1995, March 25). Evangelium vitae. In J. G. Donders (Ed.), *John Paul II: The encyclicals in everyday language*. Maryknoll, NY: Orbis Books.

Johnson, V. E. (2000). Welcome home?: CBS, PAX-TV, and Heartland values. *The Velvet Light Trap, 46*, 40–55.

Jordan, J. L. (2011, April). *The Apocalypse will be televised: The Book of Revelation, medieval apocalypticism and* Supernatural. Paper presented at the joint conference of the National Popular Culture and American Culture Association and Southwest/Texas Popular Culture and American Culture Association, San Antonio, TX.

Jowett, L., & Abbott, S. (2013). *TV horror: Investigating the dark side of the small screen*. New York, NY: I. B. Tauris.

Kagan, R. (2012, March 14). America has made the world freer, safer and wealthier. *CNN.com* [Web site]. Retrieved from http://www.cnn.com/2012/03/14/opinion/kagan-world-america-made/index.html?hpt=hp_c2

Kane, T. (2006). *The changing vampire of film and television: A critical study of the growth of a genre*. Jefferson, NC: McFarland.

Kao, G., & Copulsky, J. (2007). The pledge of allegiance and the meanings and limits of civil religion. *Journal of the American Academy of Religion, 75*, 121-149.

Kaylor, B. T. (2011). *Presidential campaign rhetoric in an age of confessional politics*. Lanham, MD: Rowman & Littlefield.

Knight, N. (2010a). Supernatural: *The official companion season 5*. London, England: Titan Books.

Knight, N. (2010b, May). Carving a niche. *Supernatural Magazine*, 39-43.

Knight, N. (2008, April/May). Do the write thing. *Supernatural Magazine*, 30–35.

Know your legend. (2008, April/May). *Supernatural Magazine*, 52–55.

Kraemer, R., Cassidy, W., & Schwartz, S. (2003). *Religions of* Star Trek. New York, NY: Basic Books.

Krauthammer, C. (2009, April 10). It's your country too, Mr. President. *Realclearpolitics.com* [Web site]. Retrieved from http://www.realclearpolitics.com/articles/2009/04/its_your_country_too_mr_presi d.html

Kripke, E. (Writer), & Boyum, S. (Director). Swan song. [Television series episode]. In E. Kripke (Creator), *Supernatural*. Los Angeles: CW Network.

Kripke, E. (Writer), & Manners, K. (Director). (2008). Lazarus rising. [Television series episode]. In E. Kripke (Creator), *Supernatural*. Los Angeles: CW Network.

Landy, M. (1994). *Film, politics, and Gramsci*. Minneapolis, MN: University of Minnesota Press.

Lears, T. J. (1985). The concept of cultural hegemony: Problems and possibilities. *The American Historical Review, 90*, 567–593.

Leclercq, H. (1910). Holy oils. In *The Catholic Encyclopedia* (n. p.). New York, NY: Robert Appleton Company. *New Advent* [Web site]. Retrieved from http://www.newadvent.org/cathen/07421b.htm

Leeming, D. (1990). *The world of myth*. New York, NY: Oxford University Press.

Lewis, C. (1992). Making sense of common sense: A framework for tracking hegemony. *Critical Studies in Mass Communication, 9*, 277–292.

Lewis, T. (2002). Religious rhetoric and the comic frame in *The Simpsons*. *Journal of Media and Religion, 1*, 153–165.

Livgren, K. (1976). Carry on, wayward son [Recorded by Kansas]. On *Leftoverture* [album].

Loflin, D. (Writer), & Boyum, S. (Director). (2013). Remember the Titans. [Television series episode]. In E. Kripke (Creator), *Supernatural*. Los Angeles: CW Network.

Loflin, D. (Writer), & Copus, N. (Director). (2012). Citizen fang. [Television series episode]. In E. Kripke (Creator), *Supernatural*. Los Angeles: CW Network.

Loomis, C. G. (1948). *White magic: An introduction to the folklore of Christian legend*. Cambridge, MA: Medieval Academy of America.

Luchsinger, J. F. (1986). Preaching as tragedy, comedy, and fairy tale: The homiletical theory of Fredrick Buechner. *Religious Communication Today, 9*, 1-9.

Luhrssen, D. (2012). *Hammer of the gods: The Thule Society and the birth of Nazism*. Dulles, VA: Potomac Books.

Maas, A. (1907). Abaddon. In *The Catholic encyclopedia*. New York: Robert Appleton Company. *New Advent* [Web site]. Retrieved from http://www.newadvent.org/cathen/01005a.htm

Madsen, D. L. (1998). *American exceptionalism*. Jackson, MS: University of Mississippi.

Maslow, A. H. (1943). A theory of human motivation. *Psychological Review, 50*, 370-396.

Massanari, A. (2005). *'Truly more than a game': Ritual, reality television and alternative religions*. Paper presented at the annual meeting of the International Communication Association, New York.

Mathews, E. (2009a, June/July). Myths & legends: Samhain. *Supernatural Magazine*, 50-51.

Mathews, E. (2009b, August/September). Myths & legends: Sirens. *Supernatural Magazine*, 46-47.

Matthews, B. (Writer), & Rohl, M. (Director). (2011). ...And then there were none. In E. Kripke (Creator), *Supernatural*. Los Angeles: CW Network.

McCain: Obama doesn't believe in American Exceptionalism. (2012, August 30). *NBCNews.com* [Web site]. Retrieved from http://video.msnbc.msn.com/msnbc/48836058

McCartney, P. T. (2004). American nationalism and U.S. foreign policy from September 11 to the Iraq war. *Political Science Quarterly, 119*, 401-426.

McKrisken, T. B. (2003). *American exceptionalism and the legacy of Vietnam: U.S. foreign policy since 1974*. New York, NY: Palgrave MacMillan.

Medhurst, M., Ivie, R., Wander, P., & Scott, R. (1990). *Cold War rhetoric: Strategy, metaphor, and ideology*. Westport, CT: Greenwood Press.

Melville, H. (2006). *White jacket*. New York, NY: Aegypan. (Original work published 1850)

Mencken, H. L. (2007). Memorial service. In C. Hitchens (Ed.), *The portable atheist: Essential readings for the nonbeliever* (pp. 143-146). Philadelphia, PA: Da Capo Press. (Original work published 1922)

Meyer, M. (2007). 'Something Wicca this way comes': Audience interpretations of a marginalized religious philosophy on *Charmed*. In K. Beeler & S. Beeler (Eds.), *Investigating Charmed: The magic power of TV*. New York, NY: I. B. Tauris.

Meyer, M. (2009). 'I'm just trying to find my way like most kids': Bisexuality, adolescence, and the drama *One Tree Hill*. *Sexuality & Culture, 13*, 237-251.

Meyer, M. W., & Smith, R. (Eds.). (1999). *Ancient Christian magic: Coptic texts of ritual power*. Princeton, NJ: Princeton University Press.

Meltzer, E. (1999). Old Coptic texts of ritual power. In M. W. Meyer & R. Smith (Eds.), *Ancient Christian magic: Coptic texts of ritual power* (pp. 13-20). Princeton, NJ:Princeton University Press.

Miles, M. R. (1997). What you see is what you get: Religion on prime time fiction television. In M. Suman (Ed.), *Religion and prime time television* (pp. 37–46). Westport, CT: Praeger.

Mirecki, P., & Meyer, M. W. (Eds.). (2002). *Magic and ritual in the ancient world*. Leiden, The Netherlands: Koninklijke Brill.

Mitchell, C.P. (2001). *A guide to Apocalyptic cinema*. Westport, CT: Greenwood Press.

Mumby, D. (1997). The problem of hegemony: Rereading Gramsci for organizational communication studies. *Western Journal of Communication, 61*, 343–375.

Murphy, J. J. (1960). Saint Augustine and the debate about a Christian rhetoric. *Quarterly Journal of Speech, 46*, 400-410.

Murphy, J. M. (2003). Our mission and our moment: George W. Bush and September 11. *Rhetoric and Public Affairs, 6*, 607-632.

Nadeau, B. (2011, June 11). Lady Gaga angers the Pope. *The Daily Beast* [Web site]. Retrieved from http://www.thedailybeast.com/articles/2011/06/12/lady-gaga- angers-the-pope.html

Nelson, J. (2009a, April/May). Myths & legends: Demons. *Supernatural Magazine*, 26-27.
Nelson, J. (2009b, October/November). Myths & legends: Rugaru. *Supernatural Magazine*, 48-49.
Nelson, J. (2009-2010, December/January). Myths & legends: Ghouls. *Supernatural Magazine*, 38-39.
Nelson, J. (2010a, January/February). Myths & legends: Vampires. *Supernatural Magazine*, 54-55.
Nelson, J. (2010b, March/April). Myths & legends: Witches. *Supernatural Magazine*, 38-39.
Nelson, J. (2010c, May). Myths & legends: Werewolves. *Supernatural Magazine*, 30-31.
Nelson, J. (2011a, March/April). Myths & legends: Fairies. Supernatural Magazine, 70-71.
Nelson, J. (2011b, June/July). Myths & legends: The antichrist. *Supernatural Magazine*, 30-31.
Nelson, J. (2013, March). Myths & legends: Japanese monsters. *Supernatural Magazine*, 30-31.
Newport, F. (2012, December 24). In US, 77% identify as Christian. *Gallup Politics*. Retrieved from http://www.gallup.com/poll/159548/identity-Christian.aspx
Newitz, A. (2009, May 21). Is *Supernatural* for atheists? *io9.com* [Web site]. Retrieved from http://io9.com/5265112/is-supernatural-for-atheists
Nielsen ratings for 2005–06 season. (2006, May 28). *TV.com* [Web site]. Retrieved from http://www.tv.com/alias/show/3451/nielsen-ratings-for-2005-06-season-90/topic/2534-252664/msgs.html
Obama, B. H. (2009, April 4). News conference by Barack Obama. Retrieved from http://www.whitehouse.gov/the_press_office/News-Conference-By-President-Obama-4-04-2009
Obama rebalances U.S. drug policy. (2009, March 17). *Christian Science Monitor*, p. 8.
O'Leary, S. D. (1994). *Arguing the Apocalypse: A theory of millennial rhetoric*. New York, NY: Oxford University Press.
O'Leary, S. D. (1997). Apocalyptic argument and the anticipation of catastrophe: The prediction of risk and the risk of prediction. *Argumentation, 11*, 293-313.
Ostwalt, Jr., C. (1995). Hollywood and Armageddon: Apocalyptic themes in recent cinematic presentation. In J. W. Martin & C. Ostwalt, Jr. (Eds.), *Screening the sacred* (pp. 55-63). Boulder, CO: Westview.
Overnight Nielsen TV ratings, Thursday, September 25, 2008. (2008, September 26). *TVbythenumbers.com* [Web site]. Retrieved from http://tvbythenumbers.com/2008/09/26/thursday-september-25-greys-anatomy-boostsabc/5332
Papi, H. (1911). Pastor. In *The Catholic encyclopedia*. New York: Robert Appleton Company. Retrieved from http://www.newadvent.org/cathen/11537b.htm
Peirse, A. (2010). *Supernatural*. In D. Lavery (Ed.), *The essential cult TV reader* (pp. 260-267). Lexington, KY: University Press of Kentucky.
Pew Forum on Religion & Public Life. (2008). *US religious landscape survey*. Retrieved from http://religious.pewforum.org/reports
Pew Research Center (2012, October 9). 'Nones' on the rise: One in five adults have no religious affiliation. Retrieved from http://www.pewforum.org/Unaffiliated/nones-on-the-rise.aspx
Primiano, L. N. (2009). 'For what I have done and what I have failed to do': Vernacular Catholicism and *The West Wing*. In D. Winston (Ed.), *Small screen, big picture: Television and lived religion* (pp. 99-123). Waco, TX: Baylor University Press.
Poole, S. (2011). *Monsters in America: Our historic obsession with the hideous and the haunting*. Waco, TX: Baylor University Press.
Prudom, L. (2012, August 3). *Supernatural* season 8: Showrunner Jeremy Carver on Purgatory and "maturing" the Winchesters. *Huffington Post* [Web site]. Retrieved from http://www.huffingtonpost.com/2012/08/03/supernatural-season-8-jeremy-carver_n_1739537.html
Rabb, J., & Richardson, J. (2008). Reavers and redskins: Creating the frontier savage. In R. Wilcox & T. Cochran (Eds.), *Investigating Firefly and Serenity* (pp. 127-138). New York, NY: I. B. Tauris.

Radish, C. (2010). Executive producer Eric Kripke and new show runner Sera Gamble interview—*Supernatural*. *Collider.com* [Web site]. Retrieved from http://collider.com/supernatural-interview-eric-kripke-sera-gamble

Reagan, R. (1989, January 11). Farewell address to the nation. *Americanrhetoric.com* [Web site]. Retrieved from http://www.americanrhetoric.com/speeches/ronaldreaganfarewelladdress.html

Rehill, A. (2010). *The Apocalypse is everywhere: A popular history of America's favorite nightmare*. Westport, CT: Praeger.

Romero, S., & Lacey, M. (2010, January 13). Fierce quake devastates Haiti, worst is feared. *The New York Times*, p. A1.

Roof, W. C. (1997). Blurred boundaries: Religion and prime time television. In M. Suman (Ed.), *Religion and prime time television* (pp. 61–67). Westport, CT: Praeger.

Rudolph, I. (2009a, July 20). *Supernatural* season 5 scoop. *TVGuide.com* [Web site]. Retrieved from http://huntersaddict.wordpress.com/2009/07/21/latest-eric-kripke-interview-tvguide-com

Rudolph, I. (2009b, July 27-August 9). Angels and demons descend on *Supernatural*. *TV Guide*, p. 32.

Rudolph, I. (2010, December 7). *Supernatural* wins *TV Guide Magazine*'s fan favorites cover poll. *TVGuide.com* [Web site]. Retrieved from http://www.tvguide.com/News/Supernatural-Fan-Favorite-1026480.aspx

Rushing, J. H. & Frentz, T. H. (1995). *Projecting the shadow: The cyborg hero in American film*. Chicago, IL: University of Chicago Press.

Schultze, Q. (2001). Touched by angels and demons: Religion's love-hate relationship with popular culture. In D. Stout & J. Buddenbaum (Eds.), *Religion and popular culture: Studies on the interaction of worldviews* (pp. 39–48). Ames, IA: Iowa State University Press.

Seidman, R. (2009, March 3). Top CW primetime shows February 23 to March 1, 2009. *TVbythenumbers.com* [Web site]. Retrieved from http://tvbythenumbers.com/2009/03/03/top-cw-primetime-shows-february-23-tomarch-1-2009/13883

Seiple, C. (2012). The essence of exceptionalism: Roger Williams and the birth of religious freedom in America. *The Review of Faith and International Affairs, 10* (2), 13-19.

Siege, J. (Writer)., & Beeson, C. (Director). (2010). 99 problems. [Television series episode]. In E. Kripke (Creator), *Supernatural*. Los Angeles: CW Network.

Signiorelli, N., & Morgan, M. (1996). Cultivation analysis: Research and practice. In M. Salwen & D. Stacks (Eds). *An integrated approach to communication theory and research* (pp. 111–126). Mahwah, NJ: Lawrence Erlbaum.

Skill, T., Robinson, J., & Lyons, J. (1994). The portrayal of religion and spirituality on fictional network television. *Review of Religious Research, 35*, 251–267.

Slatta, R. W. (2010). Making and unmaking myths of the American frontier. *European Journal of American Culture 29*(2), 81-92.

Snyder, L. (2000). Invitation to transcendence: The Book of Revelation. *Quarterly Journal of Speech, 36*, 402-416.

Soderlind, S. & Taylor, J. T. (2011). *American exceptionalisms: From Winthrop to Winfrey*. Albany, NY: State University of New York Press.

Somashekhar, S. (2007, March 24). Soldier sacrificed his life for others. *Washington Post*. Retrieved from http://www.washingtonpost.com/wp-dyn/content/article/2007/03/23/AR2007032301665.html

Stone, J. R. (2001). A fire in the sky: 'Apocalyptic' themes on the silver screen. In E. M. Mazur & K. McCarthy (Eds.), *God in the details: American religion in popular culture* (pp. 65-82). New York, NY: Routledge.

Stuckey, M. E. (1991). *The president as interpreter-in-chief*. Washington, DC: CQ Press.

Stuckey, M. E. (2004). *Defining Americans: The presidency and national identity*. Lawrence, KS: University Press of Kansas.

Stuckey, M. E. (2011). The Donner Party and the rhetoric of westward expansion. *Rhetoric and Public Affairs, 14*, 229-260.

Supernatural. (2013). *Facebook.com* [Web site]. Retrieved from http://www.facebook.com/Supernatural

Supernatural ratings 2007–08. (2007, November 18). *TVbythenumbers.com* [Web site]. Retrieved from http://tvbythenumbers.com/category/ratings/show/show-ratings/supernatural-ratings

Supernatural.TV. (2009). *In the hunt: Unauthorized essays on* Supernatural. Dallas, TX: Benbella Books.

Supernatural Wiki. (2013, June 5). *SupernaturalWiki.com* [Web site]. Retrieved from http://www.supernaturalwiki.com/index.php?title=Super-wiki

Super-wiki: About. (2012, February 26). *SupernaturalWiki.com* [Web site]. Retrieved from http://www.supernaturalwiki.com/index.php?title=Super-wiki:About

Surette, T. (2008, January 10). TV.com Q & A: Supernatural creator Eric Kripke. *TV.com* [Web site]. Retrieved from http://www.tv.com/eric-kripke/person/159154/story/10682.html

Swearingen, C. J. (2005). Homiletics and hermeneutics: The rhetorical spaces in between. *Studies in the Literary Imagination, 28,* (2), 27-42.

Sweet, L. (2010, February 10). Michelle Obama vs. childhood obesity. *Chicago Sun-Times*, p. 15.

Swine flu pandemic over says world health body. (2010, August 10). *BBC News* [Web site]. Retrieved from http://www.bbc.co.uk/news/health-10930023

Szabo, L. (2009, April 27). Swine flu: Questions and answers. *USA Today*, p. A2.

Thorburn, D. (1987). Television as an aesthetic medium. *Critical Studies in Mass Communication, 4,* 161-173.

Torrey, C. C. (1958). *The apocalypse of John.* New Haven, CT: Yale University Press.

Townshend, P. (1971). Won't get fooled again. [Recorded by The Who]. [single].

Tran, M. (2006, October 19). Bush accepts Iraq-Vietnam war comparison. *Guardian.co.uk.* Retrieved from http://www.guardian.co.uk/world/2006/oct/19/usa.iraq1

Trust, G. (2011, March 28). Lady Gaga leaps to record-tying no. 1 on pop songs. *Billboard.* Retrieved from http://www.billboard.com/articles/columns/chart-beat/472330/lady-gaga-leaps-to-record-tying-no-1-on-pop-songs

Uribe, M. V. (2004). Dismembering and expelling: Semantics of political terror in Colombia. *Public Culture, 16,* 1, 79-95.

U.S. Census Bureau. (2009). Self-described religious identification of adult population: 1990 to 2008. *2010 statistical abstract.* Retrieved from http://www.census.gov/compendia/statab/2010/tables/10s0075.pdf

Van Zoonen, L. (1994). *Feminist media studies.* Thousand Oaks, CA: Sage.

Villareal, Y. (2013, March 26). CW network revamp aims to draw wider audience. *Los Angeles Times.* Retrieved from http://articles.latimes.com/2013/mar/26/business/la-et-fi-ct-thecw-20130326

Vollick, S. (2008, April 3). The religious significance of the show Supernatural. *Telewatcher.com.* Retrieved from http://telewatcher.com/science-fiction/the-religious-significance-of-the-show-supernatural/

Whitfield, N., & Strong, B. (1970). War [Recorded by Edwin Starr]. On *War & peace* [album].

Wimmler, J., & Kienzl, L. (2011). 'I am an angel of the Lord': An inquiry into the Christian nature of *Supernatural*'s heavenly delegates. In S. Abbott & D. Lavery (Eds.), *TV goes to hell: An unofficial road map to* Supernatural (pp. 176-186). Toronto, Canada: ECW Press.

Winston, D. (2009). Introduction. In D. Winston (Ed.), Small screen, big picture: *Television and lived religion* (pp. 1-14). Waco, TX: Baylor University Press.

Winthrop, J. (1630). A model of Christian charity. Retrieved from http://religiousfreedom.lib.virginia.edu/sacred/charity.html

Wolff, R. (2010). *The church on TV: Portrayals of priests, pastors and nuns on American television series.* New York, NY: Continuum.

Wrobel, D. M. (2008). Exceptionalism and globalism: Travel writers and the nineteenth-century American West. In D. Roediger (Ed.), *The best American history essays 2008* (pp. 75-100). New York, NY: Palgrave McMillan.

Zak, D. (2009, October 12). For gay activists, the lady is a champ. *Washington Post.* Retrieved from http://articles.washingtonpost.com/2009-10-12/news/36790303_1_stefani-germanotta-lady-gaga-national-equality-march

Zezima, K. (2010, September 20). Lady Gaga goes political in Maine. *New York Times*, p. A21. Retrieved from http://www.nytimes.com/2010/09/21/us/politics/21gaga.html?_r=1&

Zompetti, J. (1997). Toward a Gramscian critical rhetoric. *Western Journal of Communication*, *61*, 66-86.

Index

Abaddon, 33
Abbott, S., 2
Ackles, Jensen, 2, 135n1
addiction, 87–88
"Adventures in Babysitting" (Episode 7.11), 35
Aesir, 131
Afghanistan, 84–85
afterlife, 23, 25–26. *See also* Heaven; Hell
agape, 74n10
agnosticism and atheism, 9, 134
allegory, 96
allies, 36–39
American Exceptionalism: beyond religion, 114–115; cowboy archetype and, 105–107; criticism of, 102; exemplarism vs. interventionism, 103; hierarchy of nations and, 132; phases and political manifestation of, 18–19; religious foundation of, 101; religious hegemony and, 110–111; sacrifice and, 112–114; secular religions and identities, combining of, 18–19; tenets of, 101–102; Winchesters as America, 104–107, 111–112
American mythos, 100, 101–104. *See also* Frontier Myth
American society, Famine as lesson for, 89–90
". . . And Then There Were None" (Episode 6.16), 38, 121

Angel, 11, 16, 127
angels: ability to defeat, 114; absence of God and, 40, 69, 115; as antagonists, 32, 33, 36, 131; anti-human attitude of, 35; Apocalypse and, 50, 78, 80, 81; Catholic doctrine and, 43; as "dicks", 70, 74n11; entrapped with holy oil, 74n9; falling, 134; in *Frailty*, 12; horror genre and, 12; human depictions of, 94; introduction and origins of, 30; Leah and, 55–56; non-Catholic Christianity and, 57–58, 134. *See also specific angels*
antagonists, religious diversity and, 27–29, 31–36
Anti-Christ, 98n10
Apocalypse: absence of Jesus Christ from, 97, 98n9; Armageddon, 30, 95, 106; Castiel on, 59; evangelicalism and, 77; homiletics and, 94–95; non-Christian gods and, 50; in popular media, 77–78. *See also* Horsemen of the Apocalypse
"Appointment in Samara" (Episode 6.11), 42
"Are You There God? It's Me, Dean Winchester" (Episode 4.2), 74n11, 129
Armageddon, 30, 95, 106
artifacts, Catholic. *See* weapons and artifacts
Atropos, 52
auction of artifacts, 51, 109–110

149

About the Authors

Erika Engstrom is Professor of Communication Studies at the University of Nevada, Las Vegas. A PhD graduate of the University of Florida, she teaches courses in gender, nonverbal, and intercultural communication. She conducts research on mass media portrayals of gender and religion. She is the author of *The Bride Factory: Mass Media Portrayals of Women and Weddings*.

Joseph M. Valenzano, III, is Assistant Professor and Basic Course Director at the University of Dayton. His research interests are on the intersection of religion, politics and mass media, and his work has appeared in the *Southern Journal of Communication, Journal of Media and Religion, Communication Quarterly* and the *Journal of Communication and Religion*. He also has co-authored two public speaking textbooks, *The Speaker: The Tradition and Practice of Public Speaking* and *The Speaker's Primer*.

CPSIA information can be obtained at www.ICGtesting.com
Printed in the USA
BVOW09*0343120214

344646BV00002B/4/P